I0814658

FROM GUERNICA TO HUMAN RIGHTS

From Guernica to Human Rights

Essays on the Spanish Civil War

PETER N. CARROLL

THE KENT STATE UNIVERSITY PRESS

Kent, Ohio

ISBN 978-1-60635-238-0
Manufactured in the United States of America

Cataloging information for this title is available at the Library of Congress.

19 18 17 16 15 5 4 3 2 1

For my sometime housemates—

Tony Geist, Fraser Ottanelli, Jim Fernandez, Sebastiaan Faber—

who've made the hard work fun and the food terrific

Contents

Preface

The Spanish Civil War entered my life not as an academic discipline, nor as the epic story that foreshadowed World War II, but because a certain woman I knew agreed to meet me in Spain in the early 1970s. The dictator Francisco Franco was alive and well; his civil guards patrolled the streets with submachine guns. Ordinary citizens we encountered were friendly but reserved. I knew there was more than met the eye. After that trip, the history and culture of twentieth-century Spain became my avocation and then an obsession.

As I moved from a tenured university position to freelance writing in San Francisco, I looked for stories related to Spain's recent history and welcomed the opportunity to interview some American volunteers who had fought in the Spanish Civil War, including writer Alvah Bessie and documentary filmmaker Abe Osheroff. I also conducted oral histories of two African Americans who served in Spain, and this work led me to other veterans of the so-called Abraham Lincoln Brigade.[1]

The term *Brigade,* let's be clear, is a misnomer. The first volunteers from the United States named themselves the Abraham Lincoln *Battalion,* which was part of the Fifteenth International Brigade. Those who came later joined the Washington Battalion and, with Canadian volunteers, the MacKenzie-Papineau Battalion, also part of the Fifteenth Brigade. Other Americans served in the John Brown Artillery, the Regiment de Tren (Transport), the American Medical Bureau, and in various other capacities. Collectively, they were known in the United States as the Abraham Lincoln Brigade. That these military semantics emerge as a matter of discussion among Spanish Civil War aficionados indicates how contentious the entire field remains.

By the end of the 1970s, Franco was dead, the number of veterans dwindling, and I was proposing articles about the Lincoln Brigade to magazines with the idea that they would lead me to write a book. I was struck by a total lack of interest among the editors I approached. For their part, the Lincoln veterans were suspicious of my interest in their history. As subjects of FBI investigations for "subversive activities," many were skeptical about revealing their stories to outsiders. Nevertheless, I went about my historian's trade, interviewing veterans of the Spanish Civil War, helping them clear out their closets of memorabilia that included books, photographs, letters, diaries, newspaper clippings, and assorted keepsakes. I began investigating archival sources in various libraries.

Time was on my side. As the Lincoln veterans entered their eighties, many understood that it was important to establish a clear historical record of their war in Spain. Several began writing memoirs and autobiographies. Many others went out of their way to assist my research. As the Cold War came to an end, moreover, the former Soviet Union allowed Western scholars to examine Spanish Civil War archives that had been transported to Moscow for safekeeping at the beginning of World War II. I had the good fortune to be among the first Americans to use these sources. Such documentary holdings, together with archives in the United States, formed the foundation for my subsequent writings.

After my book about the Lincoln Brigade appeared in 1994, I was elected Chair of the Board of Governors of ALBA (the Abraham Lincoln Brigade Archives), a non-profit educational organization founded by veterans and scholars of the Spanish Civil War. This extensive archive, now located at the Tamiment Library of New York University, remains a treasure of primary source material relating to the lives of the men and women who were involved in Spain's history, before, during, and after the civil war.

As ALBA's Chair, I received opportunities to present lectures and papers about aspects of this complicated history. Some of the essays in this book appeared first as articles; some were heretofore unpublished. Each of the chapters has its own story that I tell in brief introductory remarks. Each chapter also has its own integrity, resulting in some repetition among them. I have minimized the number of repeated quotes and contextual facts, but retained those necessary for coherence. For those who read this book cover to cover, I beg your pardon on behalf of those who will read only selected chapters.

* * *

A book that reflects forty years of writing carries a long list of acknowledgments and gratitude. It begins with Charlene and Jonathan Sharp, publishers of Alvah Bessie's books, who arranged for me to interview him for my first article about the Spanish Civil War in 1975. By the time I finished the research for *The Odyssey of the Abraham Lincoln Brigade* (1994), I'd interviewed over a hundred men and women who had been involved in that conflict. Historian Peter Stansky and editor Norris Pope helped that work into print at Stanford University Press. Subsequently, Robert Fogarty graciously published several of my articles in the *Antioch Review.* I offer big thanks to Mary Kay McCoy and Ignacio Pinedo, who translated the book into *La Odisea de la Brigada Abraham Lincoln* (Seville: Renaciamento Press, 2005).

I've worked closely on other projects with my colleagues on the Board of Governors of the Abraham Lincoln Brigade Archives, including its co-founder, Lincoln veteran Bill Susman, and with librarians around the country, most notably Victor Berch of Brandeis University and Gail Malmgreen at the Tamiment Library. Anthony Geist and I collaborated on an international traveling exhibition of children's art in wartime from the Spanish Civil War to Kosovo called *They Still Draw Pictures.* James Fernandéz co-edited the catalogue for the exhibition, *Facing Fascism: New York City and the Spanish Civil War,* at the Museum of the City of New York. Peter Glazer co-edited a remarkable found manuscript by ambulance driver James Neugass titled *War is Beautiful.* Fraser Ottanelli worked with me on articles for the ALBA website on Jewish volunteers in the Spanish Civil War and on editing the correspondence of Carl Geiser, *Letters from the Spanish Civil War: A U.S. Volunteers Writes Home.* With historian-illustrator Josh Brown, I wrote text for a graphic history called *Paul Robeson in Spain,* published as a special issue of *The Volunteer.* Julia Newman's documentary film about American women, *Into the Fire,* prompted my chapter on the motivations of those volunteers. I co-curated an exhibition of Spanish Civil War posters, *Shouts from the Wall,* with Cary Nelson. And with my friends, the late Michael Nash and Mel Small, I edited *The Good Fight Continues: World War II Letters from the Abraham Lincoln Brigade.*

Chris Brooks, director of ALBA's biographical project, provided immeasurable assistance. Others on the Board—Robert Coale, Joan Cohen, Sebastiaan Faber, and Fredda Weiss—have shared ideas and sustenance. I feel privileged that Lincoln veteran Hank Rubin and photographer Richard Bermack invited me to write forewords to their own books, *Spain's*

Cause Was Mine and *The Front Lines of Social Change.* These collaborations led to invitations to lecture at galleries and universities and to attend conferences around the United States as well as in England, Spain, Switzerland, and Canada. Some of these talks formed the basis for the articles collected here. I also want to thank Richard Bermack for his generosity in sharing his expertise about photographs of the Abraham Lincoln Brigade.

Perry and Gladys Rosenstein of the Puffin Foundation have funded many ALBA projects, not least a program for teachers that keeps me in classrooms, where I get to re-charge my batteries.

I'm particularly pleased to acknowledge the support of Will Underwood and Joyce Harrison for undertaking this on behalf of Kent State University Press.

Cynthia Young and Claartje van Dijk of the International Center of Photography in New York generously gave permission for the use of a Robert Capa photograph; Kirk Cornutt of Troy University, Montgomery, Alabama, facilitated permissions from the Ernest Hemingway Foundation; Jack Von Euw and Susan Snyder of the University of California's Bancroft Library provided the photograph of Hemingway and Milton Wolff.

My daughter Natasha Carroll-Ferrary magically transcribed dozens of pages from WordStar into postmodern text, a big step up from tearing the holes off dot matrix paper. The rest of my family stuck to moral support, for which I'm always grateful. Michael Batinski remains my close counselor and dear friend.

Everything else that matters, along with earthly pleasure, I attribute to my friend Jeannette Ferrary, who met me in Malaga and then one thing led to another.

Permissions Acknowledgments

Excerpts from letters from Ernest Hemingway to Edwin Rolfe and Donald Friede © 2015 Printed with the permission of The Ernest Hemingway Foundation.

"Facing Fascism: New York and the Spanish Civil War" was originally published as "New York and the Spanish Civil War: An Introduction" in *Facing Fascism: New York and the Spanish Civil War* (Museum of the City of New York and NYU Press, 2007) and appears courtesy of the Museum of the City of New York.

"Foreword to Hank Rubin's *Spain's Cause Was Mine*" was originally published in *Spain's Cause Was Mine: A Memoir of An American Medic in the Spanish Civil War* by Hank Rubin, copyright © 1997 by the Board of Trustees, Southern Illinois University, and appears courtesy of Southern Illinois University Press.

"The Myth of the Moscow Archives" was originally published in *Science & Society* 68:3 (Fall 2004) and appears courtesy of *Science & Society*.

"'Not Valid for Travel in Spain': The Legacy of the Abraham Lincoln Brigade" was originally published in *Las Brigadas Internacionales: 70 años de Memoria Histórica* (University of Salamanca, 2006) and appears courtesy of the University of Salamanca.

▷ CHAPTER 1

From Guernica to Human Rights

The Spanish Civil War in the Twenty-First Century

One regret I've had about leaving a traditional university position at a young age was the absence of an opportunity to give a "last lecture" that might sum up whatever wisdom I'd acquired after decades of research and teaching. I've been interested not only in my own findings, but also in how they fit into the larger cultural framework in which I have worked. How does my writing relate to more general historiographical issues? I was delighted, then, when the British International Brigade Memorial Trust in London—led by Jim Jump, Richard Baxell, Marlene Sidaway, and Paul Preston—invited me to present the annual Leonard Crome Memorial Lecture at the Imperial War Museum in March 2012. I took it as an opportunity to summarize a lifetime of work and discovery. With some revisions, it was subsequently published, thanks to my friend and editor Robert Fogarty, in the Antioch Review *70:4 (Fall 2012), 641–656. With further revisions, I also presented this last lecture as the ALBA-Bill Susman Lecture at the Instituto Cervantes in New York in March 2013 and at Stanford University in October 2013.*

▷ Writing to his mother from Spain in 1937, Hyman Katz, an American volunteer in the International Brigades, pointed to the rise of Mussolini and Hitler and the spread of anti-Semitism in Europe and said, "Seeing all these things—how fascism is grasping power in many countries (including the U.S., where there are many Nazi organizations and Nazi agents and spies)—can't you see that fascism is our problem—that it may come to us as it came in other countries?" And Canute Frankson, a Jamaica-born auto mechanic, wrote to his "Dear Friend" from Spain, "if we crush Fascism here we'll save our people in America, and in other parts of the world from the vicious persecution, wholesale imprisonment, and slaughter which the Jewish people . . . are suffering under Hitler's Fascist heels. . . ." And Carl Geiser writing to his brother in Ohio, said "The reasons I am here is [sic] because I want to do my part to prevent a second world war. . . . And because all of our democratic and liberty-loving training makes me anxious to fight fascism and to help the Spanish people drive out the fascist invaders sent in by Hitler and Mussolini."[1] These U.S. volunteers in the Spanish Civil War, together with their 2,800 comrades who formed the Abraham Lincoln Brigade, knew exactly what they were fighting for. To them the defense of the Spanish Republic against a military rebellion led by General Francisco Franco represented part of a global battle between democratic peoples and fascist aggressors.

The generation that fought the Spanish Civil War is nearly gone, and its history passes into the hands of younger generations whose sense of history is shaped in different times. If it is true that each generation writes its own history—because each generation asks different questions of the past—we might pause and consider what issues and questions appear most relevant to our own times.

While Spanish Republicans fought a war against the military rebels, who were backed by troops and munitions from Nazi Germany and Fascist Italy, the Nationalist or Franco side saw the war as a crusade against social disorder, secularism, and democracy—which reduced rhetorically to a war against socialism, communism, and anarchism. After this war and World War II ended, the Francoist view emerged as the dominant, though obviously not exclusive, idea in Western Europe and the United States. Indeed, a new Cold War ideology supplanted the notion that the Spanish Civil War was an anti-fascist war. Instead, scholars and the general public stressed the equivalence of fascism and communism, Hitler and Stalin. It was this view that led President Ronald Reagan on his visit to Spain in 1983 to say that the American volunteers had fought on "the wrong side."[2] This Cold War interpretation has outlived the Cold War. But I would suggest that the twenty-first century will see new ways to explain the events in Spain.

My understanding of the Spanish Civil War has been influenced by my own times. I confess to being a product of a Cold War curriculum. Among the more widely circulated books of my college education in the early 1960s was an anthology written by ex-Communists, *The God That Failed,* subtitled "Why Six Great Writers Rejected Communism." The first piece, by Arthur Koestler, a Spanish Civil War survivor, begins, "A faith is not acquired by reasoning. One does not fall in love with a woman, or enter the womb of a church as a result of logical persuasion. Reason may defend an act of faith—but only after the act has been committed." Louis Fischer, an early activist in the Spanish Civil War, also contributed an essay that described the life of Alexander Berkman, who did not see the evil of communism until a traumatic event—the Bolshevik crushing of a sailors' revolt at Kronstadt—destroyed his illusions. "What counts decisively is the 'Kronstadt,'" said Fischer, meaning a historical shock that breaks one's connection to an entire body of belief. Koestler and Fischer had lost their faith; or, more passively, the god had failed. In the vocabulary of the 1960s, the Kronstadt moment constituted an identity crisis that led to a reconfiguration of one's world view.[3]

Although Koestler and Fischer spoke the language of Freud and Marx, a secular version of these ideas appeared in the work of Thomas Kuhn, a historian of science, whose book, *The Structure of Scientific Revolutions* (1962), popularized the term "paradigm shift." Studying the so-called objective fields of astronomy, chemistry, and physics, Kuhn stressed that human perception of basic science depended more on scientists' cultural values than on the outside "realities" they claimed to be seeing. Consequently, a scientist's world view was so fundamentally embedded in personal consciousness that it was virtually impossible to persuade a scientist to adopt an alternative view, even when the data overwhelmingly pressed in that direction. Kuhn quoted the physicist Max Planck, who remarked, "a new scientific truth does not triumph by convincing its opponents and making them see the light, but rather because its opponents eventually die, and a new generation grows up that is familiar with it." "The transfer of allegiance from paradigm to paradigm," Kuhn concluded, "is a conversion experience that cannot be forced."[4] Without running too far ahead of myself, I would suggest that this is the current state of historical writing about the Spanish Civil War.

Arthur Koestler provides an interesting case study of identity crisis and paradigm shift and explicitly links these abstractions to his own participation in the Spanish Civil War. In 1937, the Left Book Club in London published Koestler's memoir under the title *Spanish Testament*.[5] His narrative is divided into two parts. The first describes Koestler's journey to Spain, purportedly as a journalist, then flashes back for seven chapters of Spanish history that contextualize the civil war. Part two is subtitled "Dialogue With Death" and describes Koestler's arrest, his experience of being condemned to death by the Franco side, his months in a fascist prison, and his lucky rescue thanks to the influence of his British friends.

The core of part one is Spanish history. Koestler argues that the most popular, current view of the causes of the Spanish Civil War "is the one that maintains that Spain is the battle-ground of a struggle between 'reds and whites,' between Communism and Fascism," and he goes on to say, "This is an entirely erroneous view."[6] Rather, he insists, the reforms of the Spanish Republic aimed to overcome a long history of political and economic oppression. He depicts the bombing of Madrid by Franco's air forces as a low point in Western civilization. And his terrifying captivity—during which each evening he waited for a knock at the door summoning him to his death—appears directly as the result of Franco's fascist, murderous terror. That is what he means by *Spanish Testament.*

Koestler returned to France, via Gibraltar, in 1938, still loyal to the Communist Party. But he was fatigued by the internal intrigues and political double-talk, disillusioned by news of Stalin's terror, and finally disavowed communism and the Soviet Union after the signing of the Nazi-Soviet non-aggression pact in 1939. He had reached his Kronstadt moment. Koestler's classic novel, *Darkness at Noon,* published in London in 1941, reflects his political conversion. The totalitarian jailers are no longer fascists, but communists.[7]

By 1942, as German armies stormed toward Stalingrad, Koestler's political conversion was changing his historical paradigm, witnessed by the re-publication of portions of his *Spanish Testament.* Under the title *Dialogue With Death,* he stripped the book of all the chapters of historical context. He also deleted one sentence from the first edition referring to the Barcelona May Days of 1937, which had criticized the P.O.U.M.—the Trotskyist Party. In its place, he added the following sentence: "It looked as though Spain were not only to be the stage for the dress-rehearsal of the second world war, but also for the fratricidal struggle within the European left." In a recently re-issued edition of *Dialogue With Death,* the American critic Louis Menand praises the de-contextualization of Koestler's narrative, saying "If it included details about Koestler's assignment in Spain, it would be a fascinating but dated text—a document, rather than the expression of something about the human condition."[8] The opposite of history, the opposite of remembering the past, might be called amnesia. Fascism has disappeared from the narrative.

A contrast to Koestler's transition from anti-fascist to anti-communist can be seen in the works of George Orwell, whose *Homage to Catalonia* was also required reading in my 1960s syllabus. Although published in Britain in 1938, the book did not appear in the United States until 1952 and then with an introduction by Lionel Trilling, who was identified with the Trotsky wing of Marxism and expressed contempt for the Communists in Spain. *Homage* has lived on in paperback as the one book students of the Spanish Civil War still read. Ironically, given the influence of this book, Orwell's argument with the Communist Party was not that it was a subversive, radical movement—but that the party was opposed to the social revolution in Spain. The war was lost, Orwell suggests, because the communist-led government distrusted the militia units, especially the anarchists. But what Americans read in Orwell—and continue to cite in his memoir—are the descriptions of the Communists' ruthlessness.

World War II gave Orwell, like Koestler, second thoughts about Spain. Written in 1943, his "Looking Back on the Spanish War" summarized the international stalemate that had killed the Spanish Republic: "The outcome of the Spanish war," he stated, "was settled in London, Paris, Rome, Berlin—at any rate, not in Spain." He said nothing about the role of Washington or Moscow, for in his opinion they had played small parts. Although Orwell was an eyewitness to the crushing of a left-anarchist uprising in Barcelona, he now insisted that "the much-publicized disunity" within the Republic "was not a main cause of [its] defeat." Rather, "the Fascists won because they were the stronger; they had modern arms and the others hadn't. No political strategy could offset that."[9] Orwell didn't abandon his anti-communism, but neither did he forget which sides were at war in Spain. By 1946, moreover, Orwell decided to remove the chapters describing the May events in Barcelona from the main text of *Homage to Catalonia* and put them in an appendix. Unlike Koestler, who pushed the "delete" button on his previous opinions, Orwell wanted to preserve his early thoughts, even as he repudiated them.[10]

Another writer whose reputation in relation to the Spanish Civil War has been buffeted by the political winds is the novelist Ernest Hemingway, perhaps the most famous North American to support the Spanish Republic. Hemingway made four trips to Spain as a reporter and participated in making the documentary film *The Spanish Earth*. He paid for the passage of some U.S. volunteers in the Abraham Lincoln Brigade, raised money for ambulances, and lent his name to support the volunteers and veterans. Even the cranky Lincoln volunteer Alvah Bessie, who crossed swords with Hemingway both before and after the war, acknowledged that "[t]he novelist gave freely of his substance and his spirit in the cause of Spain; he wrote and he spoke and he acted."[11]

The Lincolns admired Hemingway in Spain. His room at the Hotel Florida in Madrid was unofficial headquarters for Americans on leave from the front. After the war, they waited eagerly for the publication of the novel he titled *For Whom the Bell Tolls*. "It was going to be the greatest book," said Fred Keller, formerly commissar of the Lincoln battalion. "It was going to vindicate us all. Now somebody was going to tell the true story about why we went to Spain."[12] But the long-awaited book touched sensitive political nerves. By the time it appeared in October 1940, the world had changed. The Soviet Union had signed a pact of non-aggression with Nazi Germany, World War II had begun, France had fallen, and the Veterans of the Abraham Lincoln Brigade (VALB), most of them members of the Communist Party, opposed U.S. intervention on the Allied side.

Hemingway, though no communist, understood these issues. "The Soviet Union was not bound by any pact with Hitler when the International Brigades fought in Spain," he said. "It was only after they lost faith in the democracies that the Alliance was born."[13] This position mirrored the feelings of most Lincoln veterans. Having experienced the ordeal of war and terrible defeat because of the European policy of non-intervention in Spain, they had no desire to encourage U.S. assistance for the allies that had betrayed the Spanish Republic. Ideology, vengeance, and ignorance blinded them to Soviet crimes in Poland. The VALB announced: "this is not our war."[14]

Hemingway's novel made no claim to tell the Lincolns' story. "He fought now in this war," Hemingway wrote of his protagonist, Robert Jordan, with a bit of autobiographical candor, "because it had started in a country he loved, and he believed in the Republic and that if it were destroyed life would be unbearable for all those people who believed in it." Like Hemingway, the hero expressed little interest in politics, besides a vaguely stated "anti-fascism" and a willingness to accept "Communist discipline" for the duration of the war.[15] (It's my opinion that the prototype of Robert Jordan was not the Communist-inclined Robert Merriman, as most scholars suggest, but the non-Communist Texan Philip Detro. See chapter 6.) More generally, Hemingway depicted Communist leaders in

Spain as brutal, callous, and opportunistic, willing to launch a doomed offensive regardless of the consequences.

When *For Whom the Bell Tolls* appeared, the Lincoln veterans promptly denounced it. In a prescient comment, Alvah Bessie warned that Hemingway "will live to see every living and dead representative of the Abraham Lincoln Battalion attacked and slandered because of the great authority that attaches to Hemingway's name and his known connection with Spain." Milton Wolff, last commander of the Lincolns, exchanged nasty letters with Hemingway, calling him a "tourist" in Spain. Hemingway called Wolff a "prick," but his full response is significant: "What would you like me to have done," he pleaded, "to aid the cause of the Spanish Republic that I did not do?"[16]

Hemingway's support for the Republic cut two ways. While the Lincolns condemned his account of the Communist leaders, anti-communists criticized Hemingway's unyielding sympathy for the Republic. Most famous are the repercussions of Hemingway's break with the writer John Dos Passos, who had worked with him on *The Spanish Earth.* Following the killing of his close friend José Robles by Communists, Dos Passos reversed his politics and condemned the Republic. Hemingway refused to turn with Dos Passos. "A war is still being fought in Spain between the people whose side you used to be on and the fascists," Hemingway wrote in 1938, " . . . and for you to try constantly to make out that the war the government is fighting against the fascist Italian, German, Moorish invasion is a communist business imposed on the will of the people is sort of viciously pitiful."[17]

Scholars today appear more interested in Hemingway's relationship to communists (and women) than to his political commitments and his willingness to act on them. Indeed, he did some remarkable things on behalf of the Republic that are practically forgotten or unknown.

Consider two of them. Hemingway's companion and accomplice in Spain was the writer Martha Gellhorn, a courageous journalist for *Collier's* magazine and, coincidentally, a close friend of Eleanor Roosevelt. When *The Spanish Earth* was completed in 1937, Gellhorn arranged for a private screening at the White House in July, the first complete showing of the film. (A partial version of the film had been screened at the conference of the League of American Writers in New York, where Hemingway had spoken a few weeks earlier.) Of course, the purpose of screening a propaganda film in the White House was to awaken the interest of the most powerful man in the nation.

As he watched *The Spanish Earth* unfold on the screen, President Roosevelt remarked, "Spain is a vicarious sacrifice for all of us." Recounting the scene in a letter to the president's wife the following year, Gellhorn questioned Roosevelt's comment, remarking, "But I think Spain is maybe not a sacrifice, but a champion: and hope to God that America at least will not go on letting this country down." Mrs. Roosevelt did not address Gellhorn's point. Her own response to the film, which appeared in her regular newspaper column the following day, mentioned that three filmmakers had dined at the White House and gave her approval to using the profits from the film to purchase ambulances "to help the sick and dying in a part of the world which is at present torn by war." The word "Spain" never appeared in her article. She suggested the film's theme of land reform would seem "alien" to the American public.[18] In any case, the president was not ready to challenge the prevailing mood of "neutrality" and non-intervention in Spain. Hemingway's presence nevertheless reflected a sincere effort to influence changes in U.S. policy.

The novelist also undertook a secret and ambiguous project for the Spanish Republic, which can now be confirmed for the first time on the basis of a previously unpublished letter he later wrote to the poet Edwin Rolfe, a veteran of the Lincoln Brigade. Since Hemingway's hero (Robert Jordan) in *For Whom the Bell Tolls* performs a mission behind enemy lines, many have speculated that the novelist himself had witnessed or participated in such an expedition. One historian, William B. Watson, relied on detailed circumstantial evidence to explain how it was *possible* that Hemingway had undertaken such a mission and argued that he had.[19] Hemingway explicitly describes this secret journey in a letter written in telegraphic style in January 1940, as he was nearing the end of writing *For Whom the Bell Tolls:*

> O.K. Once I had to go to a town will not name to check personally (knew many people there) on effect of something that happened from the air and it's true effect. Also on possibility of rising there. How much dough. And to carry dough. Was scare[d] pissless all the time, really scared, woof because there is an indignity in that kind of finish that scares long in advance. On return had to report that they (1)-hate our guts. 2. It would be pouring dough down a rathole. 3-Didn't trust the bastard[s w]ho were handling what there was. O.K. Report was considered defeatism of the deepest dye. Only was true and save much lives and money.[20]

The point to emphasize is that Hemingway perceived the Spanish Civil War as a war against fascism. He certainly suspected the machinations of Republican leaders and was no fool about the chicanery of the Communists. But much as Britain and the United States collaborated with the Soviet Union during World War II, Hemingway insisted that the first order of business was winning the war. A few years later, when he read a draft of the screenplay of *For Whom the Bell Tolls*, he was appalled that the movie, released in the middle of World War II, gave no clue to explain why "a man will die and know it is well for him to die." "We are at present engaged in fighting a war against the Fascists," he said. "Throughout the picture the enemy should be called the Fascists and the Republic should be called the Republic. . . . Unless you make this emphasis the people seeing the picture will have no idea what the [Spanish] people were really fighting for."[21]

The views of Hemingway, Orwell, and Koestler, though expressed as journalism or literature, reflected important political alignments. The failure of Hemingway and Gellhorn to influence U.S. policies revealed deep fissures within President Roosevelt's coalition. His hands were tied not only by non-interventionists who opposed any international entanglements, but also by the position of his own Catholic constituents, who had followed the Vatican's endorsement of the Franco rebellion. Three months after seeing *The Spanish Earth*, the president attempted to counter what he called "isolationism" in what became known as the Quarantine speech of October 1937. Warning of the "epidemic of world lawlessness," he called for a quarantine against aggressor nations. The speech stirred up the press and enough critics that Roosevelt dared to go no further. "It's a terrible thing," he said, "to look over your shoulder when you are trying to lead—and to find no one there."[22]

By late 1938, around the time of the Munich conference and the withdrawal of the International Brigades from Spain, Roosevelt recognized he was facing a bad situation. He apparently made a secret overture through personal channels to the French government, offering to ship airplanes to France if they would transship them to Spain. The French rejected the offer. Roosevelt later called his Spanish policy a "great mistake." One of the country's most prominent statesmen, Henry Stimson, former Secretary of State in the Hoover administration, remarked in early 1939, "what a disaster the non-intervention agreement [regarding Spain] had been and how it had played into the hands of the Axis powers."[23] By then, it was too late.

Roosevelt had learned a lesson, and at the end of World War II, in March 1945, just weeks before his death, the president addressed his new ambassador to Spain, Norman Armour:

> Having been helped to power by Fascist Italy and Nazi Germany, and having patterned itself along totalitarian lines, the present regime in Spain is naturally the subject of distrust by a great many American citizens. . . . Most certainly we do not forget Spain's official . . . assistance to our Axis enemies at a time when the fortunes of war were less favorable to us, nor can we disregard the activities, aims, organizations, and public utterances of the Falange. . . . These memories cannot be wiped out by actions more favorable to us now that we are about to achieve our goal of complete victory. . . .[24]

Spain, accordingly, was not admitted into the United Nations in 1945. Two years later, Spain was excluded from participating in the Marshall Plan, the U.S. program to rebuild the economy of Western Europe. During these years, Franco received economic assistance from Argentina. But when this support dried up, Franco looked to the United States. By 1949, as the Cold War became the dominant task of U.S. foreign policy, Washington allowed private banks to extend loans to Spain. In 1950, President Harry Truman authorized additional loans through the Import-Export Bank. And in 1953, President Dwight Eisenhower used executive agreements to bring Franco's Spain into the Cold War alliance, trading military and economic aid for U.S. bases. The Cold War made the anti-communist Franco a firm U.S. ally.

For the Veterans of the Abraham Lincoln Brigade, the anti-communist campaign had begun much earlier. In 1938, Roosevelt authorized the Justice department to investigate subversive activities—by fascists, Nazis, or communists. The FBI promptly opened inquiries into the recruitment of volunteers for the Abraham Lincoln Brigade. In 1940, the FBI raided the veterans' offices in Detroit, Milwaukee, and New York and seized their files.[25] It is easy to dismiss such government harassment as mere hostility to the Communist Party—and surely only a fool would deny that such political prejudices flourished in Washington. But FBI documents reveal an additional motive that must be addressed more seriously. When American volunteers went to Spain, they did so in violation of U.S. neutrality laws and disregarding passports stamped "not valid for travel in Spain."

Only one returning veteran—a man from Brooklyn named Leo Hecht—was jailed for violating that instruction and charges against him were soon dismissed. Significantly, Hecht later became a fixture around the veterans office and then turned up as a hostile witness against the VALB during hearings before the Subversive Activities Control Board in 1954. Some have suggested that in exchange for dropping all charges he became an informer who supplied the FBI with information about the veterans' political activity.

J. Edgar Hoover, head of the FBI, was especially concerned with what happened to U.S. passports *after* the volunteers entered Spain. One field report sent to Hoover in 1942 contained a report regarding "Passports of the International Brigades, Later Used by [Soviet] Agents."[26] "One day," it said, "a batch of about 100 passports arrived [in Moscow], half of them American. They had belonged to dead soldiers. That was a great haul, a cause for celebration." Hoover made a marginal tick next to that passage. His concern about lost, stolen, and abused passports explains the FBI's obsession with identifying the names of all the U.S. volunteers and why, for instance, they raided the VALB offices. It also explains why they later tried to interview all veterans of the Lincoln Brigade, regardless of their political beliefs and affiliations. (Statistically, approximately 70 percent of the U.S. volunteers have been identified as communists.)

The FBI also alerted the State Department to look out for passport applications from persons using the names of former Lincoln volunteers, and "Refusal Notices" were put in the files of such persons. Yet the State Department reported in 1944 that "in not a single instance" had there been "any report . . . indicating that any passport was used by other than the original bearer."[27] This conclusion does not say much about the skill of U.S. authorities. From my interviews with Lincoln veterans, I learned that such abuse had indeed taken place, in small measure, both during the Spanish war and afterward.[28]

Another aspect of the government's obsession with the veterans of the Lincoln Brigade involved their close cooperation with other organizations seeking relief for Spanish refugees and groups working against the Franco regime. Cooperation between veterans and humanitarian organizations like the Joint Anti-Fascist Refugee Committee attracted the attention of government agencies. Although documents released so far are insufficient to draw a full portrait, it's clear that the FBI was concerned about the international nature of refugee aid. Such aid involved meetings and exchanges with known communists around the world as well as the transfer of significant sums of money that were inherent in the refugee aid programs.

This secret struggle between the U.S. government and the veterans existed throughout World War II and *preceded* the anti-communist campaigns associated with congressional committees and Senator Joseph McCarthy. After the German invasion of the Soviet Union in June 1941, the Lincoln veterans, like the Communist Party, demanded U.S. intervention on behalf of the Allies. U.S. officials saw that shift as proof that the veterans were merely disciples of the Soviet Union. Even when the Soviet Union was a fighting ally against the fascist axis, the U.S. military remained suspicious of the veterans of the Lincoln Brigade who volunteered to fight in their second war against fascism. The phrase "premature anti-fascists" served as shorthand for soldiers suspected of disloyalty to the United States (see also Chapter 9).[29]

These post–Spanish Civil War details represent the basic paradigm for understanding the Lincoln Brigade's place in U.S. history. Its legacy was already well-established by the end of World War II. Clearly, the veterans saw themselves as principled anti-fascists. They continued the fight after 1939 by seeking to release Spain's refugees from concentration camps in southern France, aiding political prisoners held by the Franco regime, and supporting clandestinely Spanish Republicans who continued a guerrilla war against the dictatorship. The Lincoln veterans saw World War II as an extension of that war (as did wartime Hollywood movies that addressed the Spanish Civil War, most notably *Casablanca* and *The Fallen Sparrow*), and they expected the fall of Hitler and Mussolini to lead to the fall of Franco. Meanwhile, on the U.S. home front, Lincoln veterans and their supporters worked actively to prevent the admission of Franco's Spain into the United Nations. That is half of the story.

To American anti-communists and the U.S. government, however, whatever the Lincolns did could be reduced to a single word: *Communism!* As the Cold War expanded in 1947, the Lincoln veterans became prime targets. Three groups—the Joint Anti-Fascist Refugee Committee, led by Dr. Edward Barsky; the Abraham Lincoln Brigade; and the Veterans of the Abraham Lincoln Brigade—were among the first in the country subpoenaed by the House Committee on Un-American Activities and placed on the Attorney General's list of subversive organizations. Why were they first? The passport matter was one reason; another was that Director Hoover worried about their professional military training. Their internationalism and contact with foreign officials in aiding Spain also made them suspect for collaborating with foreign agents. Truth be told, some of the veterans *were* involved in such activities. Morris Cohen, the atomic spy, is perhaps the most famous.[30] FBI wiretaps show that others violated U.S. law during World War II to make contact with Spanish guerrilla fighters in Europe. Equally interesting, the FBI files show that many veterans were willing to talk to the FBI, sometimes naming names. It had to be obvious to the FBI that the veterans' political views were not monolithic; some were skeptics, some non-communists, and some anti-communists. Nevertheless, all veterans were painted with the same red brush.

And so finally we come to the matter of history's views of Spain and the International Brigades. U.S. history textbooks of the 1940s and 1950s usually describe Franco's Spain as a fascist dictatorship, linked to Hitler and Mussolini. Charles Beard, in his 1944 history of the United States, summed it up as follows: Roosevelt supported British nonintervention while "fascist rebels were demolishing the Spanish Republic . . . and by doing so he aided, if unwittingly, in the triumph of fascism there."[31] Such ideas were common in the 1940s. But as Cold War politics rehabilitated General Franco, the views of history changed and the amount of space devoted to the Spanish Civil War diminished. Equally important, the war was seen not as a struggle between an elected government and a fascist rebellion but rather as a fight between two totalitarian systems, communism versus fascism, a prelude not to World War II, but to the Cold War.

This second paradigm continues to dominate historical writing in America—not only from the anti-communist scripts that see the Spanish Republic merely as an instrument of Soviet policy—but also from writers like myself who, consciously or not, are obliged to respond to the Cold War narrative in order to restore the historical context in which participants in the Spanish Civil War acted.

In writing about the similarity of several documentary films about the Lincoln Brigade, my colleague Anthony Geist recently observed that the prevailing story is a "response to an unacknowledged master narrative that hovers, unspoken, over all these films, and that is the discourse of the Cold War."[32] Thus the cinematic counter narrative focuses on issues that Cold War–influenced writers have introduced as evidence of communist hypocrisy, opportunism, even subversion, and argues for different interpretations. To use one of Geist's examples, since part of the anti-communist position emphasizes that communists were "un-American," the counter narrative stresses the indigenous nature of U.S. communists and places their story in the framework of particular ethnic or nationality groups. In my own work, for instance, Hy Katz speaks for the many Jewish volunteers who had reason to fight Hitler's allies; Canute Frankson for African Americans; Evelyn Hutchins for women. In addition, the volunteers appear not as Communist Party ideologues, but as independent thinkers who boldly cut against the grain of Roosevelt's neutrality policies. Such works play down the role of the Communist Party or the sectarian splits among leftist groups. Meanwhile, exponents of the Cold War narrative snipe at these works and scrutinize new archival discoveries for proof of communist evil.

I want to suggest, first, that this argument is not going to end soon. Max Planck's statement that a new idea does not convince its opponents but that eventually they die out does not account for intellectual traditions that extend beyond the grave. In fact, I should probably apologize for devoting so much space to this issue because it keeps it alive. On the other hand, I feel obliged to lay out fault lines of the existing history. And I do think that we are heading toward a new paradigm that pays more attention to diverse source materials and that appreciates multiple perspectives. The FBI files about the Lincoln volunteers, for instance, reveal the prejudices of both the federal investigators and the subjects of investigation. When a "Negro" man danced with a white woman at a Lincoln Brigade party, the FBI saw subversion (which, of course, it was, given the times) but the agents' concern about misused passports cannot be dismissed as mere bigotry. Nor can we deny that some members and veterans of the International Brigades acted as informants and spies to assist the interests of the Soviet Union. Contrary to several works of fiction and nonfiction written by Lincoln veterans, the soldiers sang not "The Star Spangled Banner" on Hill 666, but rather "The Internationale."[33] It does no good to conceal the past.

I believe, moreover, that new paradigms will move away from the national histories of the brigades and address issues of internationalism. Among U.S. volunteers, for instance, a significant number—at least 300—have Spanish surnames, indicating direct ties to Spain and Latin

America, regardless of ideology. Puerto Rican, Cuban, and Filipino volunteers had reasons for going to Spain without reference to party politics; so did the Jewish men and women who seem to have traveled disproportionately from many parts of the world. The history of the war also needs to address the diaspora of Spaniards after Franco's victory and their resistance to fascism during and after World War II. The Spanish Civil War is broader than its national boundaries.

In addition to the military narrative that focuses on soldiers, battles, and casualties, I believe it is essential to examine the "home fronts," both within Spain and in countries that responded to the Franco rebellion. In the United States, for instance, there is evidence that citizens of various persuasions participated in activities to aid the Republic or petitioned Washington to support their favored side. We know, too, that some communities, especially the Spanish immigrant groups or multi-ethnic cities like New York, were severely divided in their opinions. We know that Spain mobilized opinion throughout the Americas and served to break through the narcotic of isolationism.[34] The effect of Spain on the public consciousness throughout the world of the 1930s is critical for understanding the idealism that drove support for the big war against fascism that soon followed—even though we know that whatever the Allied commitment to internationalism was, finally, in 1945, the great powers turned their backs on Spain.

The story that remains to be told and may establish a foundation for a new paradigm involves matters that today we call human rights. Paul Preston's pathbreaking book, *The Spanish Holocaust,* focuses on internal Spanish politics in those terms.[35] We must remember that not only soldiers went to Spain to save the Republic, but also medical professionals, social workers, and humanitarians. Dr. Leonard Crome, a British doctor in Spain and in World War II, is honored by an annual lecture, which provided the opportunity for this paper. Similarly, no American volunteer showed greater heroism than Dr. Edward Barsky, who founded the American Medical Bureau to Aid Spanish Democracy, served as a frontline surgeon and a rearguard fundraiser for the Republic, and headed the postwar Joint Anti-Fascist Refugee Committee. For these efforts, he was thanked by the government with a one-year jail sentence and loss of his medical license because he refused to turn over the names of donors and recipients of humanitarian aid that, he knew, would find their way into Franco's hands.[36]

Doctors Crome and Barsky were two of thousands of world citizens who responded to the horrors of civilian bombings and forced migration of refugees, the killing of the innocent, and the sheer terror of war, by volunteering as health workers, reporters, and good Samaritans. Others stayed home and raised funds to purchase medicine, condensed milk for children, or ambulances, or wrote letters to newspapers and pleaded with politicians to intervene, warning that Spain foreshadowed a world war, and implicitly predicting what we understand today as the worst genocide of the twentieth century. Spain was the beacon ignored, the lesson unlearned by leaders of so-called democracies but not ignored or forgotten by millions of their constituents.

When at last Roosevelt and Churchill came to talk about their principles and ideals in the Atlantic Charter of 1940, they expressed the importance of people's right to self-determination and enunciated their commitment that "after the final destruction of the Nazi tyranny," they hoped to see "a peace which will afford to all nations the means of dwelling in safety within their own boundaries, and which will afford assurance that all the men in all the lands may live out their lives in freedom from fear and want."[37] The Four Freedoms laid the basis of the postwar United Nations and the Declaration of Human Rights for each and every one of us. They did not anticipate how a cold war would create everlasting uncertainties of nuclear annihilation and strategic bombings of helpless populations. We've lived to see the tragedies of Spain repeated until they seem normal.

For all the squabbling about interpreting the Spanish Civil War, however, what is undeniable is the enduring interest in that conflict. Picasso's *Guernica* immortalizes a tragedy that lives on in the twenty-first century. When the United States won the votes in the United Nations Security Council to invade Iraq in 2003, the diplomats took pains to cover up the nearby tapestry of that painting, fearing, justifiably, that the horrors of Spain would haunt their endeavors. The aerial bombing of civilians no longer troubles the universe, as it did three-quarters of a century ago in 1937. Nor does the never-ending flow of civilians from the ravages of war stop the wars. We have become inured to those terrors. But it was not always so. Every generation writes its own history because it struggles to understand its worst fears and its failures.

PART I

The American Volunteers

▷ **CHAPTER 2**

Facing Fascism

New York and the Spanish Civil War

As Chair of the Abraham Lincoln Brigade Archives, I had opportunities to collaborate on two archival exhibitions, one of Spanish Civil War posters, the other displaying children's drawings in wartime from the Spanish Civil War to Kosovo. Both were supported by grants from the Puffin Foundation, led by Perry Rosenstein. He called one day to ask if I might be interested in proposing a larger exhibition for the Museum of the City of New York, based on the ALBA holdings. The result, thanks to the enthusiastic response of MCNY's Susan Henshaw Jones and Sarah Henry, was a long-running exhibition titled Facing Fascism: New York and the Spanish Civil War. *I edited the accompanying catalogue with James D. Fernandéz and wrote the introduction to an anthology of fresh research about the response to the Spanish Civil War in the United States. The new material offered insight into ethnic and class divisions in New York and around the country and suggested that the Spanish conflict awakened the nation from the balm of isolationism to the threat of international fascism.*

▷ The opening of the Empire State Building, then the world's tallest structure, on May 1, 1931, embodied New York City's self-image as an international metropolis. Since earning huge profits during the Great War, Wall Street could justly claim to dominate global capitalism. Nevertheless, the Crash that toppled the stock market in 1929 and the ensuing economic stagnation meant that the giant tower on Thirty-Fourth Street and Fifth Avenue would remain half occupied for years. Hollywood's 1933 thriller, *King Kong,* opened with scenes of frightened people waiting on a city breadline for a meal and ended by showing imperial pretension falling apart as the exotic gorilla smashed the upper floors of the metropolis's crown jewel.

At street level, unemployment reached 25 percent, and thousands pounded the pavement looking for work or charitable assistance or scraps to eat. In 1932, weekly family relief allowances in New York City fell to $2.39, but that measly sum reached only half the eligible households. Without money for rent, evicted families could be seen standing on sidewalks surrounded by all their worldly goods. White-collar businessmen sold apples on street corners for a nickel apiece.[1] Such scenes—and worse—appeared throughout the cities of the nation and around the world. Amid raging poverty, most New Yorkers could not afford a global view of their afflictions.

International politics were less easily ignored. The same Depression that brought the election of New York governor Franklin D. Roosevelt to the presidency in 1933 also pushed the Nazi Adolf Hitler into power in Germany. Both promised economic recovery: Roosevelt spoke of a "New Deal" to save capitalism and make jobs; Hitler talked about military rearmament and international expansion. Meanwhile, in Asia, Japan sought economic stability through an East Asia Co-Prosperity Sphere that began with the invasion of China's Manchurian peninsula in 1931 and, six years later, the mainland. In Italy, Benito Mussolini, "Il Duce," pounded his chest like Kong and summoned the restoration of the Roman Empire by attacking Abyssinia and Ethiopia in 1935.

Other imperial nations of Europe—the so-called Allies of the Great War—held similar claims. Great Britain's empire stretched from Singapore and Hong Kong to India, South Africa, and Jamaica in the West Indies; France continued to rule in North Africa (Algeria, Morocco, Tunisia), Indochina (Laos, Cambodia, Vietnam), and the Caribbean sugar islands of St. Pierre and Martinique. Neither power, bled white by the world war, wanted to provoke another conflict. Instead, they adopted policies of appeasement toward the aggressive fascist leaders, Mussolini and Hitler.

By contrast, Roosevelt's America played second fiddle. Having rescued the Allies during the world war, the public recoiled from foreign politics, rejected participation in the League of Nations and the World Court, and adopted "neutrality" laws to prevent even inadvertent involvement with Europe's struggles. Instead, Washington attempted to alleviate the Depression by arranging trade agreements with other countries and extending diplomatic recognition to another second-class power, the Soviet Union, led by the communist dictator Josef Stalin. Both governments hoped that better relations would encourage business and improve their domestic economies.

The outbreak of the Spanish Civil War brought into sharp relief these global configurations. Spain's Republican government had endured explosive political competition since its creation in 1931. On one side, conservatives protected the power of the Roman Catholic church, the army, the aristocracy, and the great landowners, while republicans joined socialists in seeking reforms, such as ending the church's control of education and allowing voting rights for women and civil marriages, and more radical demands such as distributing land to the peasants. In February 1936, a coalition of left-liberal groups, the Popular Front, including the small Communist Party, won a bitterly fought election. Immediately, a cadre of army officers led by General Francisco Franco and backed by church leaders and wealthy landowners began to plot a military rebellion. The uprising began in Spain on July 18, 1936.[2]

In the first days of fighting, the rebels met stiff resistance in Spain's major cities from loyal members of the army and from militia groups formed by labor unions and political parties. Elected officials believed the insurgents would soon quit. But Franco's pleas for assistance had reached friendly ears in Berlin and Rome. Within a week, Germany and Italy sent military aid, particularly aircraft to ferry Franco's African troops (including Muslim mercenaries) to southern Spain. As the rebels marched toward Madrid, leaving a trail of destruction and death, the legal government pleaded with other nations for assistance.

Britain and France answered with a policy of non-intervention, demanding that other countries stay out of the conflict. Germany and Italy agreed to these proposals, and even participated in a Non-Intervention Committee, though both countries openly violated the agreements. Other nations understood this deception and made no changes of policy. The bombing of the Basque town of Guernica by German aircraft—immortalized in Pablo Picasso's famous painting that hung for decades in New York's Museum of Modern Art—prompted no retaliation.

Despite intense diplomatic jockeying about the Spanish Civil War, the United States and the Soviet Union played minor roles on the international stage. Although many scholars writing after World War II and the Cold War have emphasized the conflict between democratic and communist ideology, it is important to remember that, before 1945, both

Roosevelt and Stalin saw their primary enemy as fascist expansion and both directed their policies to protect their national interests. Both leaders wished they could influence the outcome of the Spanish conflict, but neither government had sufficient resources to contribute definitively and, in the end, neither perceived a major national interest in the result.

Aware of German and Italian support for the Franco rebellion, Stalin understood the importance of preserving Spain as an anti-fascist nation and began to sell military supplies to the Republic in September 1936. The communist leader also understood that Great Britain viewed such transactions as a threat to European stability and considered Soviet aid a justification for maintaining the non-intervention policy, to the detriment of the Republic. In any case, the Soviet Union, geographically distant and rebuilding its own armies, offered limited assistance. That Stalin did any business with the Spanish Republic nevertheless had vast symbolic power. The presence of Soviet military advisors and Soviet-built equipment increased the prestige and power of the Spanish Communist Party, enabling Stalinist agents to crush rival anarchist and social revolutionary parties. Outside Spain, Soviet involvement reinforced conservative fears and justified anti-Republican policies.[3]

Suspicion of the Spanish Republic permeated U.S. politics and crystallized debate in big cities like New York. Roosevelt had built his New Deal coalition on the votes of northern urbanites with roots in the white ethnic working class. Facing reelection in November 1936, ten weeks after the civil war began, Roosevelt's Democratic majority strongly opposed support for the left-leaning Spanish Republic. New York's Catholics remained sympathetic to Franco and hostile to socialists and communists. Indeed, as soon as the civil war began, the Catholic leadership opened an editorial barrage against the Republic's "villainous anti-Catholic government."[4]

Although the president's personal sympathy lay with the Spanish Republic, he lacked sufficient political support to challenge what he called "isolationist" sentiment. In January 1937, Congress extended the neutrality laws to include the Spanish conflict. Roosevelt's State Department issued a ban on travel to Spain by U.S. citizens. Such policies provided no assistance to the legal Spanish government, while Washington permitted some corporations, such as Texaco, to sell supplies to Franco on credit.

Meanwhile, the Moscow-based Communist International called upon individual volunteers to assist the Republic. The first members of the International Brigades arrived in Spain in November 1936, just in time to thwart Franco's capture of Madrid, thereby prolonging the war. In the end, some 35,000 men and women from over fifty countries found their way to Spain and served either as soldiers or as support personnel behind the lines. Among these volunteers, nearly 3,000 civilians went to Spain from the United States.

Congressional law could not prevent the clandestine recruitment of Americans eager to enter the fight. During the first week of November 1936, three Communist Party functionaries met in a small office in lower Manhattan to discuss the formation of a U.S. International Brigade. "Here was one nation standing up against the fascist dictators," recalled one of the three men, Ed Bender, in the accented voice of an immigrant from the Ukraine. "I felt honored to be asked. I felt that was something specific I could do in the fight against fascism in Spain."[5]

Word of the new brigade spread among the city's rank and file communists, who composed the first group of 86 volunteers to sail for Spain aboard the *Normandie* on December 26, 1936. By the spring of 1937, recruiters had attracted about 2,000 men, enough to form two battalions in Spain; more would follow. (The first group named their unit the Abraham Lincoln Battalion after the president who also defended the legally elected government during a civil war.) By then, the ranks had opened to non-communists—socialists, liberals, idealists—who would constitute about one-third of the Americans who joined the fight. Others served as clerks, social workers, and drivers. Collectively, they were known as the Abraham Lincoln Brigade.

Lincoln volunteers came from nearly every state, but overwhelmingly from the nation's big cities, particularly from New York, from whose port nearly all departed for Europe. Some, such as Brooklyn College English instructor David McKelvy White, were the sons of the well-born; his father had been governor of Ohio. Most were children of the immigrant generation—Irish, Jewish, Italians, Slavs, Greeks (over 70 European nationalities were represented in the ranks)—whose families had flocked to New York at the beginning of the century. For the many Jewish volunteers, Spain provided an opportunity to fight against the persecutors of their people in Europe.

The cause of Spain also appealed to a range of cultural progressives. Among the volunteers were Greenwich Village painters like Douglas Taylor and Deyo Jacobs; poets and writers like Edwin Rolfe and Alvah Bessie; students from City College, NYU, Columbia, or, more likely, the school of hard knocks. There were labor organizers, taxi drivers, and cooks, like the Japanese American Jack Shirai, and scads of "unemployed." Nearly ninety were African Americans: as Harlem resident Vaughn Love explained, "I'd read Hitler's book, knew about the Nuremberg laws, and I knew if the Jews weren't going to be allowed to live, then certainly I knew the Negroes would not escape."[6]

The volunteers weren't exactly young, either: their median age was 28. They knew what the fight was about; they saw what fascism was doing in Germany and Italy; what it threatened to do in Austria, Czechoslovakia, and Poland; what it had started in Spain. To be sure, most of the men and women who sailed from New York knew nothing about Spain, but that word—"Spain"—embodied the most passionate political cause of the decade, something for which men and women would risk their lives.

Nearly 800 of the U.S. volunteers died for the ideal of Spanish democracy. Of them, wrote Ernest Hemingway in 1939, "no men entered earth more honorably than those who died in Spain."[7] One month after those words appeared in the New York–based journal *New Masses*, Franco's troops finally entered Madrid, ending the war, and establishing a cruel dictatorship that tormented anti-fascists for three-and-a-half decades.

Those New York volunteers of the Abraham Lincoln Brigade are the most poignant example of the city's intense involvement in the Spanish Civil War. But these soldiers were by no means the only New Yorkers drawn to defend and assist Spain's elected government. While there was some support for the Francoist rebels in the city, during the Spanish war a powerful anti-fascist coalition emerged in New York, spanning both the Communist and Socialist parties; liberal small-d democrats; and the diverse ethnic communities, including the city's small, but vocal Spanish immigrant groups. Moved by images of the war's violence—the bombing of civilians by Nazi and Italian air forces—New Yorkers carried collection cans into the subways, spread blankets on sidewalks, sang Spanish songs, or organized soccer matches and basketball games to raise funds for Spain. In all the boroughs, labor unions, Spanish affinity groups, ethnic conclaves, and humanitarian aid organizations contributed money and material aid. The nascent field of photojournalism—the weekly magazine *Life* was born in 1936—brought gruesome images of the war right into the homes of New Yorkers, and in this pre-television era, the distant conflagration was experienced with unprecedented immediacy in the city.[8]

New York's artists, writers, and performers explored the war with intensity and often worked to support the embattled republic. And as casualties of the Spanish Civil War mounted, Dr. Edward Barsky, a surgeon at Beth Israel Hospital, organized the American Medical Bureau to Aid Spanish Democracy and led the first delegation of U.S. medical personnel to assist soldiers and civilians alike. Among the recruits were nurses and medical technicians from the city's hospitals, many from Jewish and Italian immigrant families, as well as Salaria Kea, an African American nurse at Harlem Hospital. Their efforts to save lives in Spain appeared frequently in news and feature articles in the New York press.

Four decades of Cold War rhetoric—a perspective that portrayed modern history as an epic struggle between communism and liberal democracy—have all but erased the complexities and nuances of the years leading up to World War II, the decisions and deeds of ordinary New Yorkers in the midst of the most profound crisis of the twentieth century. *Facing Fascism*, the Museum of the City of New York's exhibition (2007–2008), attempted to recover through archival research a sense of the lived experience of those New Yorkers who, with a mixture of trepidation and courage, saw the gathering storm on the horizon—the rise of fascism—and, in accordance with the dictates of conscience, and to the best of their abilities, chose to take action.

▷ **CHAPTER 3**

American Women in the Spanish Civil War

A Prologue

Most history written about war focuses on political issues and military actions, matters of ideology, the causes and consequences of international conflicts. By contrast, the core of the ALBA archival collections contains large quantities of personal documents: letters written to and from the volunteers, memoirs and oral history, diaries, journals, and biographical sketches. Looking at the Spanish Civil War from the perspective of ordinary people underscores their passions and commitment that explain why North Americans would venture to fight in a foreign civil war. That shift in focus from military history to personal motivation encouraged the documentary filmmaker Julia Newman to create a film about the U.S. women who served in Spain, mostly as medical personnel. She invited me to write the sample chapter for a catalogue that would accompany her work, "Into the Fire" *(2002). The written project got no further; this piece is published here for the first time.*

▷ One afternoon in December 1936, a month after President Franklin D. Roosevelt won his second landslide election to become president of the United States, one of the beneficiaries of his New Deal program was standing on a ladder in a Treasury Department building in New York when she was summoned to the telephone. Her name was Mildred Rackley. She was a slender, dark-eyed, 30-year-old painter from New Mexico and was holding a pencil or piece of charcoal in her hand when she went to the phone. She was no longer the naïve rebel from New Mexico who had first visited the metropolis on her way to Europe in 1930. Then a young bride; a veritable Daughter of the American Revolution; and an educated, aspiring painter, she had since witnessed the violence that disrupted the civility of Europe's cities, and it had changed her view of the world.

She knew the telephone call had to be important, especially when she recognized the deep voice of one of New York's premier surgeons,

Mildred Rackley, pointing to a bullet hole in an ambulance, indicating that the enemy consistently attacked non-military targets. The vehicle was donated by the International Workers Order, part of a humanitarian aid project to support the elected Spanish government. (Author's collection.)

Dr. Edward Barsky. They had met a few years earlier through a mutual friend who had encouraged the now-divorced artist to leave the painter's colony in Taos for the big city. Indeed, she and the charismatic Barsky knew each other well, pleased not only by intimate attachments but by a shared political view as well. They were, in the precise meaning of the word, not lovers, but comrades. Their passion for each other equaled a passion for people, for society as a whole, and especially for those who were suffering during the worst depression in the country's history. Unemployment rates had soared to 25 percent, and despite Roosevelt's bold language, homeless people still starved on the streets of New York. "Seeing so much injustice, seeing so much poverty," said Mildred many years later, "well. . . ." She collected her thoughts. "It was a time when you can't see these things happening and say 'la-de-dah.'"[1]

So even before Dr. Barsky put the question to her, she had a hunch about what was on his mind. And when he asked if she would like to accompany him to Spain in a few weeks to work as his secretary-translator, she never hesitated.

With that split-second decision, Mildred Rackley was going to war. She would become a worker for the American Medical Bureau to Aid Spanish Democracy, a newly formed volunteer organization whose cumbersome title meant exactly what it said. She would become a civilian-soldier, not necessarily carrying weapons of war but fighting with all her might to save the Spanish Republic from a military coup led by General Francisco Franco and supported by his fascist allies Adolf Hitler and Benito Mussolini. She would literally put her life on the line for a principle, to defend democracy from its militaristic enemies.

Rackley was not the only American citizen who resolved that winter to assist the embattled Spanish Republic. Most volunteers were young men who offered to fight in the International Brigades. By February 1937, nearly 500 civilians had sailed from the United States to Spain. There they formed the Abraham Lincoln Battalion, the American contingent of the International Brigades. They soon experienced their baptism under fire in the Jarama Valley near Madrid and many became the first casualties to be treated by Dr. Barsky and the nurses who accompanied his medical mission. Those soldiers and nurses—fewer than 3,000 of the U.S.'s 130 million citizens—forged a bond that knit them together for the rest of their lives. Whatever their duties in Spain, they would all consider themselves part of the Abraham Lincoln Brigade.

One month after the battle of Jarama, Salaria Kea—"a slender chocolate-colored girl," as the poet Langston Hughes described her—who worked as a maternity ward nurse in Harlem Hospital stood before a bulletin board reading notices that requested community medical volunteers. That week, the Ohio River had overflowed its banks, flooding Kentucky. The Red Cross put out a call for emergency medical assistance. Kea had been raised in nearby Akron and was moved to volunteer her services.[2] But when she contacted the Red Cross recruiter, she remembered, "they told me they had no place for me—that the color of my skin would make me more trouble than I'd be worth to them."[3] Utterly abashed, she repeated the story to one of her friends, who replied: "Why not Spain?" So Kea went back to the bulletin board, found a tiny card in the corner asking for help, and soon was preparing to sail for Spain.

"What!" exclaimed her friends in Harlem. "You're going to Spain in wartime. And alone?"

"Sure," she replied. "I wasn't born twins. I have to go alone."[4]

Esther Miriam Silverstein was working for the U.S. Public Health Service's Marine Hospital in San Francisco when she decided to embark alone for Spain. Most of her patients were sailors, with a strong working-class identity and an awareness of the fascist threat to peace. As General Franco led four columns of troops from southern Spain toward Madrid in the fall of 1936, the sailors on her ward taped a map on the wall and inserted pins each day to follow the course of the impending battle for Spain's capital city. By November, the rebel generals were predicting that a "fifth column" would emerge inside Madrid—traitors to the Republic—who would support the insurrection and bring victory in a few weeks. Spain's proud Communist leader, Dolores Ibarruri, rallied civilian resistance with the cry "No Pasaran!" ("They shall not pass!"). "It is better," she exhorted, "to die on your feet than to live on your knees."

Esther Silverstein (Blanc), flanked by two doctors in Spain, was a Public Health Service nurse in San Francisco before going to Spain in 1937. (Author's collection.)

The world held its breath and watched. "Spain was all everyone talked about," Silverstein recalled.[5]

As Franco launched the attack on Madrid, the citizen militia fought back. Young men on motorcycles rushed light arms to the front, and miners from Asturias used dynamite to halt the invading tanks. Then, on November 7, 1936, the first contingent of 2,000 international volunteers from Germany arrived in Madrid, marching in corduroy uniforms and steel helmets down the Gran Via, the city's prominent boulevard, as citizens cheered and shouted greetings. To everyone's surprise, the city held. Franco's armies even entered the university grounds on the edge of Madrid, but could not penetrate the hastily constructed street barriers.

In San Francisco, a desperately ill woman was wheeled unconscious into Esther Silverstein's ward. She remained asleep in a fever for a full day, then awoke abruptly.

"Has Madrid fallen?" she asked.

"No," the nurse replied.

"Are you sure?"

"Yes."

The woman fell asleep for another day.

Such drama inspired Esther Silverstein to act. At the beginning of 1937 she contacted a group called Medical Aid for Spanish Democracy in San Francisco and started the screening process to become a volunteer in Spain. She had to undergo a physical examination as well as psychological tests and a personal interview to rule out the possibility that she was an "adventuress." By the end of April, she had resigned her job and headed for New York to join a contingent of medical personnel. "The boys politicized me," she later told an interviewer, referring to the atmosphere on her ward. "They were fighting to make things better and they had a philosophy to back them up. That made sense to me."

Mildred Rackley, Salaria Kea, Esther Silverstein: What prompted these American women to leave behind the safety of their homes to join a war? Yes, as we have seen, they made individual choices. Yes, chance or luck played its part: they were women in a certain place at a certain time. But they were also part of their times, part of their country's political awakening to the threat of fascism in the 1930s. That they stepped outside the conventional roles available to most women suggests the urgency of the moment and the courage of their convictions that enabled them, that forced them, perhaps, to take a stand.

During the 33 months that the Spanish people engaged in a brutal civil war—from July 18, 1936, when General Francisco Franco led the army rebellion against the elected republic until March 31, 1939, when his troops finally marched triumphantly into the capital of Madrid—about 75 American women traveled to that embattled country to stand with the Republic. These included 46 nurses, five laboratory technicians, five other medical personnel, two administrators, one physician, and one truck driver. Others served as cooks, clerical workers, or social workers. They ranged from 21 years of age to 49, with a median age of about 26. Most were single, widowed, or divorced; a few went to Spain to be near other relatives. None of them were killed in Spain, though two were seriously wounded.[6] And they learned to live with death, to the extent that anyone, even trained nurses, can learn from such an immersion. Bullets, bombs, and hot shrapnel came too close for comfort, and all the women knew men who fought in the Lincoln Brigade who would remain forever buried in Spanish earth.

The volunteers in Spain were not fresh-faced kids looking for a kick, but women of experience. Yet, most of what they knew about war had been gleaned from weekly newsreels at the movies. They had no idea of what mechanized war meant. None had known the terror caused by a bomb screaming from the skies. Most of them had volunteered for service in Spain before such images became familiar to the world, before Pablo Picasso painted the most famous painting of the twentieth century, *Guernica,* which depicted, among other horrifying images, the shriek of a woman caught in a nightmare of fear. None of the nurses had ever treated the violent wounds of war—intestines ripped to shreds by machine gun bullets; heads split by sniper shots; tibias, femurs, and jaw bones shattered by bombs that blew shrapnel fifty feet into the air. But for days and weeks and months, such facts became part of their everyday experience.

They knew nothing of the horror they would face when they enlisted in what they considered a people's crusade, "the good fight," the battle against fascism. But they did know what they believed in. For one thing, more than half of the women volunteers were Jewish, many of them the children of immigrants who came to the United States around 1900. "I knew why I volunteered for Spain," Esther Silverstein told an interviewer. "First, I had followed the whole issue of the Jewish Question in Germany from its inception. . . . I knew very well about the persecution and what was happening in Europe; second, I was a committed anti-fascist, as was every Jew I knew; third, I was a Communist—that is, I believed in the idea of socialism."[7] Despite Hitler's claims, of course, not all Jews were Communists or vice versa, but Jews and Communists in America did share a clear understanding of what Hitler meant for their relatives and comrades, indeed for themselves. Historians estimate that Jews comprised one-third of the American volunteers who formed the Lincoln Brigade to fight against fascism in Spain; two-thirds were Communists. Most simply defined themselves as "anti-fascists." In the ranks of the other foreign volunteers who journeyed to Spain from 52 countries to join the International Brigades, Jews constituted a disproportionate number. As Esther Silverstein said, they knew exactly what Hitler intended to do. Spain gave them an opportunity to fight back.

Hitler came to power in Germany in January 1933, five weeks before Roosevelt's first inauguration. Both leaders achieved their political success because of the exigencies of the Great Depression. The unemployment, starvation, and homelessness that Mildred Rackley witnessed, matched by the failure of Herbert Hoover's administration to discover a remedy for the "hard times," ensured the electoral victory of the Democratic Roosevelt. He promptly told the nervous citizenry that "the only thing we have to fear is fear itself." He then initiated a New Deal agenda to restructure the nation's financial system, codify industrial relations, and help organized labor unions represent the interests of workers. Roosevelt also created the famous alphabet soup of relief agencies (WPA, PWA, FERA, CCC) that put able-bodied, unemployed people like Mildred Rackley to work.

The Nazi leaders in Germany also promised remedies for the Depression. First, Hitler identified the "causes" of the economic catastrophe as Germany's "enemies": Jews, trade unionists, and Communists. For Germany to recover its prosperity, he said, these people had to be eliminated, and they became the first prisoners of the infamous Nazi concentration camps. He proceeded to find work for the unemployed by rearming the German military. In 1935 goose-stepping German soldiers marched into the de-militarized Rhineland. Such violations of the Versailles treaty of 1919 might have provoked Allied opposition. But England and France feared another war and instead adopted a policy of appeasement, hoping that by consenting to Hitler's demands they could preserve the shaky peace in Europe.

Roosevelt, for his part, followed the Allied lead. Convinced that the United States had been tricked into the world war in 1917 by a coalition of bankers, industrialists, and idealists like Woodrow Wilson, a strong group of anti-interventionists demanded that the country keep out of European wars. The United States did not even belong to the League of Nations. Instead of demanding German accountability, therefore, Congress passed a series of neutrality acts that obliged the president to avoid alliances with warring countries. When the Spanish Civil War began in 1936, Roosevelt endorsed a policy of non-intervention. Although the legally elected Spanish Republic normally would have received U.S. aid, Washington avoided any commitments. The State Department prohibited trade with either side (but allowed Texaco to sell petroleum to Franco's army—on credit) and prohibited civilian travel to the embattled country.

Most Americans supported the policies of their leaders and supported neutrality. But some refused to watch passively as Franco, Mussolini, and Hitler attacked the elected Spanish government. As the Soviet Union began to ship urgently needed military aid to the Republic in September 1936, the Communist International called for volunteers. Thirty-five thousand individuals from every corner of the world responded to that plea and formed the International Brigades. Among them were nearly 3,000 men and women from the United States. Their personal motives were always individualistic, yet they shared a deep fear of and hostility to fascism on the march. They resolved to stand fast in Spain.

Mildred Rackley had been to Spain before. When Dr. Barsky invited her to join his staff in setting up a hospital, she knew the trip would be no sightseeing adventure. She had seen the face of fascism during her first trip to Europe six years earlier. In Hamburg, where she had enrolled in art school to study drawing and painting, Rackley had heard the pounding of brown-shirted men in boots who stormed down the cobblestone streets, chanting, singing, brushing people aside. She had heard the tinkle of shattered glass, the groan of people caught beneath the boots. "It scared the life out of us," she recalled.

Rackley had opened her eyes in Europe, seen the ugly Nazi politics in their inception, and felt the sting of her own poverty. She wanted to get out of Germany and began to travel. She visited museums and churches in Switzerland, Yugoslavia, and Venice, finally landing on New Year's Day 1932 on the island of Mallorca. She and her husband expected to support themselves as painters, perhaps selling portraits to the affluent tourists who idled on the beaches and swam in the blue Mediterranean. It was a fine Bohemian vision, befitting a brave independent woman, one which she would later pursue alone.

In Mallorca, she encountered another kind of traveler, the sort that would become increasingly familiar during the 1930s as the brown shirts and black shirts in Germany, Italy, and Austria persuaded good, decent people—artists, writers, and professors; trade unionists, communists, and Jews—to seek sanctuary in other countries. In Spain, ironically the land that in 1492 had forced all Jews to convert to Catholicism or abandon their homeland, Rackley discovered an unexpected cosmopolitanism as Europe's exiles arrived in Mallorca to rebuild their lives. Here, she met the German dramatist Ernst Toller and became his translator. To talk about art, literature, and politics assumed a special vibrancy.

Spain during the 1930s was experiencing a new and unprecedented freedom, something the young American came to love. Having existed for centuries under a monarchy, the Spanish people had rebelled and installed an elected government in 1931. Spain's politics remained a quagmire of rivalry and hatred. The core of the Third Republic (the first two were failures of the previous century) rested with the middle classes, who supported political rights for all citizens. The new regime initiated basic reforms. For the first time, Spanish women gained the right to vote and to divorce their husbands. Other political reforms brought an end to the Catholic Church's monopoly of the country's education system. The Republic, in other words, tried to end Spain's ties to its feudal past by introducing democratic changes. To a younger generation, the country was finally entering the modern world. They welcomed a new spirit of modernism in art, poetry, music, and literature.

These moderate or liberal reforms satisfied the urban middle classes, but aroused the anger and opposition of other groups. Among Spain's political conservatives, three groups still exerted great influence: the aristocracy of large landholders, the Church, and the military. All three objected to the republican reforms, believing, correctly, that political democracy would weaken their power and undermine their wealth. They also objected to other signs of cultural modernism—the wrenching social dramas of Federico Garcia Lorca, for example, or the startling abstract paintings of Pablo Picasso. The conservative press never accepted the triumph of republicanism. Nor did the army, whose privileged officer corps remained loyal only to itself. The threat of a military coup remained a serious and omnipresent possibility.

Meanwhile, the poorer classes—workers in the cities of Barcelona and Madrid and peasants on the great estates—as well as Spain's intellectuals welcomed the political reforms and demanded even greater changes. Many who identified themselves as anarchists, socialists, or republicans desired to end the power of the unelected groups—aristocrats, army officers, and clerics who opposed even the idea of democracy. Some radical groups urged the government to confiscate the large estates and redistribute the land to the peasants. Others wanted to dismantle the capitalist system and allow the workers to assume the control and profits of business.

Such fundamental conflicts created a volatile mix. Violence flared in the streets. Political leaders were assassinated. In 1934, the miners in northern Asturias organized a major strike; the government responded by ordering the army, under General Franco, to crush the workers brutally. The economic hardships of the world depression fueled political anger everywhere in Spain.

The island resorts at Mallorca were not spared intense debate. "It was the beginning of the Republic," Mildred Rackley remembered of her arrival, "and every political party had its own favorite café" where the discussions went on late into the night. She remembered respectable people making fun of passing priests or spitting in their direction. Others spoke of building a "new society" where all people could be equal and free. "It was really just stimulating," she said.

It was that spirit of liberation that prompted Rackley to leave her husband and then, without means of support, to return to America. She was not the naïve student who had left home four years earlier, as can be seen by the story she told, at the age of 85, when she recounted her expedition home. From Spain, she carried two books—James Joyce's *Ulysses* and D. H. Lawrence's *Lady Chatterley's Lover*—which she read on the voyage. And then she committed what she called "a daring act" by smuggling the banned books past the customs officers in New York. "Daring," she said, "because, after all, it was against the law." She later presented the books to her traditional, but sympathetic mother in New Mexico, who read them without comment and then, slightly embarrassed, burned them in the fireplace. It was, said the mature Rackley of her audacity, "the revolt of youth against parents and nonsense."

She did not stay long in New Mexico. A handsome young man from New York induced her to move with him to the nation's cultural metropolis to pursue an artist's career. In depression times, jobs were few, but her new friends helped Rackley find secretarial work, which paid for food and rent. She continued to paint. When she wanted to learn silk screening, she organized a group to rent a loft and employ an artist to teach them how. Sometimes they chipped in to hire a model. She preferred city scenes to portraits, but whatever her subject or medium, she loved the vitality of the artists' community, where art and ideas mattered. "It was like being on a champagne high day and night," she said.

In this community of young artists and intellectuals, Rackley imbibed the culture of left-wing politics. Perhaps it was the friends she made in New York that led her in that direction. But late in life, she avowed a clear continuity between her mature political views and the lessons she learned as a girl in the dry lands of New Mexico. Her family owned a ranch near the town of Las Vegas, not far from where she was born in 1906 in Carlsbad, a region in which a majority of the population was Mexican. Her father treated the Mexicans with contempt and his daughter remembered hating him for it. Her mother was more liberal, the descendant of a pioneer Texas family and an early suffragist who became the president of the local League of Women Voters. As a member of the Daughters of the American Revolution, Rackley recalled feeling ashamed of the organization's reactionary views about race. She and her mother resigned together in protest.

The daughter also found an independent path by taking up art studies in Taos, a center of the cultural avant-garde in the 1920s that attracted Mabel Luhan Dodge, D. H. Lawrence, and many painters, including Walter Ufer, who became Rackley's mentor. When Ufer asked if she ever read the leftish magazine *The Nation,* she said that was "the beginning of my awareness that there was anything besides a Democrat or a Republican." Those kinds of conversations whetted her appetite for cosmopolitan experiences, but also confirmed her sympathy for the underdog.

Her friends in New York reinforced those sentiments. She read left-wing magazines like *New Masses* and the Communist Party's newspaper, *The Daily Worker.* She attended art classes at the Workers' School, and studied painting with the famous German revolutionary artist George Grosz. Meanwhile, to support herself, she landed a job as an editor for a book publisher, and she continued to make contacts with other progressive writers and artists. She liked the company of other creative spirits, such as the filmmaker Herbert Kline, the journalist Joseph North, and the surgeon Edward Barsky.

She was still looking for something to do, something that would be both personally satisfying and socially worthwhile. One afternoon, on impulse, she marched into the Union Square office of Earl Browder, head of the U.S. Communist Party, and volunteered to help organize the farm workers in New Mexico on her impending summer trip home. That she knew nothing about organizing or farm workers didn't faze her then. Fifty years later, she admitted, "You can't get any more naïve than that."

Still, after working on the family ranch for the summer, she journeyed to San Francisco, which had just experienced a citywide general strike. It was, perhaps, the most politically radical city in the country. She found a job in a bookstore, did some sketching, and joined the Communist Party. She did not stay there long. Her New York friends telegraphed that there was a new organization forming called the League Against War and Fascism and that they needed editors and secretarial help for their monthly magazine *Fight*. Mildred Rackley took the first train east.

Fight not only named her place of work; it characterized her outlook. As part of the cultural ferment of the 1930s, artists, writers, musicians, all creative people, came to view themselves in a new light. Where the intellectuals of the previous decade—the Lost Generation that included Ernest Hemingway, F. Scott and Zelda Fitzgerald, and Gerald Murphy—considered themselves artists, geniuses, or prophets without a land, artistic producers of the 1930s saw themselves as culture workers. Although many still aspired to fame and fortune, a considerable number perceived art and literature as part of the struggle to improve society. Their credo was not "art for art's sake," but "art for the masses." In their eyes, the struggle for good art was inseparable from the struggles of "muscle workers."

Nothing so captured the attitudes of the new culture workers as their involvement with organized labor. In 1935, President Roosevelt introduced a new type of unemployment relief in the Works Progress Administration (WPA) and in the Treasury Department's Public Works Administration (PWA). For the first time in U.S. history, the WPA and PWA provided federal jobs for culture workers—writers, artists, musicians, and actors—who supposedly worked with their brains and minds rather than their backs and limbs. WPA writers received federal paychecks for writing regional guidebooks; musicologists got paid to collect folk songs; playwrights produced dramas with working-class themes. When Mildred Rackley lost her job at *Fight* in 1935, she signed up with the PWA and began to sketch murals for public buildings.

Such cultural workers were grateful for the employment, but they still saw themselves as workers. Rackley joined the New York Artists' Union in

1935.[8] Rackley became head of the Union's Unemployed Division, which helped find jobs for jobless artists. When federal budget cutting led the Roosevelt administration to declare cutbacks in unemployment benefits, she fought back, helping to organize a protest in Washington, D.C.

Activism sometimes led to unpleasant consequences. Once, Rackely was arrested for illegal picketing; another time for leading a sit-down strike at government offices. Among cultural activists, these incidents became badges of honor. They became part of Rackley's political resume, proved her bona fides within the left movement, and showed how a revolutionary artist belonged to the people. In the autumn of 1936, she returned to New Mexico and pursued her earlier fantasy of organizing workers. She might not have known a thing about farm workers, but she showed considerable talent at organizing artists like herself. By December 1936, she was back in New York. She was standing on top of a ladder in a Treasury Department building, when she was summoned to take Dr. Barsky's telephone call.

Salaria Kea's journey to Spain followed a similarly indirect, but logical route. She had been born on a farm in Milledgeville, Georgia, in 1913 and named Sarah Lillie.[9] After being orphaned, Sarah Lillie moved to Akron, Ohio, at 14 to live with her older brothers, who had gone north to escape southern segregation and find industrial jobs. But although Akron was northern, it still upheld segregation, as the young woman would discover.

Thin and spry, Kea excelled in sports. She eagerly tried out for high school basketball, but learned that "colored" girls could not join the team. "I was despondent, naturally," she recalled, "but my brother told me to 'keep going,' not to let this stop me." She transferred schools to be able to play and won medals in basketball and tennis. But segregation affected her life. Sarah Lillie chafed at color lines in movie theaters, restaurants, swimming pools, and at lakeside beaches. She had to travel to the next town just to have a swim. Soon, she would be barred from attending the local Peoples Hospital school of nursing and faced similar rejections from other institutions in the region. "I accepted it," she told an interviewer in 1979. "What else could I do? I just thought that was the world. I wasn't in heaven, this was the earth."[10]

A doctor, in whose office she worked part time, informed Sarah Lillie that New York City's Harlem Hospital provided training for African American nurses and encouraged her to apply. In 1930, she passed a special admission test, and by the beginning of the following year she was pursuing

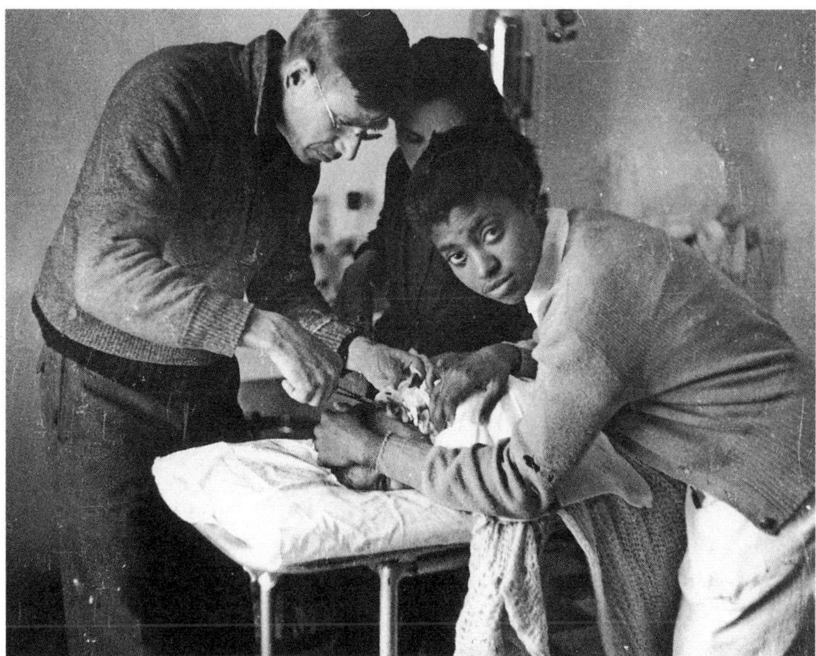

Nurse Salaria Kea working in one of the hospitals organized by the American Medical Bureau to Aid Spanish Democracy. Trained at Harlem Hospital in New York, she volunteered to go to Spain after the American Red Cross declined her services in Ohio. (Author's collection.)

her future east. By then, she was calling herself Salaria because she didn't like the fact that her mother had named her after a white friend.

Like Mildred Rackley, Salaria Kea imbibed the ferment of New York City. Having renamed herself, she found in Harlem a new kind of freedom and learned to fight back against injustice. When a waitress in the staff dining room informed a group of student nurses that they were occupying a "white only" table, Salaria and her friends rose quickly, grasped the corners of the tablecloth, and sent the silverware crashing to the floor. Their defiance created a sensation. Although older black nurses warned against "making trouble," the dissidents picked Kea as their leader and confronted the hospital administration to protest discrimination. By the end of the day, the hospital had banned segregated seating and hired a black dietician to join the staff. In her unpublished memoir, Kea described the demonstration as her "first experience in group action, in organized, planned, programmatic resistance to injustice" and said she had "emerged with a strong new feeling of group identity."

When Mussolini invaded Ethiopia in 1935, Harlem became a hotbed of protest against fascist expansion. Salaria Kea joined an Ethiopia aid society, gathering medical supplies to send overseas. Britain and France protested Mussolini's militarism, and President Roosevelt pleaded for a "moral embargo" of trade with Italy. But the war ended quickly in a fascist victory. Kea remained active in the Ethiopia club, taking the opportunity to learn more about the history of Africa and listening to invited speakers. These lectures politicized her outlook. She came to understand the menace of fascism. But her perspective reflected her personal experiences. As she explained her political development years later, she said: "We didn't know anything about Jews. For us it was all black and white."[11]

After the Spanish Civil War erupted, the Ethiopia circle focused their discussions on what they, as a group, might do to assist Republican Spain, but they found no common ground. Kea went to the hospital bulletin board looking for a mission. That, ultimately, was why she volunteered for Spain. Despite the racial insults that had blocked her applications to nursing school, despite racist practices in the north, despite the rebuff from the Red Cross, she had no quarrel with whites per se.

Salaria Kea proved to be the only African American nurse to go to Spain, but the Lincoln Brigade was racially integrated and deliberately so.[12] It was the first U.S. military group that had African Americans at every level of command, including the battalion leader Oliver Law, who was killed in battle at Brunete in 1937. In addition to black soldiers, the brigade included African American medical personnel, ambulance drivers, social workers, and journalists like Langston Hughes. Paul Robeson was the only American entertainer of any race who went to Spain to boost the volunteers' morale. The Lincoln Brigade also included Native Americans, Filipino Americans, Asian Americans, and every conceivable white ethnic group. In Spain, then, Kea would not only join in the war against fascism, but also achieve common cause with people of many nationalities and races. She would receive equal opportunity and equal treatment. And in Spain she would meet an Irish volunteer named Patrick O'Reilly and find the love of her life.

Esther Silverstein had been something of an outsider, too, before she went to Spain. Her parents were Jewish immigrants, who had landed in Philadelphia around the turn of the century, and then embarked westward to Goshen County, Wyoming, where they became homesteaders. Esther, the third of their five children, was born there in a sod house in

1913 and ever after remembered the vast spaciousness that allowed her to see the entire 360-degree horizon. Seventy-five years later, she would depict her warm family life in a prize-winning children's book, *Berchick*.[13] But a farm depression in the early 1920s took away the homestead, and her family moved to nearby Mitchell, Nebraska, a town of 2,000, where her father resumed his tailoring trade.

"My father was an ardent American patriot," she affirmed. "He knew what freedom meant."[14] Although not outwardly interested in politics her parents subscribed to the socialist *Jewish Daily Forward*. Silverstein vividly remembered the day in 1927 when the state of Massachusetts, in one of the great political cases of the decade, electrocuted anarchists Nicola Sacco and Bartholomew Vanzetti, and that her parents "honored the occasion." Hers was the only Jewish family in Mitchell, and she was aware "of a certain kind of anti-semitism." Her father befriended some Mexicans, who came and socialized around the pot-bellied stove in his shop.

Esther Silverstein left Mitchell in 1931 to attend nursing school in San Francisco, arriving in the midst of the Depression. The next year she was participating in demonstrations for universal compulsory health insurance. "We were fighting our little hearts out," she said with a chuckle many years later, "for something we still haven't gotten."[15] The ferment for social justice awakened her conscience. "I became sort of a Leftie in a gradual process," she said. "I don't think you'd call me a proper communist, although I certainly had leanings in that direction." When the great San Francisco waterfront strike erupted in 1934, she contributed to the cause, helping to raise money for the strikers and cooking gallons of spaghetti sauce for a community feed.

She was working in the Marine Hospital during a second waterfront strike in 1936. One of her patients was a young Danish sailor who had been beaten on the picket line with brass knuckles by a company goon squad. He was still wearing his Sailors Union of the Pacific strike button. His scalp wounds had become infected and meningitis had set in; he died soon afterward. With the help of another recovering patient, Silverstein prepared the body for burial. When she finished wrapping him in a shroud, she pinned the cloth with his strike button.

Soon afterward, the Spanish Civil War began. Silverstein shared her patients' enthusiasm as Madrid refused to fall. After she volunteered to join the American Medical Bureau to Aid Spanish Democracy, they threw a little party on the ward and the recuperating sailors handed her an envelope as a farewell gift, telling her to buy something pretty for herself in Paris. The envelope contained 45 one-dollar bills and a five-dollar bill. She held that money carefully as she traveled by rail to New York. There she met twenty other medical workers who would be in her travel group, including Irene Goldin from Hartford, Connecticut. The two would be inseparable in Spain and lifelong friends thereafter. On May 19, 1937, they sailed for France aboard the S.S. *Normandie.* One week later, Silverstein was in Paris, attending a big rally to support the Spanish Republic. As the organizers passed nearby carrying a Spanish flag to hold contributions, she removed the envelope she had carried from San Francisco and put the $50 into the open flag. A few days later, she was in Spain.

Like streams merging into rivers, rivers flowing to the sea, volunteers moved toward Spain, prompted by a simple desire to help. Esther Silverstein, Salaria Kea, Mildred Rackley, and those who joined them on their journeys had no idea what lay ahead. Few knew anything about Spain, only that they felt needed by the Spanish people and therefore accepted a personal obligation to answer that need. Each volunteer made an individual choice, stepping outside the rut of ordinary life because of that larger commitment to save the lives of strangers. And if most volunteers knew little about Spain, they also knew little or nothing about each other. Indeed, the only thing many of them had in common was Spain. Yet their private decisions would amount to more than the sum of their parts. And their experiences in Spain would forge deep bonds, creating a sense of common purpose, common action, and common sacrifice. In Spain, they would form a sisterhood of committed women, and the passion of Spain would cling to them for the rest of their lives.

▷ **CHAPTER 4**

Psychology and Ideology in the Spanish Civil War

The Case of the Abraham Lincoln Brigade

I began interviewing veterans of the Lincoln Brigade in the mid-1970s, just after the Vietnam War ended. Studies of Vietnam veterans by Paul Starr and Robert J. Lifton reported considerable psychological damage among the ex-soldiers, which was being identified as "post-traumatic stress disorder." Although no expert on the matter, I didn't notice such symptoms among the survivors of the Spanish Civil War. I'd heard of only two incidents of suicide and found little evidence of postwar criminal behavior (excepting the fact that the volunteers, by definition, could be defined as violators of neutrality laws). I was interested in examining how their political ideology related to their psychological responses in wartime (and vice versa). This article explores that matrix of political ideas, wartime behavior, and individual psychology. It was first published in the Antioch Review *52:2 (Spring 1994): 219–30.*

▷ "War," wrote the poet Edwin Rolfe, a soldier in the Abraham Lincoln Brigade during the Spanish Civil War, "is your comrade struck dead beside you, his shared cigarette still alive in your lips."[1] The 2,800 American volunteers who went to Spain in the late 1930s to fight fascism, in violation of U.S. neutrality laws, developed a remarkable sense of camaraderie. For one thing, about 70 percent *were* "comrades," members of the Communist Party or one of its affiliated organizations; for another, the palpable terrors of war, the high casualties (one-third of the Americans died), and the intense political stakes—all accentuated a collective identity as "fighting anti-Fascists." "We, all of us here," Rolfe wrote to his wife from Barcelona in 1938, "date a certain birth of ourselves to our arrival here, and since we didn't, most of us, know each other at home, all that we have in common is Spain."[2]

The élan of the Lincoln Brigade became legendary. Despite facing overwhelming forces; poorly trained leaders, who committed military blunders; inadequate weapons and supplies (thanks to the non-intervention agreements of the Roosevelt administration and the European powers), and a professional enemy armed by Hitler and Mussolini, the American volunteers proved themselves courageous fighters as shock troops for the Spanish Republican Army.

Their famous morale had a direct influence on the training of American soldiers during World War II. As the United States headed toward war in 1941, Professor John Dollard, a distinguished sociologist at Yale University's Institute of Human Relations, became interested in the qualities that produced good fighters. He wondered how fear acted as a psychological factor in a soldier's performance. Could fear be controlled? Was it possible to predict which recruits would overcome their anxieties and which would collapse under the stress of combat? Dollard's efforts to work with an American Legion Post in the New Haven area soon foundered. In the face of "the dive bomber, the Blitz, and the modern tank," he explained, the experience of the old doughboys appeared largely irrelevant.[3]

So Dollard appealed to the veterans of the Spanish Civil War for assistance. With a grant from the Rockefeller Foundation, the approval of the Communist Party, the cooperation of the Veterans of the Abraham Lincoln Brigade, and (unbeknownst to the veterans) the Federal Bureau of Investigation, Dollard developed a 44-page questionnaire that took about five hours to complete. He hired Lincoln veteran John V. Murra, a graduate student in anthropology, to administer the survey to 300 veterans. The results, published in 1943 under the title *Fear in Battle,* won praise from the U.S. Army's chief of morale services, who urged his officers to use its findings in the training of American soldiers.

"Fear is normal," was the report's first message. "Experienced men admit it and are not ashamed." Indeed nearly two-thirds of the respondents confessed that they had suffered moments of panic when they "lost their heads . . . couldn't control themselves and were useless as soldiers for a little while." On a positive note, Dollard suggested, this fear enhanced a soldier's instinct for self-preservation, making the men "cautious under fire."

The Lincoln veterans also described a hierarchy of wound fears: most dreaded were abdominal injuries, then wounds to the eyes, brain, genitals, legs and feet, hands and arms, face, torso. They acknowledged a range of "most-feared weapons," with bomb shrapnel deemed most frightening, bullets the least. The survivors also reported that the sounds of war—the noise of exploding bombs—produced much greater terror than any visual experience. According to the veterans, moreover, battle fear was not simply a mental phenomenon, but also stimulated specific physical reactions. These also formed a hierarchy of responses: pounding of the heart and rapid pulse, muscular tenseness, sinking feeling in the stomach, dryness of mouth and throat, trembling, sweating, loss of appetite, prickling sensations, ringing in the ears, involuntary urination and defecation; very few vomited or fainted. "Fear begins with strong bodily responses," Dollard concluded, "and is then registered in the mind." (This finding, incidentally, confirmed the nineteenth-century theories of William James's *Principles of Psychology*.)

Despite the varieties of fear, however, Dollard found that the Lincolns had learned to control their visceral responses in order to function effectively in battle. To alleviate their concerns, for example, men spoke openly about personal fear, thus sharing the knowledge of their common dilemmas. But according to Dollard, such candor was best expressed prior to going into battle. Once in combat, panic could become dangerously contagious, jeopardizing everyone. Yet the veterans observed that courage, too, became infectious. Nearly all the respondents admitted that they fought better after observing someone else behaving calmly and coolly in a dangerous situation. The best remedy for fear, the Lincolns suggested, was to focus on the work at hand, moving one's mind from the abstract to the physical. "When a man stops reacting to danger signals," Dollard explained, "he is no longer afraid."

The most important of Dollard's findings, however, revealed the power of political ideology. In a rare display of unanimity, the Lincoln veterans asserted that an understanding of the anti-fascist nature of the war and a personal identification with the cause of Republican Spain improved their battlefield reliability. "If a man knows what he is fighting for," Dollard contended, "and has an intense personal need to win, his zeal in battle will tend to triumph over his fear." Hatred and anger toward the enemy solidified morale. Although the death of a close friend might produce flashes of rage and a desire for revenge, Dollard found that a more impersonal antipathy to the enemy created "a sustained, steady anger which lasts until the final battle is won." As the guerrilla fighter William Aalto explained to Dollard, "men think of their friends, the whole social structure behind them and from that hit at the enemy . . . you hate his lousy Nazi state and his fascist bosses."[4] These motives—the result of intelligent learning, of political beliefs—lay at the center of the Lincolns' celebrated ésprit de corps. That is why they accepted the discipline of their officers, fought against overwhelming military superiority, and maintained their commitment to defeating the fascist foe.

The single female respondent in the postwar study, truck driver Evelyn Hutchins, similarly stressed the value of political self-consciousness in coping with danger. Several times during the war, enemy planes had bombed and strafed the vehicle she was driving. She also suffered exhaustion from working eighteen-hour shifts, double-clutching her truck over perilous mountain roads. "I had bad dreams all night," she told a magazine interviewer. "I'd always be driving a car and something would go wrong with it." She would awaken in a cold sweat. But in daylight, she boasted, "I've never lost my nerves yet." To Dollard, Hutchins reaffirmed her powerful self-discipline: "I just wouldn't give in to letting them frighten me. I would not permit it to happen to me." The fascists, she explained, "wanted to break our morale, and I wanted to show them that they were not going to do it. When anybody did crack, I just got mad at him for giving in." She insisted, moreover, that those who did succumb to fear were "not too clear on the issues. . . . They were there for personal reasons. Some of them were maladjusted at home. With some it may have been adventure. With some a number of their friends went, and they were ashamed not to go along—something like that."[5]

But the point Hutchins made—an idea repeated by many other Lincoln volunteers—was that intellectual understanding, correct ideology, could triumph over physical fear. "A soldier who is politically conscious that he is right," concluded guerrilla fighter Aalto, "and who has a feeling of community with his society . . . will do his job well." (Interestingly, both Aalto and Hutchins received the highest performance ratings from the Communist Party leadership at the end of the war.)[6]

The emphasis on the political underpinnings of courage in battle may have masked a deeper psychological truth: that the Lincoln volunteers, particularly the Communists, constituted a distinct type of personality. Committed to a political ideology that celebrated collective behavior, each soldier felt an obligation to validate his personal integrity in battle. "Dear," wrote Al Hawkins to his wife, in a sentiment reiterated by many of the Lincoln survivors, "I didn't turn chicken under fire the other day—

and was I surprised." Equally important, the Communist volunteer had to show his courage to the other men. "It is not bravery that keeps men from breaking," explained Ben Iceland about the ordeal of fire, "rather it is shame—shame at the thought of acting like a coward in front of your comrades—shame at being the first to give way—shame at the thought that you, who had come thousands of miles to fight, could not take it. So men act nonchalantly, when inwardly they are consumed by fear."[7]

From such testimony it is perhaps no wonder that the legend of the Lincoln Brigade depicts countless stories of individual bravery. In over one hundred interviews and oral histories of the Spanish Civil War veterans, the most frequently recounted battle memory (usually told with modest requests for anonymity) involved an individual who exposed himself to enemy fire in order to rescue a fallen comrade. Ironically, such heroes frequently joined the casualty lists themselves, requiring yet another mission of mercy.

This personal courage assumed special importance for Communist warriors. Their initial decision to join the Communist movement had often involved a genuine psychological conversion. If membership in the Communist Party transformed them into "new men," as machine gunner Bill Bailey recalled, that acquired state of grace demanded a concomitant sense of responsibility. "Comradeship" entered Bailey's vocabulary. He developed a "respect for people," stopped hustling and cheating, and sought difficult political assignments, of which Spain was one. Edwin Rolfe, who left the relatively safe newspaper offices of the *Volunteer for Liberty* to serve in the combat zone in 1938, captured the intensity of the Communist commitment. "The war has ripped all illusions from even the youngest of volunteers, leaving only the reality," he wrote from the front lines. "That reality is harder than anyone who has never been under machine-gun fire and bombs and artillery fire can ever know. Yet the men of the [Lincoln Brigade], knowing it well, chose . . . to fight for Spain's free existence . . . to be true to themselves and their innermost convictions."[8]

Beneath that bravado, nonetheless, lay great agonies of self-doubt. Just two weeks before Rolfe filed his story about American courage, the Oklahoma-born Barney Baley nestled perilously in a rocky shell hole and scrawled in his diary, "there's my self-respect to consider. If I failed to do my bit at a time like this I'd never feel right afterward. . . . I was born a rebel, a champion of the underdog. . . . May I die that way when my time comes." Observing his comrades, Baley commented on their common commitment—"a clearer, more sensitive approach and conception to life, a refusal to tolerate and accept cheapness, tawdriness. So we came to Spain. . . ." Two days later, Baley went "another round in my fight of Bolshevik determination vs. instinct of self-preservation. Again, my better angel, my Dr. Jekyll, won out. But how long, O God! how long. Standby for expected attack." To his eternal gratification, Baley held fast.[9]

Alvah Bessie, later famous as one of the "Hollywood Ten," was a highly praised novelist (author of *Dwell in the Wilderness*, 1935), when at age 34 he prepared for his first battle. Despite his political sophistication, he, too, admitted the primacy of psychological considerations in explaining his decision to go to Spain in 1938. "I wanted . . . to work (for the first time) in a large body of men," he wrote in the notebook that became the basis of his classic memoir, *Men in Battle* (1939), "to submerge myself in the mass, seeking neither distinction nor preferment—the obverse of my activities the past several years—and in this way to achieve: self-discipline, patience and resignation, unselfishness. In fine, to complete the destruction of my early training in order to build again a life that would be geared to other men and the world-events that circumscribe their lives."[10]

If the true Communist had to surrender all sense of self to fulfill the ideological imperatives of camaraderie, anti-Communists among the Lincoln veterans would later condemn those totalitarian tendencies. "To change the world totally was to change man totally," wrote veteran William Herrick in his novel, *Hermanos!* (1969, p. 100), "expunging the individual ego, overthrowing its dominance . . . and in so doing destroying . . . the tradition of personal freedom which had helped form [the Communist] as a man. . . ." More orthodox Lincolns emphasized the beneficent results of self-effacement. That is why so many veterans expressed—and still express—the honor to die, as Barney Baley wrote in his battlefield diary, "in the company of such comrades." Communist ideology, in other words, reinforced a psychological predilection; the two were inseparable.[11]

The proximity to death, however, created endless opportunities for self-deception. Sidney Kurtz, assigned to broadcast radio programs from Madrid back to the United States, confessed that he had come to Spain not only to fight against fascism, "but primarily . . . to fight against my own indolence, uncertainty and indecision." For Kurtz, the Communist movement provided coherence and direction. "Never in all my life have I felt the strength and quiet confidence course through me as I do now," he wrote. Yet Kurtz also suffered incapacitating anxieties that, he admitted, may well have saved his life. Facing his first battle on the Jarama front, he wondered "whether the coming test would bring out in me the potentialities I always thought I had, or whether under fire I would break." But before he could meet his moment of truth, Kurtz collapsed from sunstroke and diarrhea and found himself in a hospital. Then he developed appendicitis and had to undergo surgery. "If ever sickness was the result of wish-fulfillment," he conceded, "then this was it." Kurtz subsequently requested repatriation, but agreed to accept the radio job instead. From the relative safety of Madrid, he could contribute to the war effort, while boasting about how his political conversion had "changed my life so completely, redirected me into channels where there is little danger of grounding on a reef."[12] (Kurtz would be killed in action during World War II.)

Kurtz's kind of ambivalence—the tension between self-discipline and fear—permeated the brigade. Whatever inner commitments motivated people to volunteer for Spain, the conditions of war swiftly threatened their psychological defenses. Even before the Lincolns saw action, an air attack caused panic among the inexperienced soldiers. "Men ran and showed early weakness," noted a worried officer named Robert Merriman. Indeed, the battalion's first commander, James Harris, soon began to exhibit incapacitating symptoms. As he drew nearer to battle, Harris started to act erratically. Sent for treatment to Dr. William Pike, head of the brigade medical corps, Harris rambled in a hallucinatory way and defecated into his underpants. Nonetheless, he returned to the battalion, in Merriman's words, "still abnormal and talked loudly and accused me of having him confined. . . . Confused man." After Harris led the men on a midnight march through no-man's land, brigade leaders evacuated him to a hospital behind the lines. Nearly two decades later, some anti-Communist veterans would claim that Harris had been the victim of a party purge; the contemporary record shows more clearly a pattern of mental breakdown.[13]

Military action exacerbated such problems. Fortunately, Dr. Pike could help many of the casualties recover. A small-built, intense man, educated at Rush Medical College in Chicago, he had worked as a psychiatrist in a New York state hospital.[14] Soon after arriving in Spain, he began to observe distinct psychological patterns among the volunteers: many of the soldiers, according to Pike, viewed the war as an apocalyptic battleground between the revolutionary working class and the forces of fascist reaction. However much they might attempt to stifle their private egos, they perceived themselves to be daring, audacious fighters, part of the vanguard of human history. Their honor within the Communist movement confirmed that inflated self-image. "They were going to be heroes, and therefore be recognized," Pike elaborated many years later. "This was seeking gratification through recognition."

Such grandiose expectations soon crashed against the horrors of war. In Pike's words, the confrontation with "the harsh reality knocked their fantasies sky high." Soon after reaching the Jarama front in February 1937, for example, Pike encountered a small group of haggard volunteers who were living in a cave. They would appear at the entrance only for their food. As Pike reported, "they came down one by one, hands, lips trembling, faces twitching, eyes downcast, ashamed." The physician determined to bring them back to the land of the living by rebuilding their self-esteem. Through a program of "work therapy," Pike assigned these "mentally wounded" soldiers to a road-building project, safe from enemy fire, which began to restore their damaged morale. "Gradually they were brought closer to the battle lines into the second stations, then the first, and finally into the front lines—far removed from their trembling fear. They were," Pike concluded, "men again."

Such recoveries remained tenuous. During one rest period, Pike observed a sudden increase in what he called psychopathology. "Men became hysterical," he recalled," some with convulsions, weeping, mourning, reacting to the stress of war. They did not do this at the front, but once released from the burden of fighting, their emotions erupted." Pike treated the worst cases with sedatives, such as phenobarbital. With psychic defenses down, moreover, the dread of bombing assumed nightmarish forms, awakening men in terror and cold sweat. One veteran described a vivid dream of his capture by the enemy. "The fascists beat up the prisoners one at a time," he fantasized. "It was soon to be my turn. How would I take it? My brain began to work. After all, I thought, I'm just a microbe in this world—almost nothing. Supposing they torture me—so what? I began to feel happy. I don't remember being tortured in my dream, but those thoughts are still dear to me."[15] Even in this man's unconscious, the ideology of the larger cause offered solace. And, as Evelyn Hutchins said of her nightmares, "There are a lot of things worse than dreams."[16]

The tension between psychology and ideology could haunt men for years. One victim of what today is called post-traumatic stress syndrome was a volunteer named Bill McCarthy. A fatherless altar boy raised by the Christian Brothers in New York, McCarthy developed a strong class consciousness, which brought him into the maritime labor movement and then to Spain. Fighting in the seamen's machine-gun section, McCarthy experienced several brushes with death on the Aragon front, but showed no particular problems. Half a year later, however, a bomb explosion lifted McCarthy into the air and dropped him in a crash of shrapnel and rubble. He emerged in a daze, not knowing who or where he was. "I was trembling and shaking," he recalled. "And I trembled and shook for quite a while."[17]

As his battalion retreated from the front lines, McCarthy headed toward the rear. Stopped for lacking a safe-conduct pass, he was brought before the brigade commissar, who ordered him to a hospital and then, as McCarthy put it, to the "laughing academy" or "Cracker factory." Eventually the brigade approved his evacuation from Spain. But McCarthy suffered intense guilt for departing from the war prematurely. "I would get a kaleidoscope of faces," he said of the ensuing nightmares. "First eye sockets pouring out. . . . Empty eye sockets. And they would come up real close and then fade away. . . . And I figured, these are the guys I let down."

To assuage his guilt, McCarthy felt obliged to take extraordinary measures to demonstrate his anti-fascist convictions. One year after returning from Spain, while serving as a seaman in Genoa, he drunkenly launched a tirade against Mussolini. Arrested and given the notorious castor-oil treatment, McCarthy served a two-week jail sentence for insulting Il Duce. A dozen years later, while protesting against the Korean war, McCarthy climbed a lamppost in New York City to shout anti-war oratory. When he refused to come down, firemen and police beat him savagely, damaging the sight in one eye. As he got older, McCarthy began to express remorse for his participation in the war; he drew closer to his early Catholicism. He became an alcoholic. He gave away his meager savings to help other veterans. "So," he wrote, "forty five years later, lamppost, jail, loss of eye, I'm still trying to make up for my crack-up in Spain."[18] McCarthy's last request, fulfilled by his friend Bill Bailey, was to have his ashes buried amid the ruins of Belchite, his point of crisis.

The pressure of battle also forced some worried men to desert. Their exact number is difficult to confirm, but at least one hundred men, or 4 percent of the military volunteers, made the effort to escape from the trauma of the war. Many fled to U.S. consulates in Spain. But State Department policy forbade giving assistance to men who had entered the country illegally. Nonetheless, the diplomatic corps usually took the trouble to identify the disaffected volunteers. According to consular documents, the stream of men seeking repatriation rose significantly during and just after major battles. Alfred Amery, who left the war during the tragic retreats in the spring of 1938, vividly recalled his personal ordeal: "Walk, carry, run, fight, get cut off; walk, carry, run, fight again—half-starving, sleepless . . . my last thought before quitting was this: I can never help organize another battalion. I simply haven't got the strength."[19] On several occasions, groups of deserters fled together, confirming Dollard's finding that demoralization could spread through a unit. But the decision to abandon the war often was a deliberate act, rather than a spontaneous impulse. Indeed, several volunteers made the effort more than once.

Brigade policy toward deserters was generally lenient. Most who fled from the danger of combat subsequently expressed deep remorse for their failure of courage. After what one called a "pep talk" from the political leaders, they eagerly returned to their groups to preserve their self-respect. Typical punishment for deserters was assignment to a labor battalion, which required work on fortifications and trenches. Then, after interviews, deserters were attached to military units. "In 99 percent of the cases," one examining officer told Dollard, "they became very good soldiers."[20]

There were a few incidents, however, when brigade leaders deliberately determined to punish deserters severely as a warning to others. After a dozen men deserted from action during the battle of Fuentes de Ebro in 1937, including four Americans who escaped in a much-needed ambulance, the Communist leadership systematically polled the rank-and-file volunteers, who voted for harsh penalties. A two-day court-martial then heard the evidence and found the deserters guilty. Two men were sentenced to death; the others were assigned to punishment details. But then brigade leaders began to have second thoughts about the effect of the death penalties on world opinion, particularly at a time when the Spanish Republic was appealing for the end of the non-intervention policy. In the end, none of the deserters faced a firing squad; apparently most were returned to their companies to fight another day. (The whereabouts of particular men in Spain, it should be noted, is often difficult to ascertain.)

Some deserters—like the New York seaman Paul White—came to understand too late the implications of their flight from battle. His story emerges in a document I discovered in the Russian archives of the Spanish Civil War in 1993.[21] After his first taste of battle, White wrote, "I knew I was afraid to go into action again." But when a fascist breakthrough forced his return to combat, his anxieties intensified. "I tried all this time to overcome my feeling of fear," he said. "I felt we were doomed and fighting futilely. . . . I could not make it and dropped out of the line and made up my mind to desert and try and reach France. As I ran . . . my fear grew. . . . I had lost all control." White continued to run, debating with himself "whether or not to turn back." But before he could make a decision, Spanish officials arrested him in a small town near the French border. "Once I was in custody, I decided that I had been saved from wrecking my life completely," he declared. "I realize that [the] 'safety' . . . I was seeking would never compensate me for the loss of everything and everyone I value." Facing a moment of truth before a military tribunal, White pleaded "for one chance and that is to serve in the lines and wipe out this stain on my military and Party record."

"I am 29 years old," he continued, "and certain that I can serve in the ranks for many years as a class-conscious worker. I have had plenty of time to think before making this statement and sincerely believe I will be stronger in my work and devotion if given the opportunity to redeem myself. I regard my position now as the most serious crisis in my life and am ready to meet it."[22] When White faced a court-martial of his peers, however, he was too terrified to speak. He presented no defense of his actions. Just at that moment, moreover, brigade leaders had resolved to toughen the policy toward deserters. By a unanimous vote, the court sentenced Paul White to death. The next morning he was executed by firing squad.

Besides the case of Paul White, there is one other instance of a Lincoln volunteer (Bernard Abramofsky) who was shot for desertion, without benefit of a trial.[23] There is probably one more case of an unofficial execution (Albert Wallach, for whom the evidence remains inconclusive). In addition, two criminal cases resulted in capital punishments. But these were exceptional instances. Even if all the other allegations of assassination and murder within the Lincoln Brigade proved to be true, the number of Americans killed outside of combat in Spain would total less than ten. The rarity of these killings undermines the notion, made popular by works such as George Orwell's *Homage to Catalonia,* that the Communists enforced discipline by terror. Not one American, it should be emphasized, suffered punishment, much less capital punishment, for political dissent. And most deserters simply returned to their duties

The American Abraham Lincoln Brigade, led by Milton Wolff (center, without cap), at the farewell ceremony for the International Brigades, near Falset, Spain, October 16, 1938. (Photo by Robert Capa. © International Center of Photography/ Magnum Photos.)

with no one the wiser. (Surviving Lincoln veterans remained unaware of most cases of desertion.)

Long before sociologist John Dollard conducted his survey of fear in battle, brigade leaders like Steve Nelson recognized that even good soldiers might lose their resolve in a moment of panic. When possible, Nelson informally authorized the issuance of passes for deserters to allow their frazzled nerves to recuperate safely behind the front lines. But most of the Lincoln volunteers did not require such special privileges. Indeed, the historical record vindicates Dollard's findings of the 1940s. Although fear among the Lincolns appeared to be nearly universal, an overwhelming sense of responsibility to their comrades prevailed. The men of the Lincoln Brigade stuck to their guns until the doomed Spanish Republic finally ordered the withdrawal of all foreign volunteers in the autumn of 1938.

At farewell ceremonies in Barcelona at the end of October, the Lincoln Brigade paraded through a shower of kisses and flowers bestowed by the grateful Spanish people. As the remnants of the brigade reached the reviewing stand, they could hear the words of Dolores Ibarruri, "La Pasionaria" (The Passion Flower) of the Republic. She summed up their achievement and their sacrifice. "They gave up everything," she declared, "their loves, their countries, home and fortune; fathers, mothers, wives, brothers, sisters and children, and they came and told us: We are here. Your cause, Spain's cause, is ours—it is the cause of all advanced and progressive mankind." Tough veterans wept as she spoke. "You can go proudly," she told them. "You are history. You are legend."[24]

▷ CHAPTER 5

The Social Origins of the Abraham Lincoln Brigade

When the Communist International called for volunteers to support the Spanish Republic in 1936, some 35,000 women and men from 52 countries journeyed to Spain to form the International Brigades, a border-crossing movement that expressed a unique global awareness. In Spain, however, practical demands of communication required volunteers to be divided into language groups or nationalities. English speakers, for example, served primarily in the 15th Brigade. And that was the way most military records were kept. The opening of the Moscow archives relating to the Spanish Civil War in the early 1990s gave historians access to the personnel documents created by the Communist Party for each nationality group. In 1998, the University of Lausanne, Switzerland, invited scholars to present their findings on the demographic composition of the various nationality groups. I wrote this paper for that conference. The meeting became sidetracked by disagreements about the role of the Communist parties in Spain. The papers finally appeared in a French-language edition in 2008. By then, I had revised my original paper to include matters relating to Communist influence in the Lincoln Brigade. I presented this revision in 1999 at the University of Carlos III in Getafe, Spain.

▷ In her farewell speech to the International Brigades in October 1938, the Spanish Communist leader, Dolores Ibarurri, assured the departing volunteers, "You are history. You are legend." But separating that history from the legend is not so easy. Historical writing about the North American volunteers in the Spanish Civil War has followed a pattern similar to that used by historians to describe the Communist Party as a national and international institution. Ideology, not scholarship, typically serves as the guiding point both for the assumptions and conclusions as well as for the methodology of the work. Ironically, the collapse of the Soviet

Union during the 1990s and the subsequent opening of the Communist Party archives in Moscow have reinforced these trends. Rather than contributing to a consensus about the nature of American participation in the International Brigades, the discovery of new sources has encouraged a polarization of perspectives.

The first histories of the Abraham Lincoln Brigade were written by two veterans of the war: Edwin Rolfe's *The Lincoln Battalion* and Alvah Bessie's *Men in Battle,* both published in 1939, less than a year after their return to the United States and just months after General Francisco Franco's victorious armies marched into Madrid. These books depicted the war from the soldiers' perspective and, for political reasons, played down or disguised the role of the Communist Party and the Soviet Union. When Bessie described a soldier leading the battalion in a song during the siege on Hill 666, for example, he said they were singing the "Star-Spangled Banner," not "The Internationale." (Milton Wolff repeats the story in his fictionalized memoir, *Another Hill.*) Such distortions tried to deflect the interest of U.S. government officials and anti-communist witch hunters, but also contributed to the nationalist ideas associated with the Popular Front. It was Earl Browder, head of the U.S. Communist Party, who had remarked, "Communism is twentieth-century Americanism."

Anti-communist writers of the International Brigades, by contrast, insisted that communism was a monolith centralized in the Soviet Union and that the Communist Party and the Lincoln Brigade took their orders directly from Moscow. As proof, they could point to historical events that occurred in the very month that Bessie's and Rolfe's books were published, particularly the flip-flop position of various Communist parties after the signing of the Nazi-Soviet Pact of 1939. If the Brigades were spontaneous "fighting anti-fascists," as their songs proclaimed, why did they embrace the pact and become advocates for U.S. non-intervention at the outbreak of World War II?

There are two responses to this question that argue against the idea of communism as a monolith. The first is that the experiences of the volunteers in Spain—their anger at the Western European policy of non-intervention that had led to the fall of the Spanish Republic—gave them a special loathing of the Allies, England and France, and made them unwilling to support those so-called democracies when they went to war against Germany in 1939. Such sentiments were congruent with the Soviet policy of non-intervention, but were not necessarily inspired by it. The leadership of the Veterans of the Abraham Lincoln Brigade (VALB) made that point. But whatever their hatred of England and France in 1939, they swiftly reversed course, along with the Communist Party, when Germany invaded the Soviet Union in June 1941. The second reversal merely confirmed the existence of a communist monolith.

The second response is more nuanced, and that is that there were veterans of the Abraham Lincoln Brigade in 1939 who were not communists and had gone to Spain without expressing a pro-communist purpose. The numbers remain imprecise. My research suggests that two-thirds to three-quarters of the volunteers were members of the Communist Party or the Young Communist League. The others may or may not have been sympathetic to a specific party. We know that some Socialist Party members joined the Communist Party because that was the only way they could get to Spain; we know that some joined the Communist Party in Spain. But many, if not most, of the non-communists did not join the Veterans of the Abraham Lincoln Brigade (VALB) and disappeared into anonymous roles after they returned from Spain. Though veterans of the Abraham Lincoln Brigade, they seldom participated in VALB activities and perhaps felt no loyalty to other veterans or to the communist movement.

Besides these non-communist veterans, some activist veterans publicly opposed the Nazi-Soviet Pact in 1939, questioned the leadership of VALB, and voluntarily departed or were expelled from that organization. Some were labeled Trotskyists; others were considered disloyal dissidents. Some just kept their mouths shut and went their own ways. In any event, even though the official veterans group (VALB) and its leadership defended both the pact and its reversal in 1941, not all veterans followed the party monolith. Several Lincoln veterans enlisted in the U.S. or Canadian armies and sought to return to the battlefields against fascism. They remained veterans in good standing; others simply left both the party and VALB and returned to normal life. Even among loyal Communists, there is evidence of weakening support of American neutrality in the months before Germany invaded the Soviet Union.[1] One can argue, in other words, that VALB did not speak for all the veterans, though the leadership publicly closed ranks to defend the party.

World War II and its aftermath contributed to these decentralizing tendencies. Although a core of VALB activists ran the veterans office in

New York and communicated with veterans in military service and on the home front, many veterans went to war and lost contact with the national office. In the postwar years, moreover, Lincoln veterans, like so many other Americans, put aside political issues for domestic roles. They began families (note the great "baby boom"), found jobs, and abandoned, if they did not actively reject, the political Left and the Communist Party of the United States (CPUSA). To be sure, a core of VALB activists continued to run the national office in New York and engaged in many public activities to oppose the Spanish dictatorship. Many in this group were closely tied to the Communist Party and supported CPUSA positions about other foreign policy and domestic issues. Equally interesting, even outspoken anti-communist veterans of the Lincoln Brigade continued to criticize and oppose the Spanish dictatorship.

The international Cold War also ignited a domestic anti-communist Red Scare that attacked the veterans of the Lincoln Brigade. In 1947, the Attorney General's list of "subversive organizations" included both the Abraham Lincoln Brigade and VALB. In addition, leaders of the Joint Anti-Fascist Refugee Committee, including Dr. Edward Barsky, who had created the American Medical Bureau to Aid Spanish Democracy, were sent to jail for refusing to divulge the names of their contributors in the United States and the names of their recipients in Spain. The Federal Bureau of Investigation targeted Lincoln veterans, including those who were not communists or were outspoken anti-communists, for private investigation. Many were blacklisted, lost their jobs, and were threatened with jail. The Internal Security Act of 1950, passed over President Harry Truman's veto, established the Subversive Activities Control Board (SACB), which investigated VALB as a "front" organization of the Communist Party. In response to such government pressure, the entire executive committee of VALB resigned and was replaced by two active leaders, Milton Wolff and Moe Fishman, who led the fight against government repression for the next ten years and more.[2]

The effect of the Red Scare was to further separate VALB leadership from the rank and file. The 1956 Khrushchev revelations, exposing the crimes of Josef Stalin, sparked mass defections from the Communist Party and from those who no longer wanted to be associated with CP-tinged organizations like VALB. The period after 1957 saw increasing divisions among the veterans, between those who remained loyal to the Communist Party and those who repudiated its leadership. This split was not resolved organizationally until the late 1970s and remained a sensitive issue for surviving veterans until VALB ceased to exist in 2008.[3]

Despite the political fragmentation of the veterans, however, anti-communists and anti-communist historians of the Brigade continued to emphasize the monolithic nature of the veterans' political activities. Just as participation in the Spanish Civil War was considered grounds for political persecution, so the U.S. volunteers in Spain were seen merely as pawns of Moscow. It was enough to label them as communists to explain why they had gone to Spain. Any indigenous reasons for going to Spain—the persecution of Jews in fascist countries, for example—could be dismissed as rationalizations, mere cover stories that served to disguise the "true" communist motives. In the same spirit, anti-communist historians have argued that the Lincoln volunteers were not really volunteers. Rather than expressing free will in going to Spain, such historians claimed, the rank and file had been ordered to go to Spain by their communist leaders and simply obeyed their orders. Similarly, these historians insisted that the Brigades were intolerant of dissent and punished political heresy by forcing soldiers to participate in suicidal battles or by executing political dissenters.[4]

The image of a totalitarian army followed from the picture of a monolithic Communist apparatus that was based in Moscow but had tentacles spread throughout the world. Ironically, the opening of the Moscow archives during the 1990s reinforced that image. First, the very act of undertaking research in this area obliges the historian to go to the center of the Communist state, where for political reasons these archives now reside. All Western scholars have stories to tell of dealing with this former Soviet bureaucracy. Second, although many of the records in these archives are organized by nationality, like all military records they tend to emphasize transnational issues. They contain reports to headquarters, official documents transmitted from the top down and up to the top again. They include messages from the Inspector General of the International Brigades and other official records. Of course, within the nationality records there is plenty of information about the rank and file. But the weight of the evidence reinforces the perspective of the political and military leaders rather than the ordinary volunteers.

Although a few historians in the United States have written about the volunteers from the perspective of the rank and file, most studies based on the Moscow archives emphasize the perspective of the communist leadership. Books by Harvey Klehr and John Haynes, purporting to reveal the "secrets" of the Communist International, accept the view of the communist monolith and attribute all activities, military and political, to orders coming from Moscow.[5] Indeed, in several books and articles about the Spanish Civil War and other leftist movements, the word "communism" has subtly been replaced by the word "Stalinism."[6] That way, all communists can be painted with the same brush, and those who disagreed with the party line are liquidated with the same facility as a trip to the gulag. They do not exist as historical actors, but only as people who followed the dictator's orders; there is no distinction between party leaders and followers; there is no room for individuality, dissent, or personal passion. Orders are orders. It makes no difference how they were received or even if they were carried out.

Which brings me to the subject of the social composition of the U.S. volunteers, the Lincoln Brigade. To understand the complexity of the Spanish Civil War, we must begin with the individuality of those who participated in that struggle. In some ways, the task should be easy. After all, of the 125 million citizens of the United States in 1930, only about 2,800 volunteered to serve in Spain, either as soldiers, drivers, or medical personnel. What were the characteristics they shared before going to Spain?

A significant minority, as I mentioned, at least 25 percent, were not communists. Sweeping labels, like communists or Stalinists, disguise rather than reveal the demographic issues. Contemporaries called the U.S. volunteers "boys," younger in years than the soldiers from other countries. Statistical analysis partly confirms this view. The age groups with the most volunteers—the statistical modes—were 23 and 25. (The youngest were three 18-year-olds; the oldest were 59 and 60.) Other records show that 38 percent were 25 or younger; 26 percent were between the ages of 26 and 30; and 36 percent were over 30. The median age—the midpoint age—was 27 and the average age was 27.5. Separate calculations for African American volunteers are nearly identical, and a separate listing of U.S. Communists reaches the same conclusions. One study of U.S. women nurses finds the average at 26.5. The average year of birth, therefore, is 1909–10.[7]

These ages suggest that the typical volunteer was no impulsive youth. Yet very few of these men and women were married. One list of 1,249 Communists shows that only 189—15.2 percent—had ever married. Why so many adults in their late twenties were unmarried may reflect the impact of the economic Depression on family life. The most frequently listed occupations reinforce this view. As seamen, drivers, mechanics, students, or "unemployed," these people could not afford to support families. Moreover, their occupations demanded mobility, a common factor in Depression conditions, which made it harder to sink family roots.

Although U.S. volunteers came from almost every state in the Union (except Wyoming and Delaware), the great majority lived in big cities that contained large populations of European immigrants. One list of 1,745 volunteers from the United States contains over 30 distinct nationalities: Puerto Rican, Canadian, Mexican, Cuban, Guatemalan, Chilean, Ecuadorian, English, Irish, Scottish, Welsh, German, Austrian, French, Swiss, Italian, Spanish, Portuguese, Estonian, Ukrainian, Norwegian, Swedish, Danish, Finnish, Dutch, Hungarian, Greek, Bulgarian, Croatian, Serbian, Yugoslavian, Montenegrin, Romanian, Albanian, Turkish, Chinese, Japanese, Hawaiian, Philippine, Armenian, Czech, Slovakian, Lithuanian, Slovene, Polish, Russian, and Belgian. There were also over 400 people on the list whose nationality was unknown. Is it surprising that people of such international origins had an international perspective? Were they internationalists before they were communists? Didn't they have reasons, separate from their organizational memberships, to be concerned about the rise of fascism in Europe?

Consider the question of Jewish identity. The best estimates suggest that one-third of the Lincoln Brigade were Jewish, though some people suspect that figure is too low. Jews constituted a high population among the immigrant communities in U.S. cities. Their high percentage also reflects the large proportion of Jews in the Communist Party, which organized the recruitment of volunteers. It is difficult to determine whether Jewish Communists went to Spain as Jews or as Communists and whether explanations of their motives given in the 1930s differ from explanations given after they returned from Spain and especially as they got older. Thus, for example, when Milton Wolff appeared in 1940 before the notorious congressional House Committee on Un-American Activities—which was investigating communist subversion—he explained his enlistment as part of the fight against fascism. In his testimony, he stated:

> "I am Jewish, and knowing that as a Jew we are the first to suffer when fascism does come, I went to Spain to fight against it."
>
> His inquisitors then asked: "Isn't it true that you [Jews] also suffer under communism?"

Wolff replied: "I know of no instances where Jews have suffered under communism."

"Didn't you know that the government of Soviet Russia was under a Communist dictatorship just as bad as a Fascist dictatorship?"

"No"

"Didn't you regard Stalin as a dictator just like Mussolini and Hitler?"

"No."

The discussion soon proceeds to other political differences involving the Nazi-Soviet Pact.[8]

Surely, the anti-communist government investigators regarded Wolff's comments about his Jewish heritage as a cover-up. But how can anyone, even Wolff himself, decide that his heritage and his identity have no basis in explaining why he went to Spain?

When the city of Madison, home of the University of Wisconsin, dedicated a monument to honor the Lincoln Brigade in 1999, it was only the second such monument in the United States. The person responsible for this honor was a Lincoln veteran named Clarence Kailin. This is what he told a reporter for the Wisconsin State Journal:

> I was a member of the Communist party here, as many were at the time. We understood the implications of the war in Spain. We knew who Hitler was, we knew what fascism was. We knew what anti-semitism was. I'm Jewish. Here was a chance to go over there and fight back.[9]

Other examples are even more explicit. "Don't you realize that we Jews will be the first to suffer if fascism comes?" one wounded soldier wrote in 1937 to his disapproving mother in New York. "If we sit by and let [the fascists] grow stronger by taking Spain, they will . . . not stop there and it won't be long before they get to America. . . . If I permitted such a time to come . . . all I could do then would be to curse myself and say 'Why didn't I wake up when the alarm clock rang?'" Another non-Communist soldier wrote to his commissar in Spain: "I am as good [an] antifascist as any Communist. I have reason to be. I am a Jew and that is the reason I came to Spain. I know what it means to my people if fascism should win. (And I know they won't.)"[10]

Other white ethnic groups, including Italian American exiles from Mussolini's fascist regime, had plenty of reasons, besides their communism, to oppose the fascist regimes in Europe. "We will fight to the last drop of blood," declared Giuseppe Dalleo, a volunteer raised in the United States, "to demonstrate to the world that the true sons of Italy have contributed to the struggle for liberty of Spain and of the entire world." Another volunteer, Albino Zattoni, felt honored "to represent the true Italy in Spain" while fighting with the Garibaldi battalion.[11]

An additional point worth making about the immigrant communities is that the Communist Party's so-called Popular Front supported the same kind of melting pot philosophy that the children of immigrants learned in public schools around the country. That is, political and cultural leaders deliberately preached the ideology of what was called "Americanization" to encourage the blurring of cultural differences, to "uplift" the "inferior" peoples of southern and eastern Europe to achieve a common Anglo-Saxon Protestant model. A large proportion of immigrant children embraced that model; they were embarrassed by their parents' foreign names, their accents, and their unfamiliarity with American fashions and customs. But children of immigrants nonetheless remained outside the elite cultural mainstream, merely because they were children of immigrants. In the United States, however, the Popular Front's emphasis on nationalism and patriotism—the very naming of the U.S. brigade after Abraham Lincoln, for example—enabled this generation, born around 1910, to be both radicals and Americans. As American Communists they could fulfill the dream of melting pot assimilation, even as they remained outsiders. Indeed, many clung to the dream of uplifting *all* Americans to their Communist views, a type of self-idealization that suggested their superiority to other classes and groups.

The Lincoln Brigade—like all the International Brigades—also celebrated the mixing of nations and races. Photographs taken in Spain illustrate the deliberate mix of racial and ethnic groups. There were several Native Americans in Spain. Among Asian Americans, there were Filipinos, two Chinese Americans, and one Japanese American (Jack Shirai), who was clearly opposing the militaristic regime in Japan. Whether they were communists may not be the key element in explaining their commitment to Spain.

There were also about 90 African Americans, who served in this fully integrated U.S. army, the first time in U.S. history in which black officers, such as Oliver Law and Walter Garland, commanded white men in battle. Nearly all the African Americans appear to have been communists. Some, like Harry Haywood, could parrot the latest party line from Moscow.[12] But listen, too, to the voices of some African American volunteers with a more indigenous perspective. "All we have to do is to think of the lynching of our people," wrote the truck driver Canute Frankson to his wife. "On the battlefields of Spain we fight for the preservation of democracy. . . . Here, where we're engaged in one of the most bitter struggles of human history, there is no color line, no discrimination, no race hatred. There's only one hate, and that is the hate for fascism."[13]

Many African Americans spoke eloquently about their feelings of self-respect in Spain, the absence of racial prejudice, and contrasted their opportunities to serve in Spain with the second-class treatment they received at home. "I've seen lynching and starvation," said one black volunteer, "and I know my people's enemies." Another volunteer declared: "I had read Hitler's book, knew about the Nuremberg laws, and I knew if the Jews weren't going to be allowed to live, then certainly I knew the Negroes would not escape and that we would be at the top of the list. I also knew that the Negro community throughout the United States would be doing what I was doing if they had the chance."[14] Among those who did not go to Spain, the editors of African American newspapers solidly supported the Republican side and published stories by the writer Langston Hughes about the struggles among anti-fascist fighters. Later, during World War II, black and white Lincoln veterans who served in the segregated U.S. army contrasted the racist environment with the racial equality they had experienced in Spain.[15]

Anti-fascism covered a variety of social protests. Counting nurses and other volunteers, about 70 U.S. women served in Spain. Consider the statement of the truck driver Evelyn Hutchins, one of the two women from the United States who were formally attached to the International Brigades. "I remember when Mussolini issued a decree," she told an interviewer after the war, "I was just a kid at the time—he issued a decree that women were not to wear short skirts, and that they were to keep their proper places. . . . I was convinced that anybody with that kind of attitude was absolutely no good for the people generally." Communist organizers in New York did not welcome Hutchins's application to join the International Brigades; they put her off for months before she persuaded them to allow her to sail to Spain. "I never felt that I was an outstanding genius," she said, "but people had to give me a chance to think and develop whatever thinkabilities I had."[16]

The point of these examples—Jews, blacks, women, white ethnics, and the children of immigrants—is to emphasize the indigenous, home-grown motives that inspired those 2,800 U.S. volunteers to go to Spain. Nor, of course, did a volunteer have to fit into one of the ethnic, racial, or gender minorities to have motives to enlist in the anti-fascist crusade. Don Henry, born in the cowboy town of Dodge City, a former Boy Scout and church-going lad, with roots in the heart of white Anglo-Saxon America, was an undergraduate at the University of Kansas when he embarked for Spain.

On July 4, 1937, Independence Day, Henry wrote home about his traditional patriotic motives for joining the Lincoln Brigade:

> All of us here are perfectly aware of the dangers involved in this war. Yet we are positive that this method of fighting fascism is the correct method and we intend to give our lives, if necessary, to maintain the independence of Spain. Another fascist gain in the world would mean another invitation to world war and gangster government. The political situation here is not much different than the political situation of the U.S. in 1776 when the French people helped the U.S. throw off the tyranny of the British monarch because the masses believed in a democratic government. Now U.S. citizens close their eyes to an assault on a democratic people and in doing that are actually aiding the spread of fascism.

After Henry's death in Spain, the House Un-American Activities Committee delved into his possible subversive motives, but took no further action.[17]

It is likely that many of the volunteers combined such earnest patriotism with ideological desires and went to Spain to fulfill promises of the Communist International and perhaps to hasten the social revolution in Spain and elsewhere. But there are very few surviving statements of volunteers who actually said that. By contrast, nearly all did say that they went to Spain to fight fascism. Communists certainly had reasons to fight fascism. But so did other social groups.

Whatever the exact relationship between communism and ethnic groups, it is important to understand that the U.S. volunteers—and probably the volunteers from the other countries as well—did not simply respond to orders from Moscow. In fact, I have found not one person who was ordered to go to Spain. The North Americans volunteered to fight.

Their motivations need to be understood not just from the perspective of political ideology, but also as an aspect of individual and cultural identity. The Communist Party gave them a way to go to Spain. But it also expressed deeper needs and ideals that prompted those volunteers to risk life and limb to fight against fascism.

This is not to say that the Communist Party and the Communist International are not important in the story of the International Brigades, but rather that we need to place the role of the international organizations on a solid foundation of social history. The volunteers were not military robots following Stalin's orders, but deeply passionate men and women who understood the issues in Spain, who understood the stakes involved in this war, and then made the commitment to put their ideals into practice.

Without that sense of human motivation, the story of the Lincoln Brigade—and presumably the other brigades—does indeed reduce to historical mindlessness, where "impersonal forces" push people along to a deterministic fate. It is history written with a fascist view of human nature. It is history without humanity. And history without humanity is not history.

PART II

Hemingway's War

▷ **CHAPTER 6**

American Tourists in Spain

Ernest Hemingway and the Abraham Lincoln Brigade

The novelist Ernest Hemingway was the most famous American writer to endorse the Spanish Republic during its civil war. He was generous with his funds and with his words, urging the public to support the elected government. The U.S. volunteers viewed him both as a celebrity and an ally, and Hemingway reciprocated in his friendship. But his great novel of the war, For Whom the Bell Tolls, *disappointed many veterans for political reasons, and the wartime alliance between the writer and many of the ex-soldiers collapsed. Still, for many Lincoln veterans, Hemingway's presence in Spain remained unforgettable and their love-hate relationship continued long after his suicide in 1961. This paper, first written circa 1989 to attract editorial interest in my book proposal about the Lincoln Brigade, has been revised many times as new information surfaced.*

▷ "Nine men commanded the Lincoln and Lincoln-Washington Battalions," wrote Ernest Hemingway in 1939 at the end of the Spanish Civil War. By then, four were dead and four were wounded. The ninth and last commander, Milton Wolff was 23, "tall as Lincoln, gaunt as Lincoln, and as brave and as good a soldier as any that commanded battalions at Gettysburg."[1]

A native of Brooklyn, Wolff stood six feet two in bare feet and a few inches higher in the muddied brown boots he had picked up after swimming across the flooded Ebro River during the great retreats in the Aragon province in the spring of 1938, a few months before Hemingway wrote his profile. The journalist Vincent James Sheean, who, like Hemingway, wrote about the Spanish Civil War for various American newspapers, had witnessed Wolff's unexpected return after being lost for six days behind enemy lines and had seen him enter the small *chabola,* a hastily built hut that served as battalion headquarters after the recent debacles. "You built

Milton Wolff and Ernest Hemingway near the Ebro Front, spring 1938. According to Wolff, when this photo appeared in the New York Yiddish newspaper *The Forward,* his mother learned that contrary to her son's claim to be working in a factory behind the lines, he was really captain of the Abraham Lincoln battalion. (Photographer unknown; attributed by Milton Wolff to Robert Capa. Courtesy of The Bancroft Library, University of California, Berkeley.)

this thing pretty low," Wolff had deadpanned. "I guess you guys didn't think I was coming back." Then he had taken a plate of garbanzo beans cooked in olive oil, grabbed some long-delayed letters from his girlfriend in New York, and disappeared into a deep silence. "Now he sat doubled up over his beans and his letters," observed Sheean, "his gaunt young face frowning with concentration. I think he knew how glad they all were to see him, and wanted to ignore it as much as possible."[2]

Spain in wartime captured the passion and the professional interests of the finest writers of the 1930s. Most of them gave their talents to defend the Republican, or Loyalist, side against the military rebellion launched in July 1936 by General Francisco Franco and a coalition of monarchists, the Catholic hierarchy, large landowners, and fascists. Weighed against the military aid Franco received from Italy's Mussolini and Germany's Hitler, the literary voices that rallied to the Spanish Republic brought scant assistance. But perhaps, in compensation, they offered remarkably lucid prose and poetry. The English novelist Ralph Bates, who had served as political commissar of the Anglo-American Fifteenth Brigade, spoke to the League of American Writers in New York in 1937, stressing the natural sympathy intellectuals felt for the Republic, referring to "our sense of sharing the responsibility for the war." Writers "who have spread democratic ideas," he explained, "are really responsible for the fact that hundreds of thousands are now dead because they refused to live under fascism."[3]

Such feelings impelled numerous authors to visit Spain as eyewitnesses and reporters; others journeyed to the war to fight. And some who went to witness the war, such as the young journalist James Lardner, son of the celebrated writer Ring Lardner, wound up enlisting in the ranks, much to the consternation of his older colleague, Ernest Hemingway. Another Hemingway friend, the poet Evan Shipman, drove an ambulance, as his mentor had during the World War. But Lardner, wounded once in action, rebuffed requests to withdraw and disappeared into an ambush just before all foreign soldiers were withdrawn from combat. He was the last American volunteer killed in Spain.

Among the English stood the poets W. H. Auden and Stephen Spender; young writers like John Cornford and Julian Bell, both killed in battle; and the renowned George Orwell, who was wounded fighting with the anarchists on the Aragon front and returned home to write *Homage to Catalonia,* describing the conflict between local leftist revolutionaries and the central government. Orwell lived, however, to have second thoughts. In a 1943 essay titled "Looking Back on the Spanish War," he conceded, "The Fascists won because they were stronger. . . . No political strategy could offset that."[4]

French intellectuals, closer geographically to Spain and to the fascist powers, hoped to stop the aggressors on Spanish soil. None was more influential than the novelist André Malraux, who described the early months of the war in a fictionalized memoir, *Man's Hope,* portraying the conflict between political idealism and the obligations of war. "When a Communist addresses an international conference, he puts his fist on the table," the novelist said. "When a fascist addresses an international conference, he puts his feet on the table. . . . A Democrat—be he American, English, or French—when he addresses an international conference, scratches his head, and asks questions." Rejecting ambivalence, Malraux helped organize the Spanish Republic's air forces and, then, in the spring of 1937, embarked on a tour of the United States, seeking military aid for Spain. "It is good that writers and artists have their share of responsibility here," he told the Artists and Writers Ambulance Corps in New York, a group that was raising money for medical aid for Spain; "so that this swelling tide of democratic voices may be the roar which comes from the other side of the ocean to muffle the dull noise of human suffering."[5]

The words resonated for the culture critic of the *Brooklyn Eagle,* the novelist Alvah Bessie, who interviewed Malraux at his Manhattan hotel and became captivated by the Frenchman's political sensibilities. "He is that rare being," wrote Bessie, "an artist and a man of action, the one inseparable from the other."[6] Bessie was impressed by Malraux's stories of aviation. As a seven-year-old boy, Bessie had witnessed a flight by Orville Wright above Manhattan in a biplane and ever since had yearned to fly. He had recently published the novel *Dwell in the Wilderness* and written short stories good enough to appear in the annual O. Henry anthologies. Now he took Malraux as a model, joined a flying club on Long Island, and began to earn his wings. Bessie flew solo for the first time on July 4, 1937, and resolved to follow Malraux's path to Spain. Leaving behind a stormy marriage and two young sons, he volunteered to join the International Brigades to aid the Spanish Republic. He was 33, slightly older than most of the American volunteers, and some of his comrades called him Papa. He took with him a pocket-sized notebook, which he used to record his experiences in the war. When Bessie arrived in Spain, however, he learned that by then only Spanish nationals could serve in the Republican air force. Instead, he enlisted in the Lincoln Battalion.

Other American writers journeyed to Spain, bore witness, and transmitted reports to the public at home. At a time when politicians decried the financial tangles that had drawn the United States into the world war, Washington refused to support the Spanish government against the military rebellion. Rather, the White House adopted the "non-interventionist" policies of Britain and France. Those "Western democracies," as President Franklin D. Roosevelt called them, opposed the left-leaning Republic and had no interest in hastening another general war. Germany and Italy also agreed to non-intervention, but only on paper. Meanwhile, Josef Stalin's Soviet Union responded to the fascists' support of Franco by providing limited military assistance to the Republic. Since the rebels obtained abundant support from Hitler and Mussolini, the non-intervention policies served primarily to isolate the elected government.

United States neutrality, formalized by congressional legislation in January 1937, reflected widespread "isolationist" sentiments. American volunteers ignored diplomatic formalities. They applied for passports as "tourists" or "students," sometimes using false names and, in cases where those tricks failed, sneaked aboard ships and stowed away. Few people were fooled by the tourist disguise. At Le Havre, U.S. consular officials warned travelers of the risks of violating the neutrality laws. "'You're supposed to be tourists,'" Alvah Bessie was advised in Paris; "'so act the part. . . . ' We wondered," he recalled, "how we could look like tourists; eight men with identical paper parcels getting off at the same station. Eight men? Perhaps eighty men. We didn't ask."[7] By 1937, when most of the volunteers landed in Europe, France had closed the border with Spain. At sea, Italian submarines attacked coastal shipping to the Republic. Consequently, most Americans entered Spain only after a dangerous midnight climb over the steep Pyrenees, guided by experienced smugglers.

Their violation of passport laws would haunt the volunteers for the rest of their lives. But precisely because non-intervention proved to be a pro-Franco policy, most writers felt obliged to seek wider public support for the Loyalist cause. The list of names is long, including Erskine Caldwell, Malcolm Cowley, Lillian Hellman, Josephine Herbst, and Dorothy Parker. The writer Langston Hughes went to Spain to write about the black volunteers for the African American press. In the summer of 1937, he joined another poet and Lincoln volunteer, Edwin Rolfe, to send shortwave radio broadcasts from Madrid to the United States. Stressing the lack of racial prejudice in Republican Spain, Hughes warned that "if fascism creeps across Spain, across Europe, and then across the world, there will be no place left for intelligent young Negroes at all."[8] After a visit to Barcelona in 1938, the novelist Theodore Dreiser pleaded with the French foreign minister Georges Bonnet to send a few automobiles urgently needed to assist Spanish refugees across the border. "In Paris," Dreiser reported, "Bonnet said he would see what could be done. But nothing was done."[9]

The novelist John Dos Passos left Spain with a different anger. Having gone there to assist Ernest Hemingway and Joris Ivens in making a pro-Republic propaganda film, *The Spanish Earth,* he was shocked to learn that his old friend and translator, José Robles, had been killed by communist agents. His political views changed instantly, and he began to condemn the Republican cause. The reversal infuriated Hemingway, who made no apologies for the communists, but insisted that the survival of the Republic was more important. "A war is still being fought in Spain," he protested in 1938; " . . . [F]or you to try constantly to make out that the war the government is fighting against the fascist Italian, German Moorish invasion is a communist business imposed on the will of the people is sort of viciously pitiful."[10]

Later scholars and biographers of Hemingway, looking back at Spain from the perspective of the Cold War, would criticize his failure to address communist machinations while the war was being fought. By contrast, writers on the Left would denounce the novelist's portrayal of specific communist leaders in Spain, sometimes excusing his lack of ideological commitment by saying he was "naive." But it was Hemingway's unyielding dedication to Spain—not so much to the government as to the Spaniards he loved and respected—that earned him the admiration of the Lincoln volunteers. The New York–born poet Edwin Rolfe, "having heard much" of Hemingway's anti-Semitism, initially "felt like meeting him even less than he felt like meeting me—nil," but came in Spain to respect the novelist's character—"a sort of overgrown boy," he noted in his diary, "very likeable." Later, in his history of the Lincoln Battalion, Rolfe acknowledged that "the presence of this huge, bull-shouldered man with the questioning eyes and the full-hearted interest in everything that Spain was fighting for instilled in the tired Americans some of his own strength and quiet unostentatious courage."[11]

Believing that the Spanish war would be "a dress rehearsal" for a general war in Europe, Hemingway embarked for Spain, promising to write "anti-war war correspondence" to keep the United States out of the conflict "when it comes." His work on *The Spanish Earth*—Hemingway eventually wrote and narrated the film's voiceover—showed sophisticated military understanding, and his dispatches for the North American Newspaper Alliance revealed his commitment to the Republican cause. Once he visited a wounded American volunteer, Robert Raven, blinded in both eyes by a grenade, who had attended the University of Pittsburgh. "And it still isn't you that gets hit," Hemingway told readers in the United States, "but it is your countryman now. Your countryman from Pennsylvania, where once we fought at Gettysburg." Returning to America, he spoke to a Writers Congress in New York about the evils of fascism. "A writer who will not lie cannot live and work under fascism," he said.[12]

The journalist Martha Gellhorn (Hemingway's lover and later his third wife) covered the war for *Collier's* magazine. Using her personal friendship with Eleanor Roosevelt, she arranged for Hemingway and filmmaker Joris Ivens to have a private screening of *The Spanish Earth* for President Roosevelt and a few administration officials at the White House, impressing them with their commitment for Republican Spain. Like Hemingway, Gellhorn expressed no doubt about the importance of the war's outcome. "It is not a war between Spaniards," she later wrote to Mrs. Roosevelt, "it is a fight between one democracy and three fascisms."[13]

Having failed to alter Washington policy, the filmmaker-writers took a train to the west coast to raise money for ambulances. Hemingway also paid for the passage of a few Lincoln volunteers, including, the ambulance driver–poet Evan Shipman. On a second trip to Madrid Hemingway and Gellhorn lived in the Hotel Florida, subject to sporadic shelling and bombardment from Franco's forces. "All this was very strange, like movie music," wrote Gellhorn of the echoing sounds of war, "and you had to keep telling yourself that men were making this, and more men were out there half a mile away where the shells hit."[14]

Despite the shortages of wartime, the Florida tried to maintain an air of elegance—polished silverware, table linens, waiter service. But the menu seldom varied—bread, garbanzo beans, orange slices, cheap wine, and rough brandy. "There was never enough food," Edwin Rolfe would later write, "but always poetry." Hemingway's room served as a watering hole for soldiers on leave from the front. Here they enjoyed hot baths, Hemingway's private store of delicacies—hams, cheeses, even caviar—and a magical fifth of scotch that never dwindled. "No visiting American Brigader," one veteran recalled, "was ever denied the pleasure of his company or cigarettes, or a long pull at this bottomless bottle."[15]

Hemingway's other watering hole was the Café Chicote, which he remembered from prewar days as the place where "the good guys went." One warm afternoon, shortly after the fighting at Brunetė in the summer of 1937, Hemingway sat drinking at a crowded table in Chicote's with Shipman and Herbert Matthews, the *New York Times* Republican correspondent (the *Times* sent the pro-fascist William Carney to cover the other side), as well as some Lincoln soldiers on leave and some Spanish women. The 21-year-old Milton Wolff, steered there by his captain, Philip Detro from Texas, entered the bar to say hello. Wolff was then leader of a machine gun company. A high school dropout, he'd barely heard of Hemingway's literary work and remained unimpressed by the chit-chat. "Ernest is quite childish in many respects," Wolff wrote to a friend in Brooklyn. "He wants very much to be a martyr. . . . So much for writers," he concluded. "I'd much rather read their works than be with them." Wolff stuck around long enough to pick up one of Hemingway's women friends. Only later did Edwin Rolfe tell him that the novelist had arranged the affair. "I just wanted to cheer you up," a Hemingway-type character remarked in a similarly situated story, "Night Before Battle." "Grow up," the soldier replied; "what's one more?" The Hemingway answer: "One more."[16]

Wolff visited the writer again at the Florida and read manuscript pages of *The Fifth Column,* Hemingway's only play. They did not meet again until the following spring, when Hemingway covered the retreats of the Republican army on the Aragon front. Robert Capa, the legendary photographer, captured them together: Hemingway—stocky, curious, an adventurer in his half-opened, zippered jacket; Wolff—lanky in uniform, a beret covering his dark hair, but shy, hands in his pockets, face turned downward, wanting to get on with the war. "Hemingway was eager as a child," Alvah Bessie wrote of this visit to the front, "like a big kid, and you liked him. He asked questions like a kid: 'What then? What happened then? And what did *you* do? And what did *he* say?'" Bessie was flattered when the novelist recognized his name and immediately felt bad about the critical reviews of Hemingway's novels he'd written. Other writers were more sardonic about the novelist's appearance. The poet James Neugass was filling in a shell hole when "a small limousine came tearing down the road so fast I had to put on the ditchdiving act I use when the planes come near. 'That's Hemingway,' said someone pointing at the vanishing cloud of dust. 'He's a writer and I'm a writer,' I thought and went back to work."[17]

A few weeks later, the photograph of Hemingway and Wolff appeared in the photogravure section of a New York Yiddish newspaper. To her surprise, Wolff's mother finally learned what her absent son was doing in Spain. Not, as he reported in his letters, working in a factory so that a Spanish worker could fight at the front, but leapfrogging through the ranks from machine gunner at Brunеté to commanding officer of the Lincoln Battalion. A "nobody at home," Rolfe wrote about Wolff in his diary, "leader of men here." With others, Rolfe observed, the reverse had been true.[18]

While the Lincolns launched a bold offensive on the Ebro front during the summer of 1938, Hemingway returned to America to write his Spanish war stories. The news from Europe remained bad. At the Munich conference in September, the British and French capitulated to Hitler's territorial demands, agreeing to the dismemberment of Czechoslovakia. Appeasement of the dictators boded no good for Republican Spain. In a desperate effort to end the charade of non-intervention, the Spanish premier Juan Negrín appealed to the League of Nations in Geneva for the withdrawal of all foreign troops from Spanish territory, including the International Brigades. The League agreed only to supervise the withdrawal of the volunteers on the Republican side, including many soldiers who were not permitted to return to their home countries. Franco made no concessions and the war continued unabated.

Hemingway returned to Barcelona in November 1938 and planted himself at the Majestic Hotel, described by Vincent Sheean as "almost the worst hotel in Europe," but which during wartime had cultivated a "friendly atmosphere and was used to the strange hours and stranger behavior of the foreign correspondents."[19] Together with Matthews, Sheean, and Capa, Hemingway toured the battle front along the Ebro and later visited the remnants of the American volunteers at Ripoll. He met Bessie again, congratulating him on surviving the war. "I always felt responsible for your being here," he admitted. When Bessie wondered why, Hemingway mentioned the speech that Bessie had heard him deliver at the Writers Congress. Bessie, thinking of Malraux, was struck by the exaggeration.[20]

As last commander of the Lincoln Battalion, Wolff moved around more than most of the soldiers waiting for repatriation. He stayed at the Majestic, attended meetings with Spanish communist leaders, and enjoyed the writers' company. Among the hotel's other residents was the sculptor Jo Davidson, who was completing a series of clay models of the leaders of the Spanish Republic—among them the charismatic communist Dolores Ibárruri; Julio Álvarez Del Vayo, minister of foreign affairs; and El Campesino, the popular general. But he wanted an American face and when he saw Wolff's shaggy hair and gaunt features, Davidson asked him to model. Misunderstanding the image he projected, Wolff first had a haircut and a shave, nearly causing the sculptor to cancel the session.

It was this clay composition that Hemingway depicted when he wrote about Wolff at the end of the war. Both, by then, believed that Spain would be the prelude to another world war, which would surely embroil the United States. Once again, Hemingway drew analogies to the American Civil War. Wolff, "gaunt as Lincoln," symbolized that earlier battle for freedom. The name Lincoln Battalion deliberately reflected a cult of the sixteenth president that flourished during the 1930s and included Hollywood films by D. W. Griffith (*Abraham Lincoln,* 1930) and the characterizations by Paul Muni and Henry Fonda in *Young Mr. Lincoln* and *Abe Lincoln in Illinois.* From this perspective, the Lincoln volunteers in Spain were also defending the legal government from a violent insurrection. American conservatives who supported the Franco side typically appealed to George Washington, a founding father. In this isolationist decade, public interest in foreign affairs demanded a local touch.

Hemingway manipulated the symbols of Lincoln's Civil War deliberately. Just as President Lincoln resisted Confederate efforts to trade with Britain, anti-fascists criticized Washington's policy of embargoing the elected government while allowing commerce with the Franco side. Hemingway used other Civil War metaphors. His elegy "To the American Dead," which appeared in the left-wing magazine *New Masses,* evoked the timelessness of mortal sacrifice and the historical immediacy of their cause. "The fascists may spread over the land, blasting their way with the weight of metal brought from other countries," he wrote. "They may destroy cities and villages and try to hold the people in slavery. But you cannot hold any people in slavery."[21] For Hemingway, Wolff personified that tradition. "He is a retired major now at twenty-three and still alive," said Hemingway, "and pretty soon he will be coming home as other men his age and rank came home after the peace at Appomattox courthouse long ago. Except the peace was made at Munich now and no good men will be at home for long."[22]

Hemingway departed Spain in November 1938, already at work on war stories that would culminate in a major novel. His sympathies appeared unchanged. "There is only one thing to do when you have a war," he declared, "and that is win it." Driven by a desire to validate his commitment, he wrote feverishly. By the end of the year, he had written over one hundred thousand words. He also remained sensitive to criticism. When Alvah Bessie questioned the politics of one of his stories, Hemingway attacked the "ideology boys," suggesting that "what was wrong with his outfit was too much ideology and not enough military training, discipline or materiel."[23]

He nevertheless maintained friendly relations with the Lincoln veterans, helping Bessie land a publisher for his memoir, *Men in Battle,* and praising it as "a true, honest, fine book." He paid hospital bills for Rolfe's wife, sent money to others in need, and wrote letters to assist foreign-born veterans caught by immigration officials on Ellis Island. "The people . . . [who] did nothing about defending the Spanish Republic," he complained, "now feel a great need to attack us who tried to do something . . . to justify themselves in their selfishness and cowardice." When Wolff approached him for a loan to underwrite a chicken and egg farm cooperative for some unemployed veterans, the novelist advanced four hundred dollars on his word. It would be the last time they met.[24]

By the time Hemingway's classic *For Whom the Bell Tolls* appeared in October 1940, the camaraderie of the Spanish war had shattered amid the twists and turns of global politics. The novel did not tell the story of the Lincoln volunteers, as many had expected, but focused on a single volunteer, "Robert Jordan," sent on a special mission to demolish a bridge behind enemy lines. There are important parallels between Hemingway and his fictional hero. Both, as the novel puts it, "fought now in this war because it had started in a country that he loved, and he believed in the Republic and that if it were destroyed life would be unbearable for all those people who believe in it."

Like the novelist, Jordan expressed little interest in ideology other than being "anti-fascist," and accepted "Communist discipline" only because it seemed the most effective way to win the war.[25] Indeed, most scholars have assumed that Hemingway's hero, an amalgam of personalities, was based largely on the communist-leaning commander of the Lincoln Battalion, Robert Merriman, who, like Jordan, had an academic background. A more likely model, however, is the later battalion commander Philip Detro, a non-communist Texan who shared leadership with commissar Fred Keller. "Where I come from," Detro would kid Keller, "we shoot communists." Hemingway, in a letter to Milton Wolff, described "A guy named Detro with no more politics than Robert Jordan [who] commanded that battalion before you did."[26] In any case, Hemingway's fiction showed the communists not as heroes but as foolish, selfish, hypocritical leaders, a necessary evil perhaps in real life but near villains in the book. There was ample reason for the Lincoln volunteers, somewhere between two-thirds and three-quarters of whom were affiliated with the Communist Party, to despise the book's political views.

"It was going to be the greatest book," Fred Keller recalled. "It was going to vindicate us all. Now somebody was going to tell the true story about why we went to Spain." Instead, the novel tripped sensitive nerves.

During the summer of 1939, as Europe plunged toward a second world war, liberals like Hemingway and communists like Bessie, Rolfe, and Wolff shared a common anti-fascist position. When Hemingway privately expressed interest in enlisting in the French army, Bessie wrote to Rolfe, "He loves [war], the dope. We'll be in before you can count the letters in totalitarian," he predicted.[27]

The surprise announcement of the signing of a German-Soviet Non-Aggression Pact in August 1939 rapidly altered the political context. The liberal literary critic Alfred Kazin chided those who remained in the Communist Party as "ideologues," lacking "moral imagination."[28] Hemingway was no communist. Yet he had no trouble rationalizing the diplomatic reversal. "The Soviet Union was not bound by any pact with Hitler when the International Brigades fought in Spain," he said. "It was only after they lost any faith in the democracies that the Alliance was born."[29] This analysis mirrored the feelings among most Lincoln veterans. Having experienced the consequences of Anglo-French non-intervention in Spain, they had no desire to encourage U.S. assistance for the allies who had strangled the Spanish Republic. Thus, as President Roosevelt moved to increase U.S. aid to the allies, traded American destroyers for British naval bases, and supported the first peacetime conscription laws in U.S. history, the organization Veterans of the Abraham Lincoln Brigade (VALB) announced "This is not our war."

Arriving in the middle of this heated political climate, Hemingway's Spanish novel aroused a bitter controversy among the Lincoln veterans. Already facing government harassment for their political beliefs—summoned before the House Committee on Un-American Activities, their offices raided by FBI agents who confiscated papers, charged with political offenses on the state and local levels—Lincoln veterans viewed *For Whom the Bell Tolls* as an anti-communist work. "What emerges from your book," VALB declared in an open letter, "is a picture so drastically mutilated and distorted . . . as to slander the cause for which we fought, which the great majority of the democratic people of the world supported, and which you yourself honorably sustained both by your writing and your personal action." In a series of particulars, the Lincolns charged Hemingway with placing all the atrocities on the Republican side; using the real names of leading communists for the purpose of criticizing their decisions; and maligning the role of Soviet advisors in Spain. In a prescient comment, Alvah Bessie also warned that Hemingway "will live to see every living and dead representative of the Abraham Lincoln Battalion attacked and slandered because of the great authority that attaches to Hemingway's name and his known connection to Spain."[30]

In the continuing debate, Milton Wolff, Hemingway's heroic civilian-soldier, stood with his battalion, accusing the novelist of having been a "tourist" and a "rooter" in Spain. Hemingway fired back. "What would you like me to have done to aid the cause of the Spanish Republic that I did not do?" Indeed, Hemingway's personal efforts outside of journalism were not known to the Lincoln veterans in 1940. News of his visit with Martha Gellhorn to the White House did not circulate in Spain. And the novelist's secret mission behind enemy lines—not, like Robert Jordan's, to blow up a bridge but to provide intelligence about the prevailing political climate in an unnamed town—was not something Hemingway would admit or discuss publicly. Instead, in anger, he called Wolff "a prick." Then within a month he retracted the insult. The Lincolns went on denouncing the book, even holding a public symposium to criticize the novel and the novelist.

The release in 1943 of the movie version of *For Whom the Bell Tolls*, starring Gary Cooper and Ingrid Bergman, perpetuated the antagonism. Hemingway, possibly responding to the Lincolns' earlier complaints, had criticized the Hollywood script, written by Dudley Nichols, for its lack of political clarity.[31] "It gives *nothing* of the reason for which a man will die and know it is well for him to die." He proposed that "the enemy should be called the Fascists and the Republic should be called the Republic. . . . Unless you make this emphasis the people seeing the picture will have no idea what the [Spanish] people were fighting for." His complaints produced no results. And Lincoln veterans like Alvah Bessie and Milton Wolff, even the former guerrilla fighters in Spain William Aalto and Irving Goff continued to scorn Hemingway's work. "The green boy-scouts are the fanatical dopes. (Hemingway)," said Aalto; as for the movie, "it stank."[32]

Despite the sniping and Hemingway's deep resentment of what he considered unjustified criticism, Lincoln veterans understood the power of his reputation and often appealed for his assistance. During World War II, the U.S. Army had treated Spanish Civil War veterans as potentially disloyal soldiers, labeling them "premature anti-fascists."[33] As the Cold War with the Soviet Union intensified after 1945 and government agencies launched a domestic anti-communist campaign, the veterans, both as a group and as individuals, faced condemnation and harassment for their political views. Nevertheless, they remained outspoken critics of the victorious Franco regime in Spain and of the U.S. foreign policy that supported his dictatorship. To commemorate their continuing defiance of fascism, VALB planned a tenth-anniversary celebration on Lincoln's birthday in 1947 and invited Hemingway to New York to read his eulogy "To the American Dead in Spain." Wolff made the phone call, but the novelist had other commitments. Instead, he offered to send a recording of his reading.[34]

In his dry, Midwestern voice, sharing an old camaraderie, he mentioned first his pleasure to be in the company again of "premature antifascists." He said that the soldiers of World War II likely would have been able to stay at home if Washington "would have let us win in Spain." It was knowing that, Hemingway said, that "made a man a premature antifascist." Hemingway could not resist pointing out that having to wear World War II army helmets had turned "many premature anti-fascists prematurely bald."

Hemingway afterward maintained an occasional correspondence with Lincoln veterans, particularly Rolfe, Wolff, and Irving Fajans. When Rolfe sent him an elegy to the city of Madrid, the novelist wrote back that it had made him cry. Wolff also appealed for his assistance to help Lincoln veterans facing imprisonment for defying anti-communist committees in Washington. Hemingway kept his distance, acknowledging that Dr. Edward Barsky, a frontline surgeon in Spain and head of a Spanish refugee aid committee, was a "saint," but feeling that others did not deserve his friendship. "You guys sort of bought this anyway," he said. "You hired out to be tough and then somebody gets hit and says you can't do this to me."[35] Wolff ended this round of their correspondence lamenting Hemingway's failure to speak out against the raging anticommunist atmosphere. "What we all need from you," he wrote, "is a handful of brave words."[36]

It was this lingering antagonism that prompted a contingent of Lincoln veterans to oppose the inclusion of Hemingway's eulogy in an anthology of literary works about the Spanish Civil War, eventually published under the title *The Heart of Spain* in 1952.[37] After Wolff led a formal vote to exclude Hemingway's work, Fajans resigned as editor, leaving Bessie, now facing prison for contempt of Congress as one of the Hollywood Ten, to explain the decision. "Under the name and prestige of

Hemingway," he concluded, "important aid was thus given to humanity's worst enemies." "Bessie," Hemingway said, "I consider to be a jerk on the best day he ever lived."[38]

Nor did the quarrel cease. The controversy between Hemingway and the Lincolns was no literary debate, but rather addressed issues of responsibility. Were the Lincolns responsible for alleged communist crimes in Spain? Did their commitment to the Republic justify persecution at home? For their part, the veterans demanded accountability from Hemingway for the plight of the Spanish people living under Franco. To what degree had his novel contributed to the pro-Franco sentiment in the United States? Should Hemingway have spoken out? Should he have accepted journalistic assignments in the dictatorship during the 1950s?

"I don't know one damned thing about [André] Marty," Wolff assured Herbert Matthews twenty-five years later, referring to Hemingway's prime villain, the head of the International Brigades. "And *that's* significant."[39] Whatever the machinations of the Communist Party in Spain—and Hemingway knew about some of them—Wolff argued that the Lincoln volunteers had fought primarily as anti-fascists—and were ignorant and innocent of Stalinist politics in Spain. No evidence exists showing that Lincolns killed anyone in Spain on political grounds, except fascists. Moreover, Wolff insisted that Hemingway neither faced the risks of warfare in Spain nor saw best friends and comrades killed nearby. "He was a 'tourist' in Spain," Wolff told Bessie in 1981, "a voyeur who darted in and out of action as it pleased him. . . . Which is not to say Ernest Hemingway was not on our side. He was. And his contribution was considerable. . . . But his commitment was not as ours." Unlike the Lincolns, Wolff advised another comrade, Hemingway "was free to choose where to go, when to go, when not to go. . . . In other words his commitment was such that he could write For Whom the Bell Tolls without taking into account what was truly best for la causa." The result, said Wolff, was that for Hemingway "the essence of commitment to the struggle did not exist."[40]

Ironically, despite Wolff's criticism of Hemingway, it could be said that the Lincoln volunteers were the real tourists in Spain, at least at the beginning. Unlike the novelist, who had long shown his love of the Spanish people, most of the Lincolns knew almost nothing of the country they went to help: not its geography, customs, food, language, or culture. They went to Spain, as Hemingway stated, for reasons of "ideology."

They might have gone anywhere to fight fascism (later, during World War II, they did just that). But in Spain their ideology did mature into love, leaving them with a passionate desire to see Spain free.

"Ideology," to use Hemingway's word, made all the difference: it motivated the Lincolns to take action, to risk their lives to affirm anti-fascist principles and the idea that an elected government should be protected from aggression. Unlike the many sympathetic writers in Spain who struggled to awaken the public mind in America, the Lincolns faced genuine deprivation, exhaustion, injury, pain, and death. Over eight hundred Americans were buried in Spain; nearly all were wounded at least once. For them, the war was literally a struggle between life and death, a struggle, therefore, they could never abandon.

"Ideology" also carried the Lincolns outside the American mainstream. Unlike Hemingway, they were never welcomed back home. While he was writing a best-selling novel and earning an enormous sum for the film rights, they endured endless harassment from government agencies and employers. And while Hemingway eventually made peace with the Franco regime, the Lincolns fought to prevent Spain's admission into the United Nations, opposed the mutual aid agreements made between the United States and Franco, and struggled to send aid to Spanish refugees in concentration camps in France and political prisoners caged in Franco's cells. Indeed, "ideology" could thwart their best interests: expunging Hemingway's work from their anthology offended the very people they wanted to reach.

Those attitudes dominated the rest of their lives. "If you lose [a war]," Hemingway wrote in 1939, "you lose everything and your ideology won't save you." Most of the Lincolns—Hemingway's "ideology boys"—clung to the opposite view. Although they "lost the war," Milton Wolff insisted, "neither the Spaniards nor the [International Brigades], nor anti-fascists of any mettle, lost their ideology, much less 'everything.'" To Wolff, writing twenty years after Hemingway's suicide, the novelist's lack of political commitments meant "he had no ideology to save him in the end and contrary to what he says it is exactly that that saved us. And may yet save the world." It was this spirit of commitment—unswerving optimism in the face of political defeat and personal tragedy—that distinguished Lincoln veterans from many literary observers and reporters. To be fair, there were also many writers, Hemingway's ex-wife, Martha Gellhorn among them, who remained outspoken critics of the Franco regime. For them, Spain was the touchstone, symbol of anguish and hope that gave continuity to their lives.[41]

And the world moved on. After Franco's death in 1975, veterans of the Lincoln Brigade returned to Spain, individually and in tourist groups, old men and women come to testify about their role in history and to celebrate the anniversary of their youthful struggles. Fifty years after the war began, as Alvah Bessie prepared a second literary anthology of Spanish Civil War writings, the veterans were proud to include Hemingway's elegy "To the American Dead in Spain." By then, the Spanish dictator lay in his grave and a parliamentary government had taken the first steps toward a modern democracy. To be sure, the transition hinged on a so-called "pact of silence" by which the incipient democracy agreed not to discuss, much less redress, the enormous crimes committed by the Franco regime during and after the Spanish Civil War. Nevertheless, it seemed time to make peace with the past. For the veterans of the Abraham Lincoln Brigade, the war was finally over. "The dead do not need to rise," Hemingway said. "They are a part of the earth now and the earth can never be conquered. . . . It will outlive all systems of tyranny. Those who have entered it honorably, and no men ever entered earth more honorably than those who died in Spain, already have achieved immortality."[42]

▷ CHAPTER 7

Ernest Hemingway, Screenwriter

Letters About For Whom the Bell Tolls

Living with a writer is a touchy matter, and when one writer lives with another writer, as I do with the culinary writer Jeannette Ferrary, you learn to form sturdy, but permeable walls of separation—lines of demarcation that sustain privacy and independent creativity and yet permit the sharing of insight and phrasing and correction. We make sure to work on different terrain. But sometimes, fortuitously, our interests overlap. As I embarked on a history of the Abraham Lincoln Brigade and the Spanish Civil War in the 1980s, my mate began work on a biographical study of her friend, the writer M.F.K. Fisher. When I traveled to Brandeis University to read archival letters from Spain, she drove down the road to peruse Fisher's correspondence from the same era at the Schlesinger library in Cambridge.

It was oral history that produced the most splendid convergence. One day, we found ourselves focusing on the same source, the highly respected editor and publisher Eleanor Friede. She was a strong-voiced woman of about 70, living in a fine, old, red-brick home in Greenwich Village, and had the distinction of being the fifth wife and widow of the remarkable impresario, publisher, and agent, Donald Friede. And the late Mr. Friede, in his diverse incarnations, held the strands that brought us three together. For Mrs. Friede's marital predecessor—the fourth of Donald's wives—was none other than Mary Frances Kennedy Fisher. But even before he had wed either of these women, Friede had made his mark in literary circles as co-founder of Covici & Friede, publishers of John Steinbeck, William Faulkner, Dorothy Parker, and Ernest Hemingway, among other luminaries. In addition, Friede had acted as the Hollywood agent on behalf of Hemingway's Spanish Civil War novel, For Whom the Bell Tolls, *which Paramount bought in 1940 for the record-breaking sum of $100,000 plus ten cents for each copy of the book sold.*

"Did he have much of a relationship with Hemingway?" I inquired on a sunny Saturday afternoon, as we sat in Mrs. Friede's tiny backyard patio consuming Brillat-Savarin cheese, French bread, and white wine.

"For a while," she responded.

"By any chance," I dared to ask, "were there any letters from Hemingway about the Spanish Civil War?"

Indeed there were. But because of the circumstances by which Donald Friede left his employment with Myron Selznick, himself a Hollywood agent and brother of the famous producer David Selznick, there existed only copies of the originals. Addressed to Donald Friede, the correspondence was actually intended for Dudley Nichols, screenwriter of the movie version of Hemingway's novel. Carlos Baker, in his magisterial biography, Ernest Hemingway: A Life Story *(1969), used Friede's copies but did not quote from them directly. My own comments about Hemingway's impassioned critique of the screenplay follow the last letter, below. These letters are printed through the kindness of Eleanor Friede and with the permission of the Ernest Hemingway Foundation. Variant spelling is in the original; typos are corrected by brackets.*

Myron Selznick & Company
Beverly Hills, California
Telephone — Cable Address
Crestview 19171 — Selco"

September 5, 1944

Mr. Donald Friede
A. and S. Lyons, Inc.
356 No. Camden Drive
Beverly Hills, Calif.

Dear Donald:

In accordance with Mr. David O. Selznick's request, I have gone thru our files and am sending you copies of the original letters Mr. Hemingway addressed to you in care of this office. These letters are dated March 3, March 16, April 21, and again April 21, all in 1942, pertaining to the script of "For Whom The Bells Toll".

Regards,
Cordially,
Mary Rechner
Encl.

* * * * *

cc: Mr. Selznick
FILE.

March 3, 1942

Mr. Donald Friede
c/o Myron Selznick
Beverly Hills, Calif.
Dear Donald:
I am studying the Nichols' script very closely. I am sorry that you sent it to me under the circumstances which you did. There is a war on and no one has any right to send a script as confidential when the way it is handled can have such wide implications and be so dangerous. It is my duty to protest against various things in the script and sending it to me confidentially while we are at war can not relieve me of the responsibility for protesting.

What I am anxious for and always have been anxious for is for Paramount to make a good picture. I am not protesting because I want to make any money coming into the thing at this time. But there are certain points about the Nichols script which are really dangerously bad from the standpoint of making a picture which will be useful to our country's war effort at this time. There are also a number of things which are simply stupid and which I can easily correct myself. Principally, these are things dealing with Spain where he has made changes without knowing what he was talking about so that the resulting dialogue could be ludicrous to anyone in a Latin American country. Also reference etc. and great errors in fact and probability. I am reading the script carefully and will write you a letter telling you the various things which I find to be dangerous. If Paramount would send Nichols down here, I could go into all of the other things with him. As it is, I think you were extremely over-enthusiastic about the script. In spite of the very bad dialogue, much of which could be corrected, it could be a good script with certain things put right. As it is, unless certain changes are made I will have to protest against it through the medium which will give my protest the widest amount of circulation, which would be, I imagine, an interview with the Associated Press correspondent here in Havana.

Will you please write me your reactions as soon as you receive this letter. Please believe, Donald, that I have no intention of creating difficulty or causing trouble because I am an author who does not want to see any changes made in his work when it is transmitted to the screen. It is simply that I can not allow a book which has had over 500,000 readers and which on the screen can be an extremely valuable asset in our fight against Fascism, to be presented in any other way than that, without doing everything that I can to keep the book from being sabotaged.

I will write you later when I have completed a study of it. There is no sense in my doing a rewrite job for nothing for Paramount, but I would be glad to do that rather then see the book sabotaged.

Best to you always,

Ernest (Hemingway)

Unless corrections made, will also protest immediately to Cooper who accepted Nichols script on my guaranty Nichols would write a script which would not distort the true significance of the book.

FINCA VIGIA SAN FRANCISCO DE PAULA CUBA

March 16, 1942

Mr. Donald Friede
c/o Myron Selznick
Beverly Hills, Calif.

Dear Donald:

I was glad to get your letter, but somewhat amazed at your attitude about the script. You should never have sent it to me, nor should Dudley Nichols have expected you to send it to me without expecting me to do something about the ignorant, the inept and the dangerously wrong phases of it. To send something like that and then say you cannot comment on it or do anything about it except through Nichols himself, who is an excellent fellow but really only an employee of Paramount, without exposing him and yourself to trouble, is very bad for me. I suggested Dudley Nichols doing the job because I thought he would write a good script and would keep it straight. The excuse that it is not so bad as Bromfield or a thousand times better than Bromfield, is not what we are after. What we are after is to make a fine picture out of what was, at least, a good book. The book had to have certain definite elements of popular appeal to sell the number of copies that it sold. People go to a picture because a certain star or stars are playing in it and if the star is good enough to carry it, a great number of people go to see it anyway. Other people go simply because it is all they have to see and they have a habit of going to pictures. If it is really a great picture with a great star an indeterminable number of people go to see it. But the book costs, this one anyway, $2.75 and when six or seven hundred thousand people pay that out the book must have certain things to make that many people buy it. If this sounds like a kindergarden explanation it is because I am trying to get the whole thing straight to you so that you can let Dudley see the letter and see what I am trying to get at. To make it really clear I have to make it very simple and not skip anything.

"For Whom the Bell Tolls" had three things that sold it to people. The best thing it had was to show what men and women would die for and it concentrated and made come really true what one man would die for. The second thing it had was the true relation in bed between two people. This was all concentrated into the short space of four days. The third thing that it had was a fine action story in which the movement progressed steadily from the beginning to the end and all details were made so truly that the reader felt that he had lived the things that happened in the book.

I can see how much worse Dudley's script could have been. There is no question about it at all, nor that he has tried to follow faithfully much of the book. Where his script fails is that it gives nothing of the reason for which a man will die and know it is well for him to die. It gives nothing of Pilar's true feeling for the Republic which is the animating motif for the whole band. That is the first and greatest loss and the thing which will make it essentially a second-rate rather than a first-rate picture.

I understand his problems in the treating of the relations between Maria and Jordan, but that does not excuse him for having been inept, sometimes ridiculous and often grotesque in the writing of his love scenes. I can truly say that they are really weak and bad love scenes and the dialogue about the twins is enough to kill the picture. I have tried conscientiously to see the good effect of where he is writing for Gary and how Gary would handle the lines, but much of it is really terrible. So, we have two-thirds of the picture, the strength of it, all of which could be retained in spite of any Hays office [r]ulings, already thrown away. I can see how a man can have to vulgarize some things under orders and how to earn his money he will substitute his own bad dialogue for good dialogue, which if he were not paid to rewrite he might have stolen or imitated as has been done often enough in the past. But there is no reason to condone fatal ignorance, bad writing and bad construction in the script of a picture which means as much as this picture means. It can be a great picture or a disastrous flop and Dudley has taken a terrible responsibility in the way he has bitched it up.

The good part that he has done is to write good action. Bu[t] in his action he has neglected the other two things that made the book, and one, at least, of these could very well have been included.

The other thing which is extremely important is his treatment of all of the people of Pilar's band. If you know Spaniards you can kid them in writing about them or projecting them, but if you do not know them and are simply visualizing the long line of phonies that have appeared in all such disastrous films as the last "Blood and Sand," you're headed straight for disaster. The Spaniards in this book are not out of Carmen. There are no picturesque rags, no bandanas, none of the ghastly falseness of that last flop of Mamoulian. The clothes should be dignified and hard. The whole note is dignity. The men should be dressed in grays and in blacks and whites, and for Christ's sake let there be no "bright colored bandanas" worn around the heads as there are in Dudley's script.

I have many more points to make but I should start now to take up some of the script to show you what I am talking about technically. You realize, Donald, that by your lovely handling of this you have forced me into doing a gratis partial rewrite of the Nichols script simply as a protest against its ignorance and ineptness. That is a piece of agent-ship that you ought to be eternally proud of. The way you have handled it, Dudley is bitched if I protest to Paramount; I am a s.o.b. if I say anything about having seen the script; and I can not make suggestions to Paramount but only to Dudley. I hope you will at least arrange to get some money out of Dudley for yourself for my services in correcting his script for him. Seeing this handling certainly makes me feel good that I closed the deal with Paramount in Chicago myself over the telephone rather than leaving it in anybody else's hands.

To start with the script, following Nichols' apologetic note about length, there is a page headed, "People." Under the band of El Sordo one character is called Rinaldo. This is an Italian name, not a Spanish one. Evidently, it is a hang-over in Dudley's memory from, "A Farewell to Arms." I suggest the substitution of the name Paco or Enrique or Segundo. In the same list of characters General Golz is described as a German who directs the offensive for the Loyalists. Golz in the book is a Russian who has taken that nom-de-guerre which was that of a great German general. I suggest that he be described as an officer from the Soviet Union. In the same list of characters, Andre Marty is described by his own name as a French political commisar who is an insane fanatic. I used the true name Andre Marty in the book. In a year or so I will be broke and neither Andre Marty nor his descendents, if they sue me, will be able to obtain any damages. The Guaranty Trust tell me that Paramount probably will not be broke for some time and I suggest that you change the name of Andre Marty in order that they do not have another Youssopoff suit on their hands. I suggest you change the name to Paul Massart or Paul Carre or Andre Massart.

In sequence A, where Jordan and Kashkin blow the train they would never have been alone. There would have been supporting guerrilla troops with at least one machine gun to fire on the train after the explosion in order to cover the retreat of the men who had used the exploder and to kill as many of the troops as possible when they got out of the cars. This whole scene is badly visualized and for it to be done right you should see the guerrilla troops hidden behind the rocks, Kashkin handling the machine gun, Jordan with the exploder, and then far away the train, first small in the distance, then getting larger and larger as it comes up the track and the tightening of the people who are expecting it and then the train blowing its whistle, you seeing the steam, then hearing the sound come, and then finally the train closer and closer, and the roar of the explosion, and then the blown up engine, the derailed cars, the troops swarming out, the machine gun hammering, the officers trying to form them up in some kind of order, the toll the guerrillas take, and finally their break for the hills and the firing of the troops and the pursuit. When Kashkin is hit and wishes to say goodbye to Jordan, he would never say, "adios," which was a phrase used only in old Spain and never under the Republic. In that extremely dubious scene of Nichols' I would have said, "salud," and Jordan would have used the same word. Even that way it is ham but at least salud is the proper word and the other word in such a place in the mouth of anyone fighting for the Republic is ridiculous. Also, when Jordan shoots Kashkin he would not fire three times into his head. Anyone shooting a person who is being shot willingly or asking to be shot would shoot them once in the back of the head, putting the muzzle close to the head. The three shots in Dudley's script are horrible and ridiculous. This scene could be written so clearly and so effectively and instead it is a botch in the dark which will only confuse people and lose all the advantages of making the picture real to those who see it rather than phony and foggy.

After this first scene, Jordan meets Golz in a scene which seems to come straight out of "Blood and Sand." Why could Nichols not have had Jordan meet the general in the latter's headquarters rather than in a completely irreal and impossibly phony situation in Madrid. For a general to meet a man carrying out guerrilla operations behind the enemy lines in a cafe and in that cafe to show a map and the plans for an attack is as unreal as for a girl to be raped in St. Patrick's Cathedral during a High Mass. One of the finest and best things about American pictures is their fidelity to how things would be and how they actually are. But this scene of Dudley's is extremely and utterly ridiculous and sets a note of silliness and unreality for the whole picture. Golz' language in speaking to Jordan is amateurish and stupid. All the effects which are needed could be made by clear, hard-spoken military language which would be clearly comprehensible to any audience rather than the type of mush that is put in the mouth of Golz. I can correct this language for Dudley and will do so if you and he wish, otherwise I refer him to the book. As it is it is very bad. The only way he could keep his cafe stuff would be for Golz and Jordan to meet in the cafe and then go around corner to Golz' headquarters, which would be guarded by sentries in a side street.

And now skip to page A-17 where Pablo says, "But every day the vermin gets stronger." Why not say Fascists instead of vermin. We are at present engaged in fighting a war against the Fascists. It was always the Fascists that were referred to in Spain and to make the issue clear it is best to use this term. No one in America knows what a Falangist is but everyone should, or will by the time the picture comes out, know what a Fascist is. On the same page where Pablo says, "Before the war I worked in the bull ring." This does not give a clear picture. It would be better to say, "I looked after the horses in the bull ring." On page A-18 the sentence, "lifts his arm to Pablo." This is the Fascist salute. He should raise his clenched fist to Pablo.

The next sequence where all of the band are working very comically around a machine gun is really very bad. These men have been fighting guerrilla actions for a year and a half and if they have been using a Lewis gun, any of them should be able to take it apart and put it together blind-folded in the dark. The idea of making them simply ridiculous figures in order to make Jordan more of a man is part of the whole silliness of the treatment of Spaniards which insists that any foreigner must be a fool. Remember that practically all the people in this picture except Jordan are Spaniards and these are the people you are fighting a battle with and you should not make them idiots at this stage simply for the sake of a misplaced laugh. This sequence is infinitely stronger if it were written this way: The men are grouped around the gun which has been taken down and the parts spread on a blanket. Remember, these men expect to defend their lives with this gun and no one would take it down and scatter parts about or have the ludicrous jigsaw puzzle complex which has been inserted for a gag. Actually, Cooper would look down at the gun and say, "What happened to her?" One of the men answers, "We had a jam on it at the last train and it wouldn't eject." Cooper draws in his upper lip, stoops and looks closely at the parts that are spread out on the blanket. He says, "How are you getting along with it?" One of the men answers, "All right. We had to make a piece but it doesn't quite fit." They go on working on the gun. Cooper leans down and picks up one of the pieces. He says, "Let me see the extractor." They all look up at him with varying shades of doubt and distrust on their faces. He takes out a worn leather case attached by a leather thong to his pocket and extracts a file and works on the piece with the file, bringing his lower lip up over his upper lip as he works. They all watch him. "I always carry an extra extractor in the butt plate," he says. "There was an extra one," the gypsy says, "but it cracked at the last train." "They'll all crack if you fire too long bursts," Cooper says. "This one is going to be all right. Try it now." He turns away and Primitivo starts fitting the gun together. Continue with Nichols.

On page A-24 where the gypsy says, "I am a trapper, Roberto." There is no such thing as a trapper in Spain. A man may trap a few things but he is not a professional trapper as in America. The line should be, "I do some trapping too."

On page A-32 at the bottom of the page where Pilar says, "How are you and how is everything on the other side of the lines?" It should be, "How are you and how is everything in the Republic." This is to establish as soon as possible her fixation on the Republic and her illusion that everything is fine and which is her motive for what she is doing and for what they are all fighting for. It is extremely important that this be established as soon as possible, for otherwise what are all these people doing fighting in the hills after a year and a half and what is Jordan doing? There must be something established which they believe in and for which they are fighting. In the book it is the Republic and it is the use of that word which is something that we also in America believe in and are now fighting for and which gives the word a dignity so that it gives a true symbol of what the fight is all about. Throughout the picture the enemy should be called the Fascists and the Republic should be called the Republic, not simply ourselves and the enemy. This in the script is a hangover from Bromfield's treatment whereby the whole action was to take place in Limbo and no one was to be offended in any way. But now we have had Pearl Harbor and various other things and by the time the picture is released it is perfectly possible we will have an expeditionary force fighting in Spain. You take a much greater chance of ruining the picture by not having the names clearly stated and issues clearly drawn than you do in trying to muddle along in order to appease the enemies of our country and please Jock Whitney and any of his Fascist inclined relatives. I mean specifically his brother-in-law, Charlie Payson.

On page A-34 the same observation holds true when Pilar says, "Now we have horses. Let's blow all the bridges and get out." She should continue, "Let's go to the Republic. I am sick of this place," and so on.

On page A-38 the scene with Anselmo and Jordan where they watch the sentry at the bridge is horribly ham. Anselmo says that the sentry looks like a man from his village and then whispers, "Yes, he looks like the son of Sanchez. He is very young." Sanchez is as common a name in Spanish as Smith here. Even if Anselmo were to make such a ham remark he would say, "The son of Domingo Sanchez or Rodrigo Sanchez," but never "the son of Sanchez" any more than you would say, "the son of Smith of Chicago." The whole scene is very bad and should be rewritten. It loses all tensity through the bad philosophical blah-blah uttered at a time when men would only whisper to each other about the most practical details. That type of talking is only justified after the action has taken place and people are let down, as when Anselmo and Jordan were climbing back to camp after inspecting the bridge.

Because I am so severe where the script is wrong, do not think that I do not appreciate the good parts that Dudley has done, but this is like a battle, and there is no time for praising something that has gone properly. The defects must be corrected and where no censure or praise is given, it means that one understands what the man has done with what he has had to work with.

On page 46, the last line should go for the same reasons I have mentioned before, "I am for the bridge and for the Republic." Unless you make this emphasis the people seeing the picture will have no idea what the people were really fighting for. Since it is told which side is which, the emphasis must be made in order for there to be any emotional basis at all for what they are doing.
On page 51 the description of Jordan's robe should read, "covering of warm green balloon silk," rather than "silk." Also where does he get the folded blanket for a pillow? Why not have him fold up his jacket? The man can't carry a ton of stuff around with him.

On page 55 Rafael says, "Can he be allowed to live now, after what has been said?" It is much better to have him say, "Why don't you kill him before he kills you?" And for Jordan to answer, "He won't kill me."

On page 58 where Jordan says, fed up, "Go to bed. I told you I am no assassin. It is much better to say, "Go to bed. There is no need to kill now." He would not chuck that word assassin around, offending everybody and talking in such a high faluting way. If you are to make the picture credible, Jordan must have some sense in his handling of the people and also I am against these horrible hammy phrases, such as on page 59, "You know Pablo better than I do. Is there danger of treachery?" This should read, "You know Pablo better than I do. What will he do?" This has equal menace in it without the use of such hammy words in conversation as treachery.

On page 61, why should Jordan say, "Yes. More safe."? Why not say, "safer?" He is supposed to be able to speak both English and Spanish without having to go into pidgin English to show that he is speaking in a foreign language.

On page 62, where does Pilar get this bed in the cave? Wouldn't she have a simple blanket bed like anyone else? Where would such a bed come from? If you can figure out where it would come from and see how they hauled it up there and put it in, then it is O.K. to have it. As a matter of fact, if they made tables, they could make a bed or loot one, so Dudley can have his bed if he needs it, although I do not remember any bed.

On page 71 please use the word "planes" or the Spanish word, "aviones" instead of "air machines." Air machines is as idiotic and corny used in Spanish or with Spanish people as if you would have someone referring to flying machines instead of planes in the American Army. The same holds true for that horrible corniness about the "machinery gun." The audience know that these people are Spaniards and are foreigners and it is not necessary to make them idiots.

On page 73, why not say Fascists instead of Falangists. Not one out of 200 Americans will know what a Falangist is in spite of the Dies Committee and for the South American trade they can always put Falangist in the sub-titles. In the English-speaking version it should always be Fascist.

On page 78, I must express my admiration for the phrase, "climbing as hurriedly as they can through gigantically beautiful scenery." Don't you think it would be better to indicate what the scenery is like that they are climbing through or don't we learn anything from such films as "The Grand Illusion?"

On page 85, Gustavo is middle aged and wears long mustaches. I think this is the same Italian influence that got the other guy called Rinaldo. There haven't been any long mustaches on a Spaniard in the last 100 years. Please keep long mustaches off everybody in the picture unless you are prepared to furnish little cartons for the audience to vomit in for the South American trade.

Reading over the Maria and Jordan scenes up until page 121, they are probably the best that Dudley could get out of what he was ordered to do. They are quite unreal and not at all credible but they are in motion picture tradition of what happens between two people of the opposite sex and have been carefully styled to Gary. People forget what a good actor Gary is and how many things he can do besides hesitate and seem embarrassed at the thought of any emotion. I think he had hoped in this picture to get away from this but Dudley has fed steadily to those two abilities of his rather than to what he is really able to do. It makes me sick to see what has been done and how a picture which can be a great picture and still not run afoul of any Hays office, has been cut in all the love part up until page 147 into the stupidest conventional shy-dope-meets-pure-young-thing-who-has-suffered. Neither of these people had much time for shyness but I can see how well Dudley has been cutting it to what they said they would take. If that was not the circumstance, then he ought to be shot.

On page 138, if this scene is not to be simply a brutal massacre, there should be an insert after the line, "Don Federico Gonzalez who came next was a Fascist of the first order." The insert should tell in the words of the book why he was a Fascist. It needs only to be a sentence in length, otherwise no one knows why any of these people were killed, or what the towns-people had against them, and the whole killing is a meaningless butchery. I know that Dudley did not inten[d] it to be this way and it is simply a matter of an insertion of one sentence which he can find in the book.

Throughout I am not criticising construction since the script has reached a phase where it would be useless for me to do that. I am simply trying to supply certain things which are necessary and which are missing and to correct certain things which demand correction if it is not to be misleading and ridiculous.

On page 151 I think it is much more effective if the line reads, "Cavalry don't ride alone," instead of, "Soldiers don't ride alone."

I will give you the rest of the corrections and a general summing up in another installment. Will take the script with me to Mexico City where I am going on Wednesday and will dictate corrections, etc., on the rest of the script from there. You can reach me by wire and airmail until April 2, c/o William Davis, Uruguay 69, Mexico, D.F.

If I sound bitter in this, please throw it out, the bitterness or any rudeness or insults. I am trying to be accurate and correct in a hurry and it is like being on a boat. There is no time to say, "please cast off this," or, "Please make this fast." The politeness is understood and throw out the rudeness. But everything I say I mean absolutely and sincerely. Only do not be offended by the fact that I have to be tough and say it in a hurry.

Best regards to yourself and to Dudley Nichols. Yours always,

(Signed) Ernest (Hemingway)

cc: Dudley Nichols
cc: Mr. Selznick, FILE

* * * * *

FINCA VIGIA SAN FRANCISCO DE PAULA CUBA

April 21, 1942

Dear Donald:
Have just received your wire and am rushing comments on Dudley's script from page 157 on. There is probably not much that I can do about the El Sordo fight as I understand all that has already been shot. So I will not tear it down but will only make a few corrections on obvious errors which would be damaging to the film in Latin American countries or anywhere people understand anything about Spain and Spaniards.

On page 163, can't the long moustachios be removed from this man? They have long moustachios on Italians but never on Spaniards. It is an absolutely phoney touch. As phoney as calling one of the men in Sordo's band, Rinaldo, which I have already written about. Rinaldo is an Italian name and is not Spanish.

On page 165, he should say "That's our comrade, El Sordo." Not "Our friend."

On page 170, why must Dudley make the boy Joaquin feeble-minded? Of course he knows they would attack with planes. Hadn't he seen the planes of the day before? I hope in the cutting Dudley will eliminate some of the awful talky-talky about death and dying that has been put into the mouths of the characters. People can have thoughts in their heads but no one talks that phoney poetry about dying, that he has put in their mouths. It is really ghastly stuff.

On page 172, why does he have Jordan coming back from his defensive position, disarming himself and the camp to come back down to the cave, while the Sordo fight is still going on? This is nonsense, kills the suspense of that fight, and will be ridiculous to anyone seeing the picture. Remember this picture is being made in war time and will be seen by people who are war minded, and it cannot have muzzy thinking and construction in it.

Sequence F is almost the worst thing so far in the script. In it Dudley manages to lose all the suspense and all the tension which in the book is maintained steadily until the blowing of the bridge. He does this by a mishandling of the whole progress of the action after Sordo's command is destroyed on the hill. When he reads it over, I am sure he will see how wrong the structure is and how the suspense is lost.

Until I reach that point, will note various things wrong on the way. On page 190 Jordan bawling out the Gypsy for taking the wrist watch is absolutely phoney. All people in all armies loot the enemy dead and Jordan in the position he is in would never be such a silly prig as to bawl out the Gypsy for taking a wrist watch off the dead cavalryman. What does Dudley think Jordan would want done with the wrist watch? Bury it with the body or send it to the boy's dead mother or his sweetheart or what? If there was a wrist watch on the body, it belonged to the first person who found it. It is a lack of understanding of such things which makes phoney scenes; and phoney sequences make a phoney picture.

On page 191, Dudley has Jordan say "the dead cavalryman is from Tafalla." This is a town in Navarre in northern Spain where the people are fanatical Carlists. Navarre produced some of Franco's finest troops and best fighters. It is a symbol of the fanatical troops on Franco's side. Dudley then has Maria say that Joaquin comes from that same town. This is an impossibility, because Joaquin is a boy from Valladolid, a town where there were many Republicans who were butchered at the start of the war. If Joaquin would have come from Tafalla, he would have been a Carlist and fighting on Franco's side. This is the sort of thing which seems unimportant to anyone not knowing Spain, but would make the picture ridiculous to a Latin American audience.

On page 192, he makes Jordan into a prig again with the gypsy over the business of the letters. There is plenty of opportunity for business between Jordan and the Gypsy without this priggishness.

It is on this same page that Pablo comes in from having found the bodies and Dudley's construction goes all to pieces. The whole point about Pablo is that he is a man who is frightened and actually this business of Sordo being killed, and the heads cut off, really comes to him with such a terrible shock that he deserts that night on account of it. But Dudley brings him in, high spirited, jovial, and absolutely untouched by the terrible thing which has happened on the top of that hill. All of that, on page 193, is completely false and phoney and destroys the character of Pablo and the structure of the picture. Why in God's name not tell the thing visually, and have Anselmo watching the troops ride down with the officers bodies lashed over the horses, as what is left of Berrendo's command rides along the dusty road into Segovia? And then Anselmo coming onto the hill, instead of this phoney business of Pablo rushing in in that preposterous way? What in the hell is the matter with the way that sequence is handled in chapter 29 of the book? When Dudley improves something, okay; but when because he was tired or not feeling so good that day he makes an absolutely silly sequence, it is bloody awful. For instance, it is obvious that Berrendo would take Sordo's machine gun in with him. Remember he is the only officer left out of those sent out on that mission. He has plenty of explanations that he will have to make and he's got to bring in something concrete to justify his losses. That is the reason for the heads business and it is nonsense to have Pablo make that speech at the bottom of page 193, about the gun. When I suggest that Dudley read Chapter 29 for the handling of this whole sequence, it is not a case of the author thinking that no changes can be made in his work. It is just that he gets his own changed version into a childish jam, which absolutely distorts the character of Pablo and by sending the man off to Golz seemingly sure that the attack will be called off, he loses his suspense then and there.

On page 196, where Jordan says "you're crazy with the heat,"!! I thought that phrase had gone out of use along with "Twenty-three Skiddoo." The whole conception and movement is falsified by Dudley's handling of this situation. Jordan would naturally take steps instantly to send someone to Golz to warn him of the preparations to meet the attack, indicated by the movement on the road. That is why his conversation with Pilar on page 199 is so phoney. For God's sake, get Dudley to read chapter 29 on this. And on the rest of that sequence. It is a really terrible sequence. I am not being paid to rewrite it, or I could rewrite the whole thing. What I am trying to do is indicate to Dudley where he has done it wrongly.

Will rush you the rest of it tomorrow. Dictated this to Marty. As before

(Signed) Ernest (Hemingway)

cc: Dudley Nichols, Mr. Selznick, Mr. Marcus, FILE.

* * * * *

FINCA VIGIA SAN FRANCISCO DE PAULA CUBA

April 21st

Dear Donald (Friede):

To continue on with Dudley's script from page 205 Sequence "G":

On page 206 at the bottom of the page Dudley says in an explanation "He looks off, not wanting to tell her the truth, that perhaps even Golz couldn't stop it now; or perhaps Golz knows about the counter attack and will make a holding attack; so many contingencies he knows as a soldier.

But NEVER has Dudley made this clear either in conversation or in action. How does he propose to translate this aside of his into film?

On 211 it should be Comrades instead of Friends. This should be changed throughout.

On same page instead of bomb it should be grenade.

It should be I'm a comrade of yours I tell you—*not* I'm a friend.

On page 215 after Maria's sentence "to make a gag." It should follow. Then they ran a clippers across my head.

On the same page where it says "I stumbled over the barber lying dead in the doorway," it should continue "They had shot him because he belonged to a Union." Otherwise what was a dead barber doing in the doorway.

I will refrain as much as possible from commenting on the love talk between Jordan and Maria. There was human, believable, credible talk in the book that he could have taken. Instead he has written the most revolting slop I have ever read. I know that there are parts of the book which could not be screened but why make Jordan and the girl talk such utter worthless sickening, maudlin blah when there is real, tender and believable dialogue which could be used? Or does Dudley think he writes better dialogue than I do?

On page 218 he says Gomez still looks like a barber despite his uniform. This is incorrect. The man I had in mind had been a barber but was a fine looking soldier. He is in the Spanish Earth in the fighting inside the house and in another sequence where Republican soldiers are being shown how to take down and assemble a rifle. He is the officer who was doing that instruction.

Could Sam Wood be induced to look at the Spanish Earth to see what these people actually look like in order to avoid making the sort of fake Spaniards that appeared in Blood and Sand?

On page 223 you are liable to get a laugh with that The Earth moved—Sequence H.
I already wrote you about the danger of using Andre Marty's name and suggested other names. If he doesn't sue Paramount it would be possible for his wife or his children to. Tell them to remember the Yousupoff (you spell it) suit and lay off of it. Also the man in question for dialogue purposes on page 224 is *not* a commandant. A look at the book will show you how to fix that.

Pages 227–228–229–230–231 are a part of the Jordan-Maria stuff I have objected to. It is not that it is changed. It is that it is no good.

If you would have fixed a deal for Dudley to come down here to work for awhile on this with me I could have fixed all the weak places and he could have had all the credit. I don't want any credit. All I want is a good picture. And it is hell to see weak and inept spots that could be wonderful. Where Dudley has done a marvelous job is in all the action in the actual bridge blowing and the fight at the roadmenders hut and the sawmill. All his work there is marvelous. Don't think that I do not appreciate fine and wonderful stuff just because I did not write it myself. But I do know bad stuff and all I can do is try to point out when it is bad. I could make it right.

On page 237 why not use the good, tender and practical stuff about how she would look after his pistol etc. that is in the book instead of this weak dilution?

On page 239 it should be Comrade Karkov—Comrade this—Comrade that.

On same page dialogue is false where Karkov says—Not a party member like you, etc. He would never possibly have said such a thing. Please ask Dudley to cut that out.

On 240 it is much stronger if Karkov says I hope all men will speak to me always. I come from Stalin. (Otherwise how did Karkov have any authority over Marty, a head political commissar.) The sentence "I am a journalist and am going to write about the activities of some of our political commissars" should go out. He would never have said such a thing. It is silly talk. Like the party member business.

On page 245—after Maria says Is there no other way to explode the charges? It is absolutely out of character of either Jordan or Cooper to say I've got to find a way! I've got to! If Golz attacks the bridge has got to go! That is cheap melodrama talk and spoken like a hysterical girl. Jordan would say Yes. Sure. There's a bad way. But I can do it. (Then thinking of Pablo) Oh that rotten filthy swine!

Maria: What is the way, Roberto?

Jordan: Shut up. I'm thinking of it now.

Then go into the hand grenade business as Dudley has it.

On page 250 Jordan's last speech is lousy. Do I have to write it?

One page 263 after Golz says Nous sommes foutus. Comme toujours. Oui. C'est dommage. Oui. It is absolutely necessary that after that his face should smile with pride, happiness and delight as he sees the planes coming on and he should say "But how it could have been! And how it will be some day!"

Without this the Golz business is weak instead of strong and all the glory of the possibility of victory the reason for which Jordan is blowing the bridge is unexpressed.

On page 271—There are no smoke puffs with modern rifles shooting smokeless powder. There are flashes. The smoke puffs are a hangover from Dudley's Indian fighting days.

On page 272. There is no slit in a tank through which the gypsy could insert a hand grenade. The way to work this business is to have the gypsy roll a grenade in under the tread after the explosion when the tank is stalled he works in close beside it as Dudley has him doing for the grenade business and slams this bottle he has been carrying in his grenade bag alongside the slit in the turret. He lights the wick in the end of the bottle as he is crouched before he makes his rush. There is a sheet of flame when he smashes the bottle and the tank blazes.

You can write in how he prepared it before. It can be one of El Sordo's whiskey bottles and Fernando could get it filled with gasoline and used motor oil for him on one of his nightly trips into La Granja. Or he could have syphoned the gas out of a car at night in La Granja with a rubber tube. This bottle can be the gypsy's pride and secret for a long time. You can show him fooling with it and hiding it before the attack. He doesn't want anyone to know he has it because he is afraid he will not have nerve enough to ever use it.

On page 274 Fernando would say Comrades not Brothers.

On page 283—Tank guns have semi-automatic fire—The shells are loaded in a clip in much the same style as for an anti-aircraft gun. So you had better check that reload business or I suppose it possibly could be an old enough style tank to get by with that. Otherwise it should be when they change clips.

If Dudley is convinced that it is better to have the girl going to America (impossible) rather than Madrid and that he can write a better farewell scene between Maria and Jordan tha[n] I can there is nothing I can do about this part except protest. When you have something wonderful why do you have to change it for something silly just because you are paid to put the book into film? When you have something that is good and right and can be used why change it? He has done a wonderful job writing that action of the fight why not then leave something that is good and not ruin it. And please don't have Agustin on page 289 say With My Life—It is by saying something quiet in a case like that that you get dignity and pathos instead of 10 20 30 melodrama. Actually he would say something quiet and each one would try to comfort the other. Not that awful "With My Life!" sort of craperoo.

Well will get this off now so as to get the practical observations to Dudley as quickly as possible.
What has happened to you all of a sudden that you can't write a letter.
(Signed) Ernest (Hemingway)
cc. Dudley Nichols, Mr. Selznick, Mr. Marcus, FILE.

* * * * *

FINCA VIGIA SAN FRANCISCO DE PAULA CUBA

August 13, 1942

Mr. Donald Friede
Myron Selznick & Company
Beverly Hills, California
Dear Donald:
I just got your letter today and am so happy to know that Bergman is to play the Maria. I see nothing about it in the papers, so will you please let me know the details. So far it seems so much too good to be true that I am afraid to count on it. It is so wonderful to think that Zorina, looking like

a cross between Pavlova's legs mounted on an okay body with a dachund's face, will not be ruining that picture. There are always enough things against it when a man is directing who refuses to be told anything about how things actually should look, without inserting that combination.

I will be very happy to see Dudley's script and if there is anything I can do to help out, please let me know. The reason I had not written before was because we had come to sort of a dead-end matter. Because of having to make many points in a hurry I hope I was not offensive to Dudley. It is sort of like the old story of the man who took his bride out sailing and shouted to her, "Let go that sheet." She didn't let go of the rope and the cat boat turned over. Later on it turned out that the trouble was that he had not said, "Please." I did that work on Dudley's script under such a press of hurry that many times when I should have said please it was omitted. I know that looking back on it he will understand. I appreciate all the difficulties he works under.

When you get this will you please wire me so I will actually know that Bergman is to play the girl and will not be like the time I thought we had won the lottery in Valencia and spent all the money before the official list came out.

The boys are here and send their best to you. Patrick says if you would come down here he would get drunk. He has only been drunk twice in his life and they were both when you were there.

Best always,

(signed) Ernest (Hemingway)

cc. Messrs. Selznick, Henigson, Marcus, Townsend, Ryan, Rose, Graybill, Howell, Powell, King, Donahue, Holbert, FILE.

* * * * *

Ernest Hemingway, famous for his clipped style, does not mince words. We are struck first in these letters by the intensity of Hemingway's feelings. After reading Dudley Nichols's script, the novelist has reason to be angry about "fatal ignorance, bad writing and bad construction." He expresses more than a little annoyance at the politics of the Hollywood studio system, which prevent him from communicating directly with the filmmakers. And he is utterly disgusted by Friede's "piece of agent-ship" that obliges him to correct the flawed script, gratis, "as a protest against its ignorance and ineptness." But Hemingway's anger, we soon come to see, is no wild rage, but a calculated, disciplined, professional response to the adulteration of his work. As the movie begins to be shot, he rushes to save the story from being "sabotaged" by a multitude of technical errors, silly misunderstandings, and clumsy, stilted dialogue.

His eye for detail is extraordinary. He is concerned that bad costuming may replicate "the ghastly falseness" of director Rouben Mamoulian's 1941 movie *Blood and Sand*. He laments the poor choice of fictional names, scoffs at Spaniards with long, Italian mustaches, and labors to correct seemingly slight errors of fact, such as identifying the gypsy as a "trapper." And he worries, prudently, that the naming of real people, such as the French Communist André Marty, will open the studio (and himself) to a lawsuit. (The Youssopoff case, to which he refers, involved a Russian émigré couple, who saw themselves depicted in the 1932 MGM movie *Rasputin and the Empress,* and successfully sued the studio in England for defamation. It was this case that led to the famous disclaimer that "any resemblance to anyone living or dead is a coincidence." Hemingway had ignored the precedent in his novel, but perhaps feared now that the assets of a Hollywood studio added to his more meager estate might make a juicy legal target.) His comment later—"Dictated this to Marty"—refers, however, to another "Marty," his wife Martha Gellhorn.

Amid these many details, Hemingway attends to the political ramifications of his work. "There is a war on," he asserts less than three months after Pearl Harbor. And "there are certain points about the Nichols script which are really dangerously bad from the standpoint of making a picture which will be useful to our country's war effort at this time." Is the novelist merely posturing? Does he really believe that a movie of a novel can affect the outcome of the war? From his home in Cuba, he identifies the importance of winning Latin American audiences to the Allied cause.

Just a few years earlier, Hemingway had joined the Dutch filmmaker Joris Ivens in producing the propaganda film, *The Spanish Earth,* which he acknowledges in the second letter of April 21 to be the source of one of the characters in the novel. Yet American public opinion in 1937 remained sufficiently ambivalent about the Spanish Civil War that Hemingway omitted the term "fascist," lest it provoke a zealous censor to ban the documentary. So, apparently, the original Hollywood treatment of *For Whom the Bell Tolls* by Louis Bromfield had perpetuated what Hemingway calls a political limbo "and no one was to be offended in any way." Now with the United States in the war, Hemingway rejects his former restraint. "Throughout the picture," he advises, "the enemy should be called the Fascists and the Republic should be called the Republic." No longer, he says, is it necessary "to muddle along in order to appease the enemies of our country," among whom he mentions socialite Jock Whitney and "his Fascist-inclined relatives." Nor should Nichols hide behind the Spanish term "Falangist"—the Iberian version of "fascist"—because few Americans will recognize the word, despite the incantations of Texas Representative Martin Dies's House Committee on Un-American Activities.

Such proposals reflect a certain political agenda, but we should not miss Hemingway's primary motive for correcting the ideological vocabulary. "The best thing" about his story, he avers, is that it shows "what men and women would die for . . . and know it is well for [them] to die." That insight suggests a subtle convergence between the psychology of character and a particular historical circumstance, the intertwining of an individual and a moment in time. Hemingway's novel had been criticized by the American veterans of the Spanish Civil War for distorting a certain historical "truth." In condemning Marty and the Communist leadership, in depicting the savage execution of Spanish elites by vengeful peasants, in elaborating the romantic relationship between the American guerrilla fighter Robert Jordan and the female victim of fascism, Maria, the novelist, according to the veterans of the Abraham Lincoln Brigade, had distracted attention from the more systematic evil of fascist atrocities.

Here, however, Hemingway shows a deeper understanding of the aversion to fascism as "the animating motif for the whole band" of resistance fighters. Similarly, he explains, the victims of peasant rage need to be identified as the fascists they were because otherwise "the whole killing is a meaningless butchery." In this way, the hatred of fascism and the passion for the Republic serve two purposes: providing a political rationale for the war and the emotional reality that motivates action. "Remember," Hemingway concludes, "this picture is being made in wartime and will be seen by people who are war minded, it cannot have muzzy thinking and construction in it."

Hemingway's last missive refers to the abrupt change in the film's cast. Although the novelist strongly favored Gary Cooper playing the role of Robert Jordan, he cringed at the studio's choice of Vera Zorina, a dancer, to play Maria. Donald Friede persuaded David Selznick to interview Ingrid Bergman for the part, and Hemingway enthusiastically endorsed the change. "She should be marvelous in the role," he exclaimed.

To his editor Maxwell Perkins, Hemingway described the many changes he had recommended to Dudley Nichols. "In the end he rewrote it," the novelist stated, "and incorporated almost everything that I had suggested." But after the movie premiered in New York on July 10, 1943, Perkins attended a screening and offered the author a mixed review. Hemingway replied that he hoped he would never have to see the damned film!

PART III

Legacies

▷ **CHAPTER 8**

"Not Valid for Travel in Spain"

The Legacy of the Abraham Lincoln Brigade

Spain under General Franco's dictatorship did not encourage critical discussion of the Spanish Civil War. The government presented its version of events and suppressed publication, even private conversation, from the other side. Even after Franco's death in 1975 and in the years of so-called transition to democracy, a "pact of silence" discouraged commentary from those who had supported the Republic. The war was not taught in schools; families of both sides did not want to relive the events that had occurred during wartime and afterward. But a third generation of Spaniards, grandchildren of participants in the war, expressed a growing interest in their family histories. Increasingly, Spanish scholars are publishing books and articles based on archival research that questioned the official version of the war. During the 70th anniversary, historians at the University of Salamanca organized a conference examining the role of the International Brigades. My paper, which was published in Las Brigadas Internacionales: 70 Años de Memoria Historica, *edited by Antonio R. Celada, Danial Pastor Garcia, and Rosa M. Lopez Alonso (Salamanca, 2007), addresses the changing views of the Spanish Civil War in the United States in scholarly circles and among a larger public.*

▷ Nine months after Martha Gellhorn and Ernest Hemingway brought the documentary film, *The Spanish Earth* to the White House, Gellhorn addressed a letter to her friend Eleanor Roosevelt, recounting the president's spontaneous remark, "Spain is a vicarious sacrifice for all of us." Now Gellhorn recoiled from Roosevelt's comment. "I think Spain is maybe not a sacrifice," she pleaded, "but a champion: and hope to God that America at least will not go on letting this country down."

Gellhorn's letter was written during the military crisis in the spring of 1938, when rebel forces ripped through the Republican army's ranks. She had just spent a day "at a quiet part of the front," visiting the American volunteers who formed the Abraham Lincoln Brigade and whose numbers had been dramatically reduced in the recent fighting. "I find that I love them immeasurably," she wrote, "am immeasurably proud of them, individually and collectively, and proud of their record and proud of the reasons that brought them here and keep them here. I never saw better men in my life in any country, and what they are willing to die for if need be is what you . . . are willing to live for."[1]

Gellhorn had hoped that her missive might succeed where the screening of the movie had failed: to persuade Washington to change its non-interventionist policy toward the Spanish Republic. But Roosevelt had other priorities and obligations, not least to preserve the support of conservative Democrats in Congress, who were influenced by their Catholic, pro-Franco constituents in the nation's large cities. Roosevelt sympathized with the Republican side, but he had no intention of challenging his political allies in a battle he believed he could not win. The United States did not assist Republican Spain, Franco won the war, and the volunteers of the Lincoln Brigade, so admired by Martha Gellhorn, returned home in defeat.

Arriving in New York in the late autumn of 1938 they met with what must be called a mixed reception. Before they could debark from the ships that carried them across the Atlantic, they were greeted by officials of the U.S. State Department, who interviewed them briefly and confiscated their passports—the official travel documents whose prohibition of travel to Spain they had violated.

Then, as the *Daily Worker* headlined the story, "Crowds Roar[ed] Welcome to Lincoln Veterans." The article reported, "No enemy marksmen sniped at them from the heights. . . . Today they marched through the canyons of New York while their supporters showered them with homemade confetti, raised their fists, gave them a hearty welcome home." However, when the procession of veterans reached Madison Square Park with the intention of laying a memorial wreath at a monument to the nation's war dead, the Lincolns were met by a small army of policemen, some on horseback, who refused to allow them to perform the ceremony.[2] Not everyone in New York City approved of the young men and women who had volunteered to fight for the Spanish Republic or sympathized with the legacy of those who had died.

"You can be afraid to come home," confessed James Benét, a truck driver in the Regiment de Tren who returned to his job as a reporter for the liberal weekly magazine *The New Republic*, "and we were afraid, that the folks wouldn't understand, that we had changed too much or they had, that Hitler and Mussolini had fooled them, that Chamberlain had fooled them, that maybe they just wouldn't get it, wouldn't be fighting the way the Spanish do." Some veterans looked forward to continuing the Spanish war on another front; some feared being dragged into another war that would end in another defeat. "The war of bullets and steel would be left behind," wrote Edwin Rolfe seven months after his return from Spain, "and the war of nerves and incessant threats would begin."[3]

Subsequent history has enshrined this mixed legacy. The Lincolns were simultaneously loved and despised, honored and feared, and their reputation in history is, to put it mildly, a complicated story. Their legacy—and the history of the Spanish Civil War in the United States—needs to be seen in three interrelated dimensions.

First, there is the specific historical legacy of the volunteers who participated in the war—how their lives were affected by the decision to embark for Spain in violation of U.S. neutrality laws, how they engaged in the subsequent history of their country and the world, and how their individual actions influenced other people in the larger society. This personal legacy is actually quite impressive.

A second aspect of the legacy of the Lincoln Brigade and the Spanish Civil War can be seen from the perspective of subsequent historical writing—what scholars call historiography: How have historians explained the Lincoln Brigade? How have they portrayed the experience of the volunteers, and how does this writing itself express the context of both the veterans and the times the historians were writing in? And third, the legacy of the Lincoln Brigade needs to be seen as a function of public memory, the unofficial stories that survived the experience and typically survive outside the academic mainstream.

I will address each of these topics in what follows, though it's apparent to me and I hope to you, too, that they are not really separable. Rather, the history that we come to accept, to believe, reflects not so much the experiences of the *participants,* but the existential experiences of the *observers,* who approach the historical data with agendas of their own. I had a teacher once who said that history was the mythology we believed, mythology was the history we didn't believe. History is not outside ourselves, but something that lives within—perhaps it is a singularly human reality, to think in terms of time. The history of the Lincoln Brigade and the Spanish Civil War creates obligations for all of us.

Let me begin with some stories of the veterans themselves. Consider, for example, the work of one of the ambulance drivers, James Neugass, who returned from Spain and resumed his career as a writer. He published excellent poetry about his experiences in Spain and wrote a fine novel based on his family in New Orleans, but died suddenly at the age of 44 in 1949. He left behind an unpublished manuscript, titled "War Is Beautiful," in which he describes his feelings: "We killed naturally and with constant gnawing desire to kill more and more, but we hated death and war and we could never manage to think of ourselves precisely as soldiers."[4]

Another cultural worker was the musician Conlon Nancarrow, who was educated in classical music, played jazz trumpet, and studied orchestral composition before going to Spain. He served in an anti-aircraft battery in Spain and was one of the last Americans to cross into France. He spent eight excruciating days in a refugee camp and expressed outrage at the U.S. government's antagonism to the Lincoln veterans. When the State Department refused to reissue his passport in 1940, he moved to one of the few countries he could reach without a passport and became an exile in Mexico City. He continued to experiment with musical composition, but could find few musicians capable of playing his complicated work—until he discovered an alternative form of presentation. He realized he could compose for the mechanical player piano. He returned to New York in 1947 for the purpose of purchasing a player piano and a machine to make piano rolls. The result was the creation of incredible polyharmonic music—some of it too complex to be played by human hands. He eventually achieved an international reputation as a composer. In 1992, the American Academy and Institute of Arts and Letters elected Nancarrow as a "Foreign Honorary Member." Obviously, the decision to go to Spain had changed his life forever.[5]

Similar stories proliferate among the 1,500 or so veterans who returned to the United States. James Benét resumed his career as a journalist; the medical professionals continued to work as nurses, doctors, and technicians; others returned to school, joined labor unions (sometimes as organizers), or took what jobs they could. Some also faced job discrimination because they had served in Spain.

While few Lincoln veterans, as James Neugass remarked, thought of themselves "precisely as soldiers," as a group they remained politically active, paid close attention to world events, and remained skeptical about the policies of the Western allies—Britain, France, and the United States—

who had allowed, if not encouraged, Franco's triumph. The French government's callous treatment of Spanish refugees and International Brigaders—Germans, Swiss, and Hungarians, for example—who could not return to their home countries outraged the veterans. Most of the Lincolns remained Communists and praised the Soviet Union for its defense of the fallen Republic. Indeed, many quietly undertook various activities, acting as couriers and even as secret agents in other countries to assist the Soviet Union. Some seamen helped illegal refugees and other stowaways to enter the United States with the help of forged maritime papers and passports. In early 1939, one veteran compiled a list of 1,600 names—"American Communists and Sympathizers Who Fought for Loyalist Spain"—because, he noted, "a great many of them are party to a scheme of helping Soviet Russia secure passports to use at a later date."[6] What, if anything, he did with the list is not known. But clearly some veterans were suspicious of the pro-communist leanings of the organization which now called itself the Veterans of the Abraham Lincoln Brigade (VALB).

These political attitudes crystallized with the announcement of the Nazi-Soviet non-aggression pact in August 1939. Although the news shocked the veterans, most Lincolns justified the agreement. "The USSR is a socialist state, protecting herself from highly antagonistic surrounding states," wrote James Benét in *The New Republic*. "This does not appear to a socialist as an act of alliance with fascism."[7] Some Lincoln veterans rejected this reasoning and withdrew or were expelled from VALB.

The outbreak of World War II five days later brought the contradictions into focus. "This is not our war," declared VALB, in an echo of the Communist Party, "the present European war is not an anti-fascist war but an imperialist war." Soon, the veterans adopted another Communist slogan: "The Yanks are NOT coming!" In this way, the famous "fighting anti-fascists" found themselves opposing President Roosevelt's effort to assist Britain and France in the war against Germany and Italy. "I justified it," explained Milton Wolff, the last commander of the Lincoln Brigade. "Everything I said was based on the Spanish experience—who had helped us; who had not helped us; who had been part of the sellout [of Spain]."[8] Not all veterans shared Wolff's position; several broke with VALB publicly, others more quietly.

Nor did Wolff's rationalizations impress the leaders of the U.S. government. Prior to the outbreak of World War II, President Roosevelt had authorized the Department of Justice to conduct investigations of possible subversive activities—whether by fascists, Nazis, or communists—and with that mandate the FBI opened inquiries about the recruitment of volunteers for the Lincoln Brigade. In February 1940, the FBI staged a coordinated raid of the veterans' offices in Detroit and Milwaukee and arrested 11 people for possible violations of laws prohibiting recruitment of soldiers for foreign armies. Other FBI agents went to VALB headquarters in New York City armed with an arrest warrant and proceeded to search file drawers, desks, and waste baskets. After the federal authorities left the office, the veterans prudently removed their mailing lists from the office and took records to a veteran's apartment and burned them in the fireplace.[9] What they did not know—and what I have discovered from FBI files that have been declassified—is that the earlier raid in Detroit gave the government all the relevant information about the members of the Lincoln Brigade.[10]

Government harassment reflected widespread suspicion of Communist activities in the United States and elsewhere. FBI documents reveal particular concern about the abuse of U.S. passports by Spanish Civil War volunteers both in traveling to Spain in violation of neutrality laws and their subsequent use by Soviet agents. Only one returning American veteran—Leo Hecht from Brooklyn—was jailed for violating passport laws and charges against him were soon dismissed. Hecht later testified as a hostile witness against VALB before the Subversive Activities Control Board in 1954. But if the State Department was generally not aggressive about punishing passport violations, FBI Director J. Edgar Hoover exhibited intense interest in what happened to U.S. passports *after* the volunteers entered Spain.[11] One field report sent to Hoover in 1942 contained the following passage from a book written by the turncoat Soviet agent V. G. Krivitsky regarding "Passports of the International Brigades, Later Used by OGPU [Soviet intelligence] Agents to Visit Foreign Countries":

> One day, a batch of about 100 passports arrived [at the OGPU office in Moscow], half of them American. They had belonged to dead soldiers. That was a great haul, a cause for celebration. The passports of the dead, after some weeks of inquiry into the family history of their original owners, are easily adapted to their new bearers, the OGPU agents.[12]

This concern about lost, stolen, and abused passports explains the FBI's obsession with identifying the names of all the U.S. volunteers—why, for instance, they illegally raided VALB's offices in 1940. Moreover, Hoover personally sought to identify those who had died or been taken prisoner in Spain because it was most likely that their passports were being used.

The FBI alerted the State Department to be on the lookout for passport applications from persons using the names of former Lincoln volunteers, dead or alive, and "Refusal Notices" were put into the files of such persons. Yet the State Department reported in 1944 that "in not a single instance" had there been "any report from any one of its Foreign Offices indicating that any passport was used by other than the original bearer, nor was it found that a photograph and signature appearing in a passport failed to compare satisfactorily with the photograph and signature appearing on the correlative passport application." Nevertheless, from my interviews with Lincoln veterans—Sydney Levine and Jack Bjoze, to be specific—I learned that passports of dead men were used by Soviet agents both during and after the Spanish Civil War.

The government also investigated the close cooperation between Lincoln veterans and other organizations seeking aid for Spanish refugees around the world and working against the Franco regime. Ever since the Lincolns had departed from Spain—or, in some cases, like that of Conlon Nancarrow, from French concentration camps—the veterans had lobbied actively to find safe homes for the Spanish refugees incarcerated in France. During the winter of 1940, only six weeks before Germany would attack and defeat France, the veterans learned that the French government had decided to terminate the problem of Spanish refugees by ordering their return to Franco's Spain.

VALB joined a coalition of left-wing groups, the Emergency Conference to Save Spanish Refugees, to protest the new policy. And because the ex-soldiers were more tempestuous than others, they organized public demonstrations outside the French consulate in New York. These rallies resulted in their arrest, but also won publicity in the international press. Such pressure persuaded France to reverse its policy and permit the Spaniards to remain in the camps.

Continuing cooperation between VALB and refugee aid groups like the Joint Anti-Fascist Refugee Committee (JAFRC) further attracted the attention of federal authorities. The FBI was especially concerned about the meetings and exchanges with known communists around the world and the transfer of money that were both inherent in the refugee aid programs. Convinced that this project to aid Spanish refugees was part of an international conspiracy, the FBI bugged the homes and telephones of leading figures in the movement.[13] From one such eavesdropping case they learned that a Lincoln veteran named Felix Kusman, one of the activists in the refugee aid program, had made an illegal trip to Europe in 1943 and met with the members of the Spanish underground. The wiretap also found evidence that Kusman, or others close to him, were involved in shipping what the FBI believed were explosives to the anti-Franco guerrillas. Other tapped telephone conversations in the early postwar years indicate that the FBI knew about the subterfuges used by Lincoln veterans to disguise their assistance for comrades in Spain and elsewhere. There was no secret about their political sympathies. But what is interesting is how much the FBI was aware of those sympathies and watched what was occurring. Surveillance of the Lincoln veterans continued throughout World War II and preceded the famous anti-communist investigations associated with congressional committees and Senator Joseph McCarthy. Indeed, FBI-gathered evidence lay at the core of most congressional inquiries into communist activities in the United States.

After the German invasion of the Soviet Union in June 1941, VALB, like the Communist Party, demanded U.S. intervention on behalf of the Allies. U.S. officials saw that simultaneous shift as proof that the veterans strictly followed the Communist line. Even when the Soviet Union was a fighting ally of the United States against the fascist axis, therefore, political and military leaders in Washington remained suspicious, if not hostile, to the veterans of the Abraham Lincoln Brigade who volunteered to fight against Hitler and Mussolini.

The day after the Japanese attack at Pearl Harbor, Milton Wolff sent a one-sentence telegram to President Roosevelt: "We who fought the Fascist Axis in Spain proudly volunteer to march shoulder to shoulder with our fellow Americans for the final crushing of this menace to the independence and democracy of America and all peoples."[14]

By then, numerous Lincolns were already serving in the military, having enlisted in defiance of VALB's original non-intervention position or been drafted under the national conscription laws. Like Lincoln veterans in civilian life, they expressed a sense of relief that the tensions between their political beliefs and national policy were over, at least for the duration of the war. During the following weeks, dozens of the veterans enlisted for what they were confident would be the final battles against fascism. Most believed that the destruction of Hitler and Mussolini would also bring the downfall of General Franco. By the end of the war, at least 425 Lincoln veterans had served in the U.S. armed forces and another one hundred in the merchant marine and nursing corps.

Despite their knowledge that participation in the Spanish Civil War alarmed government officials, Lincoln veterans were surprised to discover that the military had adopted policies that treated them as potential subversives. Instead of being assigned to training programs to prepare for war, many Lincolns found themselves placed in limited service units that included pro-fascists, Nazis, and German and Italian nationals who refused to fight against their homelands, as well as assorted misfits. "I hadn't looked forward to being in the Wehrmacht," Jack Lucid wrote from Camp Ripley, Minnesota, but "that is what I am in here."[15] Angered and disgusted by such circumstances, the veterans pleaded for transfers into regular army groups, without success.

By early 1943, however, VALB leaders realized that their problems were not local or "accidental" but the result of a government policy created in Washington. "It is simply and DEFINITELY A POLICY established by the heads to effect us not as individuals under a microscope, but as a whole on principle," concluded Milton Wolff, himself a target of army intelligence.[16] In January 1943, VALB leaders wrote directly to President Roosevelt to describe incidents of discrimination as well as examples of the loyalty of Lincoln veterans in the war effort and concluded:

> We think it is now clear to all liberty-loving Americans that the cause of Spain was the cause of Democracy and was our cause. This treatment of our Veterans, and there can be no other conclusion, is being meted out because we fought in Spain, then certainly some steps must be taken to correct this situation.[17]

Gathering additional testimony from other Lincolns, VALB's Executive Secretary, Jack Bjoze, went to Washington to meet with sympathetic political leaders, including cabinet member Harold Ickes and the influential journalist Drew Pearson.[18] The result was a series of news stories, beginning in April 1943, that described the cases of Lincoln veterans who had been denied the right to fight as equals in the U.S. Army. A New York newspaper, *PM*, headlined the problem in May 1943: "'Premature'

Anti-Fascists Still in Army Doghouse." That phrase—premature anti-fascists—would become sarcastic shorthand to refer to the Lincoln Brigade. A few congressmen demanded that the army explain its policy.

Such publicity broke the dam, somewhat. To be sure, the War Department continued to deny that political discrimination existed and cited as evidence the well-known examples of Lincoln veterans who had served overseas and won medals for their courage. But after the articles appeared, many Lincolns now found that the army approved their applications for regular service, and they began to be sent overseas. Nevertheless, the discrimination against Lincoln veterans in the military did not end in 1943, as many of their letters show. Through 1944 and 1945, outspoken members of Congress, including the House Committee on Un-American Activities, continued to challenge the commissioning of specific Lincoln veterans as military officers.

These contradictory experiences reinforced the Lincolns' self-identity as a special group. Whether celebrated as heroic "fighting anti-fascists," as their songs proclaimed, or hazed as "premature anti-fascists" by government leaders, the Lincolns understood that their service in Spain had made them unique. Many veterans saw themselves as exemplars of what a good soldier ought to be. "All in all," wrote Jerry Weinberg, after entering the Army Air Corps in 1942, "it's a tough job living up to what's expected of a vet, but I'm trying." The persistent Weinberg was shot down in a raid of the Ploesti oil fields in 1943, but managed to escape from an internment camp in Turkey and returned to England to fly again, only to be shot down and killed in another raid, becoming one of the Lincoln heroes of World War II.[19]

That some of their contemporaries opposed their principles and harassed their efforts to serve in the U.S. Army merely confirmed the Lincolns' distinctive identity. "And if I ever doubted whether I've done (and am doing) my share for progress," wrote the frustrated veteran Adolph Ross, "I no longer have any uncertainties. These reactionaries in Washington have reminded me that I haven't done so bad after all."[20]

What I've been trying to suggest with these post-Spain details is that the basic paradigm for understanding what the Abraham Lincoln Brigade meant to Americans and the nation's political identity was already well-established by World War II. Clearly the Lincoln Brigade veterans saw themselves as principled anti-fascists—the only 2,800 of a population of 130 million who had stood up during the 1930s to fight the fascists in

Spain. They saw World War II as an extension of that war. They expected the defeat of European fascism to lead to the overthrow of the Franco regime and the rescue of Spanish Republicans from Franco's labor camps and prisons. But to the U.S. government, the Lincoln veterans were nothing more than tools of the Communist International and Josef Stalin.

Sometimes this simplicity had remarkable consequences. For instance, the Lincoln Brigade in Spain was the first fully integrated army of American soldiers in which whites and blacks, as well as Asians and other nationality groups, served equally. For the first time in U.S. history, the Lincoln Brigade allowed African American officers to command white soldiers in battle. Racial equality, by the way, was one of the fundamental principles of the Communist Party. Therefore, when Lincoln veterans appealed for a racially mixed army in the United States during World War II, military leaders and the FBI found further evidence of their subversive communist intentions. African American soldiers, who had fought in the racially integrated army in Spain and had even served as officers, found themselves during World War II in a segregated army that prevented them from obtaining combat assignments but expected them to do the dirty work of cleaning, cooking, digging, and carrying. They were embittered, to put it mildly. But their complaints proved to the government that they belonged to a dangerous class, best kept in their place.

During the early years of the Cold War, the FBI gathered evidence about the veterans of the Abraham Lincoln Brigade to strengthen the government's case against the U.S. Communist Party as an illegal organization. To prove that domestic Communists advocated the overthrow of the government "by force and violence," Director Hoover circulated a memorandum in 1948 claiming that the Communist Party had created the Lincoln Brigade, which "was specifically sent to Spain to engage in force and violence [i.e. to fight in a war], fundamentally for the purpose of advancing Communism. Here, then, is a concrete example of the Communist party of the United States . . . engaged in overt acts leading to force and violence."

The memo further claimed that the Lincoln veterans, "by virtue of their loyalty to Communist principles and practice, are an actual menace today to the security of the United States because of their willingness to engage in *espionage*." Even more serious, in the eyes of Director Hoover, was that their military training in Spain and World War II made them "a potential menace as saboteurs."[21]

With such powers against them, the Lincolns remained embroiled in the struggles of the red scare through the 1950s and 1960s—the so-called McCarthy period. They were summoned before various government investigating committees on the national and local levels; some were imprisoned for sedition or subversion. Many were blacklisted in the private sector, lost their jobs and careers, and faced the stigma of police oversight. They spent immense energy, both as individuals and collectively, defending themselves from political attack and clinging to the hope that they might yet see General Franco removed from power in Spain. As individuals, many of the veterans continued the good fight—working for improved race relations, participating in the civil rights movement, and being active in labor unions. Even as more of them left the Communist Party, sometimes becoming strongly anti-Communist, most held to their principles about Spain and about larger issues of social justice.

Not until the 1970s—after the U.S. fiasco in Vietnam, the revelations of Watergate, and the death of the Generalissimo in 1975—did the veterans begin to feel some justification for the positions they had taken. As opponents of U.S. foreign policy during the Cold War, they were well equipped to protest U.S. intervention in Vietnam, Cuba, and Central America during the 1980s. To their delight, they found support among young leftists who learned about their politics during the 1960s. But nothing pleased them more than the welcome they received from the people of Spain. The transition to democracy in Spain, whatever its problems on a domestic level, validated their faith, in the words of Abraham Lincoln, "of a government of the people, by the people, and for the people." The love of the Spanish people for them has meant more than anything else.

This historical background establishes a framework for understanding the place of the Lincoln Brigade and the Spanish Civil War in U.S. history, at least as it appears on the printed page and in academic books. The emergence of the Cold War in the 1940s had a powerful effect in determining how historians looked back to the 1930s. Although some historians sympathized with the Lincolns politically, the prevailing anticommunist ideology dominated the issues of the Spanish Civil War. Like the U.S. government during World War II, historians of the Cold War era looked at the veterans of the Lincoln Brigade primarily as communist subversives who flouted U.S. laws and sympathized with the Soviet Union. Other principled reasons for going to Spain—the fight against fascism, opposition to racism, outrage at the policies of appeasement and anti-Semitism—vanished before the anti-communist crusade.

This is the political context for historical writings about the Abraham Lincoln Brigade. To be sure, in the years before the outbreak of World War II, two veterans of the brigade—the poet Edwin Rolfe and the novelist Alvah Bessie—wrote remarkable works of history and memoir that saluted the motives of the Lincoln volunteers.[22] During World War II, articles in the liberal press continued to praise their role in anticipating the fascist threat. Even the Hollywood production of Ernest Hemingway's novel *For Whom the Bell Tolls* in 1943 (starring Gary Cooper and Ingrid Bergman) made the American volunteer appear as a great hero in Spain, though the film industry refused to use the word "fascist" in identifying the opponents. The 1945 film *Fallen Sparrow* (featuring John Garfield) specifically linked Spanish Civil War veterans to the struggle against Nazi groups within the United States.

The most influential book of the postwar era, however, proved to be a memoir of a different sort: George Orwell's *Homage to Catalonia,* published in the United States in 1952 with an introduction by Lionel Trilling, who was identified with the Trotskyite wing of Marxism and expressed contempt for the role of Communists in the Spanish Civil War. The book won praise from great numbers of reviewers and has lived on in paperback as the one book students of the Spanish Civil War still read. Ironically, given the book's influence, Orwell's argument with the Communist party was not that it was a dangerous, subversive, radical movement—but that the party was opposed to the social revolution in Spain. The war was lost, Orwell suggested, because the communist-led government distrusted the militia units, especially the anarchists. But what Americans read in Orwell's finely written memoir—and continue to cite—are his descriptions of the Communists' wickedness.

To my professional surprise, few people, even scholars, were aware of another essay by Orwell titled "Looking Back on the Spanish War." Written in 1943, as German bombs fell upon the cities of Europe, Orwell wrote perceptively about the international stalemate that had killed the Spanish Republic: "The outcome of the Spanish war," he stated, "was settled in London, Paris, Rome, Berlin—at any rate, not in Spain." Rather, he explained quite simply, "the Fascists won because they were the stronger; they had modern arms and the others hadn't. No political strategy could offset that."[23] Orwell subsequently requested that the chapters describing the Communist crushing of the anarchist rebellion in Barcelona in May 1937 be removed from the main text of his book and placed in an appendix.[24]

Toward the end of the Cold War, a few more works focused on the history of the Lincoln Brigade. Some, like Robert Rosenstone's *Crusade of the Left* (1969), expressed sympathy for the U.S. volunteers; others, like Cecil Eby's *Between the Bullet and the Lie* (1969), perpetuated the Cold War prejudices. By the 1980s, documentary films like *The Good Fight* (1984) and *Forever Activists* (1991), together with my book, *The Odyssey of the Abraham Lincoln Brigade,* tried to place the communist issue into the context of the 1930s, emphasizing the economic strains of the Depression, the prevalence of racism, and the rise of Hitler and Mussolini as motivations for ordinary Americans to become involved in radical politics and to enlist in the fight in Spain. Such works did not deny communist influence, but insisted that there were good, indigenous American reasons for people to adopt those kinds of political views. These later works implied that the Cold War had distorted the lens through which people were looking back at the Spanish Civil War.

But instead of staunching those criticisms, post–Cold War scholarship—disparagingly called "revisionism"—has led to a proliferation of more Cold War history: numerous books by Harvey Klehr, John Haynes, Ronald Radosh, a reissue of Eby's book, and Anthony Beevor's popularization of these earlier books. Such works, however much they are criticized by academic professionals, continue to dominate the popular media in America, particularly *The New York Times,* the *Wall Street Journal,* and the hearts and minds of ordinary citizens.[25]

But the most striking thing about the Lincoln Brigade and the Spanish Civil War in U.S. history books is the silence. U.S. textbooks in high school and on the university level do not mention the Lincoln Brigade and barely deal with the Spanish Civil War. The average educated person in the United States cannot distinguish the Spanish Civil War from the Spanish-American War of 1898. Recently, a group of high school students in Massachusetts developed a project on the Lincoln Brigade for a program called National History Day. They won first prize on the local *and* the state level. But when they went to Washington to compete nationally, the judges admitted that they thought the project was about the U.S. Civil War and with no further apology moved away to examine another project![26]

And so we come, finally, to the third aspect of the legacy of the Lincoln Brigade, the survival of the Lincolns in public memory—which is the major work of ALBA, the Abraham Lincoln Brigade Archives. Side by side with the condemnations of the Lincoln Brigade or, in a different kind of attack, the widespread amnesia about it, comes something more vital. The significant element of amnesia is not only that someone forgets, but that they forget that they forgot. In the words of another victim of the Franco years, the German Jewish philosopher Walter Benjamin, "every image of the past that is not recognized by the present as one of its own concerns threatens to disappear irretrievably."[27]

The Lincolns were always concerned about preserving their history. In his poem, "Postscript to a War," written in February 1939, two months after his return from Spain, Edwin Rolfe says:

> we must remember cleanly why we went,
> clearly why we fought; and returning, see
> with truth's unfilmed eyes what remains constant,
> the loyalties which endure, the loves that grow. . . .[28]

In that spirit, the African American poet, Langston Hughes, who went to Spain as a journalist to write for the black press about the Lincolns, asks:

> What does your heart hear,
> Poet,
> What songs unfurl?
> Bright banners
> Made of words
> . . . to fly
> Over the trenches,
> And over frontiers
> And over all barriers of time. . . .[29]

In addition, the songs of the Lincoln Brigade have been recorded in many versions since the 1940s. The veterans have also held annual reunions in New York, California, and Chicago, attracting huge audiences between the 1970s and 1990s as a younger generation, influenced by antiwar protests and sentiment, swelled the ranks to protest U.S. policies in Central America.

History and memory can be deliberate acts, but there's something about history and memory that is also spontaneous, revealing deep, unspoken truths that are too subtle or too dangerous to articulate. Among the most popular films made in the United States—according to nearly every poll taken by film critics—is *Casablanca,* made in 1942 and released in 1943 around the time Churchill and Roosevelt met in Casablanca and announced a policy of "unconditional surrender" toward Nazi Germany.

Why is *Casablanca* so important? *Casablanca* is the story of an American veteran of the Spanish Civil War, played by Humphrey Bogart. As the movie begins, we learn that he has opposed Mussolini in Ethiopia and supported the loyalists in Spain, but has become disillusioned by defeat and betrayal and refuses to get involved in foreign affairs. He embodies American isolationism. Laszlo, the resistance fighter, begs him to change his mind. The movie is set in December 1941. When Bogart hears the Nazis singing the Horstwessel song, the Nazi anthem, at Laszlo's instigation he allows the band to play—not the "Internationale," nor "The Star-Spangled Banner," but "La Marseillaise"—and so Bogart rejoins the fight. At that moment, everyone in the movie theater in 1943 knows that this time the war against fascism will succeed.

I would argue that Bogart represents the nation's guilty conscience. If only the world had listened to the Lincoln Brigade in 1937, all the subsequent calamities might have been averted. He is the manifestation of what no one wants to admit about the Lincoln Brigade: they were right! They were right and Roosevelt was wrong. The Lincoln Brigade has been silently removed from the textbooks of U.S. history—but *Casablanca* lives on.

One final point. The Lincoln veterans took history into their own hands by creating ALBA in 1979 to ensure that their past would not disappear. At this point, I could do a song and dance about how busy ALBA has been during the past 35 years to preserve the history of the Lincolns. I could tell you to visit the website [www.alba-valb.org]. Or I could urge you to subscribe to the quarterly journal *The Volunteer.* Or I could ask you to contribute your children to the cause. But I don't have to ask. You understand the importance of historical work, of sustaining history in the face of the abyss, of finding one's personal meaning by acknowledging the power of time to destroy everything and then defying that power by acts of creative memory. You understand—you and I both—we are all in this together. History matters.

▷ **CHAPTER 9**

Premature Anti-Fascists, Again

Six months after General Franco led his army into Madrid, the same German air forces that had bombed Guernica in the Basque country in 1937 were flying over Poland heralding the onset of World War II. The linkage between these events suggests that Spain was indeed the first battlefield of the larger war, though Britain, France, and the United States chose to avoid direct involvement. In any case, the connection between the Spanish Civil War was crystal clear to Congressman John Coffee (D-Washington) in a speech at Madison Square Garden in January 1945. His speech also reflects a more general view that the Lincoln Brigade had been correct in trying to stop fascist aggression in Spain. That others disagreed with Representative Coffee is also apparent; these critics still promote a different view of the Spanish Civil War in the twentieth-first century. When two commentators dismissed my research for dubious reasons, I wrote this brief essay as an alternative to suing for slander. It was published in The Volunteer *(December 2003).*

▷ By going to Spain to fight fascism, the men and women who served in the Abraham Lincoln Brigade stepped outside the political consensus to defend the principle of democratic government in a foreign country. Their own government did not thank them for the effort, even after the United States found itself at war with the same fascist enemies after December 1941. Public opinion apparently supported their cause in Spain, though the inaccuracy of polling practices in the 1930s limits the value of numbers showing that 75 percent favored the Spanish Republic. In any case, many conservatives criticized their breach of isolationist neutrality. Following the signing of the Nazi-Soviet Non-Aggression Pact in 1939, when Communists and most Lincoln veterans loudly opposed U.S. intervention in World War II, the Lincolns drew outraged criticism from the non-Stalinist left for reversing their position and standing with isolationist conservatives. Pearl Harbor seemed to end the public debate, though Communists, by definition, continued to attract widespread suspicion.

The political flip-flops continue to haunt the reputation of the Lincoln Brigade. In a collection of essays, John Earl Haynes and Harvey Klehr raise the argument that the term "premature anti-fascist" was *not* used by the U.S. government during World War II to classify, pejoratively, the veterans of the Abraham Lincoln Brigade who served in the armed forces of the United States. Rather, the authors say, the term was invented by Lincoln veterans "in a proudly sardonic way" to conceal the fact that they actually opposed U.S. intervention in World War II during the era of the Nazi-Soviet Pact (September 1939–June 21, 1941). They base their claim on the absence of contemporary documentary evidence showing the use of that phrase by wartime government officials. Indeed, for failing to provide adequate evidence in my book, *The Odyssey of the Abraham Lincoln Brigade: Americans in the Spanish Civil War,* they charge me with "scholarly malpractice."[1]

Never mind, for the moment, that the destruction of nearly all military personnel records from World War II in a fire in a St. Louis archive in 1973 precludes the discovery of likely documentary sources. Never mind, too, that U.S. intelligence agencies, such as the FBI or army intelligence, have not rushed to divulge their full archival holdings. Such documents may or may not exist to enlighten future detectives. But as early as May 1943, the phrase appeared as a headline in a New York newspaper, *P.M.*, and similar wording (e.g., "prematurely anti-fascist") showed up in the *New Yorker* magazine during the war. But there is a more specific document on record that explains not only the origins of the phrase but also how it entered the national vocabulary in 1945.

On January 2, 1945, as U.S. troops were recovering from the German counteroffensive known as the Battle of the Bulge, Representative John M. Coffee, a Democrat from Washington, spoke at a public meeting in Madison Square Garden to urge the U.S. government to break diplomatic relations with the Franco regime in Spain. His speech was broadcast on national radio networks, and within days people were using the language attributed to the Washington bureaucracy.

In his address, Representative Coffee placed the contemporary situation in Spain within a historical context and had it printed in the *Congressional Record.* It follows here with my italics added:

We meet tonight as allies of the democratic peoples of Spain, and we meet in a hall which echoed to the heroic words of the Spanish people during the years 1936 to 1939. Perhaps some of you still remember how, in 1936, the people of New York filled this very hall to greet the first delegation of spokesmen for the Popular Front Government of Spain. . . .

I recall how this pioneer delegation from embattled Spain pleaded for our aid; how for night after night they told new American audiences that the fighting in the streets of Madrid was the start of the Axis war against the free world; how they pledged that if we aided them then, the Spanish people would come to our side when we were attacked by their German and Italian invaders.

Later, to these Spanish voices, were added the voices of Americans who had gone to Spain to fight the Nazi monster, and who returned, wounded, to tell us of what they had seen. They, too, were voices crying in the night. The Spaniards and the Americans told us that if Madrid fell, Paris and London—and Pearl Harbor—were next. Here at Madison Square Garden, and at hundreds of similar meetings throughout the United States and Canada, the rafters rung with the cry of the Spanish Republic—the cry "Make Madrid the Tomb of Fascism."

Perhaps our voices were not strong enough. . . .

I know that it is a hard thing to say, but these are hard times, when only cowards refuse to face facts. For the fate of Spain, we have no one to blame but ourselves.

We, who saw; we, who knew; we, who understood—did we really fight hard enough?

There is, of course, no honor high enough for those few thousand gallant American men and boys (*they call them premature anti-fascists in some nasty Washington circles today!*) who made their way to Spain and fought and suffered in the ranks of the Abraham Lincoln Brigade. They more than did their best to stop the third [sic] world war before it hit their native land. Never in the history of our nation has a group of Americans fought so heroically and received so little recognition from our own people as have the men of the Lincoln Brigade. I am indeed moved tonight to know that among the organizations sponsoring this meeting is included the Veterans of the Abraham Lincoln Brigade. They, of all Americans, did their share.

Coffee proceeded to appeal to the 16,000 people in attendance to express their opinions directly to their congressional representatives. With enough public pressure, he said, *"the appeasers will run for cover quicker than you can say premature anti-fascist."*

After this speech, the phrase "premature anti-fascist" began to appear widely in public statements and in private letters by Lincoln Brigade veterans. For example, when the Lincoln veteran Herman Bottcher was killed in action in the Pacific in January 1945, a former comrade in arms, Captain Robert Thompson, himself a decorated World War II hero, declared: "Herman Bottcher was a man whom cynical political dilettantes have dubbed a premature anti-fascist. He grew up fighting fascism. He fought it in Germany and in Spain and he died fighting it on Leyte Island."[2]

There is nothing sardonic in that statement. And as Bernard Knox, a veteran of the British battalion, who was also labeled a "premature anti-fascist" by a Yale professor, has said: "If you were not premature, what sort of anti-fascist were you supposed to be? A punctual anti-fascist?"[3]

But why is this tempest important?

For the Lincoln veterans who served in the U.S. Army during World War II, "premature anti-fascist" put a tag on what they had experienced for years. On August 24, 1945, for instance, Archie Brown was stationed in France when he received a copy of the West Coast Communist Party newspaper, *People's World.* There he found "an article about the investigation of the 'premature anti-fascists' by a congressional committee. . . . The funny part," said Brown, "is that we had been discussing the thing today about discrimination."[4]

From the beginning of the war, the military had treated the Lincolns as subversives, denying them opportunities to become commissioned officers, to obtain overseas assignments, or to attend technical schools where they might gain skills useful for civilian life. (As ever, military bureaucrats were not always efficient in screening out these alleged subversives, enabling some Lincolns to slip through the system.) When the Lincoln veterans questioned the denials, commanders told them the orders came from higher up. Brown's first sergeant blamed military intelligence (G-2) for keeping him out of radio school. In this way, "premature anti-fascist" foreshadowed the discrimination, harassment, and persecution associated with the anti-communist crusade of the Cold War era.

For historians like Haynes and Klehr, the claim that the Lincolns invented and glorified the term "premature anti-fascist" reflects the veterans' duplicity in concealing their opposition to U.S. intervention in World War II prior to the German invasion of the Soviet Union. They are correct in stating that the Veterans of the Abraham Lincoln Brigade (VALB) participated in the Communist Party's campaign, "The Yanks Are Not Coming." They err in assuming that all Lincoln veterans, or even all Communist Lincoln veterans, adopted that position. Some, like Sydney Levine, left the Communist Party but remained active and in good standing in VALB. Others, like Jack Shafran and Harry Schoenberg, ignored the jeers of their communist comrades and enlisted in the army. Still others were drafted. Whatever their motives, they all faced the same discrimination by the military leadership.

My critics err more grievously in claiming that veterans who opposed U.S. intervention were, as they put it, "interim pro-fascists." Such language simplifies to distortion the complexities of the period before U.S. entry into World War II. Having seen the consequences of British and French non-intervention in Spain—and, equally important, having seen the continuing brutal treatment of Spanish refugees in French concentration camps after the fall of the Spanish Republic—many Lincoln veterans had no sympathy with the plight of the Western Allies. In November 1940, for instance, Lincoln veterans were trying to raise money—futilely—to send an American rescue ship to liberate Spanish refugees from Vichy France. In February 1941, a veterans' delegation tried, without success, to meet with the British ambassador in Washington to arrange for the SS *Lovcen* to take 450 Spanish refugees from French Morocco to Mexico.[5]

To be sure, many veterans, including the VALB leadership, actively supported the Communist Party's pro-Soviet line. Yet even within those ranks, they articulated various positions about their opposition to intervention. For most, Spain remained the touchstone of their politics. "If you ask yourself, who were the enemies of Spain," veteran Alvah Bessie advised a writers' and artists' congress in June 1941, "you will know your enemy today."[6] Some even considered aligning with the conservative non-interventionist America First movement. Others expressed ambivalence about war in general. These were hardly "pro-fascist" sentiments.

Yet the Lincoln veterans paid dearly for their political views. Texas Representative Martin Dies, chair of the House Committee on Un-American Activities, considered them dangerous subversives. So did FBI Director J. Edgar Hoover. Congressman Coffee's "nasty Washington circles" may well refer to these architects of the red scare. Against their allegations of un-Americanism, however, stands a small mountain of World War II letters in the Abraham Lincoln Brigade Archives at New York University that demonstrates a remarkably intense commitment to democratic, anti-fascist beliefs. That is why the Lincolns were so indignant at the discrimination they faced in the military. That is why they pulled every string they could to obtain battlefield assignments. That is why they served so bravely, so heroically, in every theater of the war. And that is why, eventually, they grasped the term "premature anti-fascist" as a badge of honor.[7]

▷ **CHAPTER 10**

The Myth of the Moscow Archives

Nothing more clearly reveals the continuing influence of the Cold War on Spanish Civil War studies than the response to the opening of the Soviet archives during the 1990s. With remarkable alacrity, American students of communism leaped to explore some of the key spy cases of the postwar era and arranged to publish important documents previously hidden away in Soviet files. In 1993, the Abraham Lincoln Brigade Archives sent me to the Communist Party repository in Moscow to explore its holdings. I didn't know what to expect: a hundred documents, a thousand, ten thousand? It turned out to be more than 100,000. I spent nearly a month going through the papers and arranged for large portions of them to be microfilmed and eventually deposited in the ALBA collection, originally at Brandeis University and now at New York University's Tamiment Library.

Gathering the material was hard, interpreting it more complicated. As ever, researchers—me included, no doubt—brought to the table their biases and perceptual limitations. That is not the same thing, however, as cherry-picking evidence, by which I mean using only documents that reinforce one's point of view and pretending that counterevidence does not exist. I wrote this article, which was published in Science & Society's *Fall 2004 issue, in response to several publications that deliberately ignored parts of the documentary record for the convenience of pre-existing ideology.*

▷ During the past decade, a flurry of commentary on the History Channel, in book reviews, and in slick magazines has asked our literate public to consider the relative goodness of "the good fight" waged by the U.S. volunteers who formed the Abraham Lincoln Brigade to save the embattled Spanish Republic from fascist-backed military rebels in the Spanish Civil War (1936–1939). Mostly a rehash of worn arguments about the evils of communism in Spain, these pieces pay homage, not to George Orwell's anarchist Catalonia, but to supposedly new and startling evidence culled from the archives in the former Soviet Union, first opened to Western historians during the 1990s. Treated as sacred texts, these bits of de-contextualized history now serve as paltry evidence that the Lincoln Brigade fought, in the immortal words of Ronald Reagan, "on the wrong side."[1]

The honorable history of the Lincoln Brigade is thus replaced by myths of the Moscow archives. For decades after 1939, the keepers of the flame in the Soviet Union denied the existence of such archives, fanning inflated claims about murky agents and mysterious events that may or may not have actually occurred in Spain. The opening of hitherto "secret" papers promised to put to rest several contentious historical issues and finally quell debates about communism, the Lincoln Brigade, and the Spanish Civil War.

As one of the first researchers to view these archives, I can say that we now have much more evidence to play with than ever before, though even such elemental questions as to who actually fought in the Lincoln Brigade remain elusive. And, alas, as any good researcher must admit, the archives do not speak for themselves. Only people speak. And people who use the archives in Moscow (or anywhere else) do not ordinarily go empty-headed into a room full of historical materials and emerge full of wisdom. What happens instead is that they approach the historical archives with their own ideas, beliefs, and biases, which limit what they actually notice when they read the historical records. The result is that even though they do not start out empty-headed, their "research" often appears just so. They neither learn nor do they forget.

Among the most egregious examples of such pseudo-research are a pair of volumes published by Yale University Press under the rubric "Annals of Communism"—*Spain Betrayed: The Soviet Union in the Spanish Civil War,* edited by Ronald Radosh, Mary R. Habeck, and Grigory Sevostianov (2001), and *The Secret World of American Communism,* edited by Harvey Klehr, John Earl Haynes, and Fridrikh Igorevich Firsov (1995)—and a widely read article, "Innocents Abroad," in the September 2001 issue of *Vanity Fair,* written by the biographer of Whittaker Chambers, Sam Tanenhaus. Such efforts appear to have the trappings of bona fide scholarship, but to a remarkable degree stand instead as examples of unvarnished ideology and polemic.

Posing merely as compilers of documents—"the facts"—these writers assume that the Moscow archives are the final truth because their existence proves that during the 1930s someone wrote certain words on paper and these papers were filed and saved, waiting for self-revelation. After all, a document is real and its words may be quoted. But a historian should also ask about the origin of the sources themselves. Although many scholars talk about the "Russian" documents, the adjective properly refers to where these documents may be found today, not where they were created or by whom. Nor, with few exceptions, are these "official" documents, in the sense that they contain government or legal authority. Reports sent to the Kremlin by Soviet generals can hardly be taken at face value or treated as statements of policy without considering that reporters serving under the dictator Josef Stalin would, to put it mildly, attempt to place themselves in the best light.

The so-called Russian archives are the effluvia of war. The largest collection in Moscow relating to the Spanish Civil War, at least as far as we now know, consists of documents that originated in the International Brigades in Spain. These were military records that included the personnel files of individual volunteers. Most of the documents were written by members of the brigades in their native languages; very few were written in Russian. During the course of the war, many records were lost or destroyed; some undoubtedly wound up in enemy hands and will emerge some day from the former fascist archives. In 1939, as the Spanish Republic was collapsing before the advancing armies of General Francisco Franco, record keepers within the International Brigades, including New Jersey volunteer John Tisa, trucked tens of thousands of documents across the French border. Tisa helped to organize some of these records before he returned home in the spring of 1939. A handful of items were added to the files as late as 1940. And some time around then, probably just before or after the German invasion of France, the archives were shipped for safety to the Soviet Union.

For a military archive, a surprisingly large amount of material consists of lists of names—the members of a company, battalion, hospital ward, nationality group, and the like. The editors of *The Secret World of American Communism* make much of the lists of deserters and "bad elements." It is appropriate then to ask what such lists mean. The editors of the volume propose that they indicate the evils of communist leadership in Spain. One such list (Document 48) described dozens of volunteers as deserters, demoralized, suspicious. No doubt, such epithets suggest serious problems of morale within the ranks. But what army has been without complainers or delinquents? More to the point is the willingness to exaggerate the punishment meted out to such "bad elements." I've always wondered what happened to a soldier named Virgil Morris, who was put into a labor punishment battalion for misconduct and subsequently brought to a military court for making a racist remark to African American battalion commander Oliver Law. In Document 48 he is listed as a "spy." Sixty-three years later, I received an email from Morris's grandson, attached with a copy of his honorable discharge from military service in 1938. Other FBI files show that Morris returned to his home in Oregon along with other veterans of the brigade. So much for the horrors of communist-led military tribunals in the Fifteenth Brigade.

According to Tanenhaus, however, labels such as "Defeatist," "Agitator," "Suspicious Trotskyist," "were loaded epithets and potential death sentences." No one likes to be called bad names, but the operative word in that sentence is not "death" but "potential." What does it mean when a person's name, as the writer says ominously, "disappears from the records"?

Consider the case of a volunteer named Edward Carter. When his family contacted the Abraham Lincoln Brigade Archives, an educational nonprofit organization, seeking information about him, the archival records provided only one item: his name. Except for that isolated entry, there is no evidence that he was ever in Spain. Perhaps he entered with a false passport and used someone else's name? Perhaps, as was the case with many others, he fled during the Great Retreats of 1938 across the French border, as family testimony implied? Or perhaps he was recaptured by the Soviet secret police, taken to a dark and dirty dungeon, interrogated, shot, and his files effaced from the records? The Moscow archives do not say.

Another type of document frequently used by critics of the International Brigades is the end-of-the-war evaluation form, in which military and political leaders (the latter usually, but not always, commissars in the army) graded the rank and file from "excellent" to "muy malo." These subjective accountings apparently tried to assess the value of individual volunteers to the Communist Party after their return home. The evaluations often said nasty things about individuals, but despite the rhetoric they do not foreshadow how people were treated in Spain or afterward. Praise did not necessarily lead to a party position; criticism did not always affect a person's postwar standing. And, for the one-third of the volunteers who were not party members, the grading system appeared even less meaningful.

So when Tanenhaus, as part of his "research," e-mailed me a list of ten names without any indication of where his list had come from and asked if I knew their fate, I noticed one who had come home and one who I thought had died in Spain, and decided that the writer could do his own research to ascertain the whereabouts of the others. Of course, not really being interested in the question, Tanenhaus dropped his inquiry, but in print he audaciously postulated that these men, in disappearing from the records, had joined a line of those who faced "potential death sentences."

Which brings me back to the mysterious Edward Carter. Thanks to another more tenacious researcher, Carter's daughter-in-law Allene Carter, who conducted her search not in Moscow but in Washington, D.C., among other places in the United States, the man with only a single two-word entry in the Moscow archives served in the U.S. Army during World War II; killed a bunch of Germans in a fantastic one-man exploit in 1945; subsequently returned to his hometown, Los Angeles; attended a social event featuring Paul Robeson in 1946; and ultimately became one of the seven African Americans who posthumously received the Congressional Medal of Honor from President Bill Clinton in 1996. In June 2001, in a ceremony near Norfolk, Virginia, the U.S. Navy proudly christened a ship after Sgt. Edward A. Carter, Jr.

That's the difference between "death" and "potential," between history and speculation, authenticity and nonsense. A careful researcher must also be wary of assuming the omniscience of these archives. *The Secret World of American Communism* makes much of a statement written by volunteer Morris Cohen when he entered the International Brigades in 1937: "When the war is finished, I would like to return to activity in the American Labor movement. However, if circumstances require my presence elsewhere, similar to the Spanish struggle against fascism, then I would go there."[2] Claiming that no other volunteers made such a clear offer of future services elsewhere, the editors conclude: "Cohen's answer illustrates why Soviet intelligence officers spotted him as a potential recruit." Cohen went on to become part of the Soviet Union's international spy network. But interviews I conducted with the person who actually recruited Cohen for such work made clear that they were old friends in New York City and the above-quoted statement had nothing to do with his selection.

While the Moscow archives can provide an immense amount of raw data, the records do not necessarily make anyone more knowledgeable.

Facts are easily bent; fictions easily reified into history. The specious allegations, repeated by Tanenhaus, that the African American battalion commander Oliver Law was a victim of fragging by his own men is a particularly blatant example of deceit, especially after all the counter research that has been offered.[3] But the more such false stories are repeated, the more the value of any historical scholarship is deflated and the purposes of inquiry reduced to arrogant self-promotion.

PART IV

Postscripts

▷ CHAPTER 11

Spain and "Spain Again"

An Interview with Spanish Civil War Veteran Alvah Bessie

After six years as a history professor, with three published books, I became a freelance writer in San Francisco in 1974, contributing book reviews and articles to a weekly alternative newspaper, The San Francisco Bay Guardian. *My first significant piece, published in October of 1975, was based on an interview with Lincoln Brigade veteran Alvah Bessie, notorious as one of the Hollywood Ten, screenwriters and producers who refused to testify before the House Committee on Un-American Activities in 1947. Bessie served a year in prison when the Supreme Court refused to consider his First Amendment claims. He had recently published a book titled* Spain Again *about his return to Spain to work in a fictional movie about an American veteran of the Spanish Civil War. His publisher, Jonathan Sharp, arranged for me to meet Bessie at his home in Marin County. I probably asked him more questions than he wanted to answer, but he did anyway. Bessie's statistics about the Lincoln Brigade are inflated, largely because such data were not widely available in the 1970s.*

▷ Nearly 40 years after the Spanish Civil War ended, Franco's Spain is still ripped apart by political discord. The execution of five revolutionaries by the Franco regime last month reopened the deep fissures that divide the country, and the international protests that followed are exacerbating the crisis. In San Rafael, one survivor of the civil war, author Alvah Bessie, is enthusiastic about the new anti-government demonstrations.

"I'd like to be in Spain," Bessie told me. "This is what I've been waiting for."

Bessie, now 71, has been waging war against General Francisco Franco since 1938, when he enlisted in the Abraham Lincoln Brigade, a unit of American volunteers who violated the American Neutrality Act to fight for the Spanish Republic against the armies of Franco and his fascist allies Hitler and Mussolini. Bessie later achieved even greater notoriety as one of the Hollywood Ten, who refused to testify to the House Un-American Activities Committee (HUAC) in 1947 and went to prison for his principles.

Bessie's confrontations with political power provide the background for most of his writing—four novels, three autobiographies, and one anthology. In his latest book, *Spain Again,* Bessie weaves the entire story together, tracing his career from the 1930s to his recent return to Franco's Spain.

Bessie first described his wartime experiences in Spain in a powerful, gripping narrative, *Men in Battle,* published in September 1939—in the week that Hitler invaded Poland—and recently reissued [in 1975]. It is an extraordinary account of battlefield conditions, written with drama, passion, and sensitivity:

> . . . these men behind these fragile rocks, these men whose tender flesh is torn to pieces by the hot and ragged steel; they could not accept their death with such good grace if they did not love so deeply and so well—were not determined that love must come alive into the world. What other reason could there by for dying? What other reason for this blood upon your hands?

Bessie's descriptions of battle and the horrible toll of warfare are outstanding and the political commentary that runs through the narrative provides insight into the motives and reasoning that turned a "small" war of rebellion into the staging ground for World War II. The Spanish Civil War—with its splits between Trotskyites, Stalinists, Anarchists, Socialists, and Republicans, not to mention Catholics, Monarchists, and Fascists—remains one of the most confusing ideological struggles of modern times, but *Men in Battle* goes a long way toward clarifying the issues. It offers a healthy antidote to George Orwell's pessimistic *Homage to Catalonia* and is far more honest about political passion than Hemingway's *For Whom the Bell Tolls.*

Of the 3,000 Americans who fought for the Spanish Republic, only 1,300 survive. Bessie emerged from the war with what he called "a morbid obsession" about his survival and a burning commitment to vindicate the sacrifice of his closest friends and comrades. "The war was not actually lost," he insists today. "The struggle goes on. No people can be suppressed forever."

Alvah Bessie, veteran of the Abraham Lincoln Brigade, wrote numerous books of fiction and nonfiction about the Spanish Civil War. He was working on an anthology of writings by veterans of the Lincoln Brigade when he died in 1985. (Photo by Abraham Aronow. Reproduced with permission)

The veterans of the Lincoln Brigade returned home just in time to become involved in World War II. According to Bessie, 1,200 served in the American armed forces or the merchant marine.[1]

But as sympathizers of the Spanish Republic, over which the Communist Party had a strong political influence, the survivors discovered that they were "suspected of disloyalty" by the U.S. Army and so denied military promotions and combat assignments.

Those suspicions followed the veterans into civilian life. Bessie went to Hollywood as a screenwriter, worked on films like *Objective Burma*, and was nominated for an Academy Award in 1946. Since the Soviet Union was a military ally during the war, Communist sympathizers could be tolerated, if not actually welcomed, in the entertainment industry.

But in 1947, as part of a shift toward the Cold War mentality, Congress began to ferret out Communist subversion in all areas of American life, and HUAC, one of whose freshman members was Congressman Richard Milhous Nixon, began to investigate the motion picture industry. When summoned to testify about their political beliefs and affiliations, Bessie and nine other Hollywood writers refused to talk.

They were convicted of contempt of Congress and, after the Supreme Court refused to review the case, went to federal prison. Senator Joe McCarthy, with whose name the witch hunts of the 1950s are indelibly associated, had not yet arrived on the national scene. But when the Hollywood Ten were released from prison—Bessie served ten months in Texarkana—they quickly learned they were blacklisted within the industry.

Bessie describes these events in an autobiographical work, *Inquisition in Eden* (1965), and in a bitter, ironic novel, *The Un-Americans* (1957). The latter work, though hardly noticed in this country, has survived underground in Latin America and Spain, passing from hand to hand and, according to Bessie, has even been smuggled into the cells of Franco's prisons.

In *The Un-Americans,* Bessie best articulates the intimate connection between the fascist victory in Spain and the anti-Communist crusade of the Cold War. The events are only nine years apart—something that the notion of a "McCarthy era" tends to obscure—and the protagonists on both sides are often the same people. Bessie's personal need to testify about the war in Spain undoubtedly explains his subsequent refusal to testify before the suppressive elements within his own society. In whatever form, he declares, "fascism is fascism."

Bessie's tough stand against HUAC, like his engagements in Spain, has haunted the remainder of his life. Banished from Hollywood, Bessie scratched out a living, first as a publicity writer for San Francisco's longshoremen's union, then as a stage director/light man at the hungry i nightclub. His books—with the exception of a weak Hollywood novel, *The Symbol*—have been ignored by the media, and the cause for which he fought has been consigned to romanticism and nostalgia.

Bessie's new book, *Spain Again* (Chandler and Sharp), is suffering a similar fate—which is too bad, because it presents one of the clearest and most persuasive explanations of the current situation in Spain. It is the story of Bessie's return to Catalonia in 1967 as a consultant for a Spanish film based on the civil war. The film, *Espana Otra Vez* (Spain Again), describes a Lincoln Brigade veteran who returns to the scenes of battle and confronts the "new" Spain. Though nominated for an Academy Award for the Best Foreign Film in 1968, it never found an American distributor.

Like Bessie's other autobiographical work, *Spain Again* is a strong, touching account of the meaning of survival and the burden of vindication. Here is Bessie searching for the grave of his comrade Aaron Lopoff and witnessing, partly through his own life, the continuation of the struggle for Spanish freedom. It is a political narrative, in the fullest sense, but it preserves the compassion, poignancy, and delicacy of a fine novel:

> I could visualize the picture and it sickened me. We would find [the grave] and it would be untended, bare of any name. . . . We would paint the masonry, paint the name and dates of birth and death, clean up around it, place flowers in the new metal containers on the wall—and send the color picture to his father and mother in Los Angeles!

Bessie never found the grave. But he learned later that the bodies of anti-fascist soldiers probably had been removed by the government because they symbolized resistance to the fascist regime. "Other Brigade men who had visited Spain," he recalls, " . . . invariably discovered that the local peasants had been caring for these graves for over 20 years, and placed fresh flowers on them regularly."

It is this enduring spirit for liberty, Bessie argues, that makes the fall of Spanish fascism inevitable. "Your murder . . . of five heroic antifascist Spaniards," he wrote in an open letter last month to "El Puto," General Francisco Franco, "signed the death-warrant of your putrescent regime. . . . Now it will die."

Mussolini and Hitler were eliminated in World War II, Bessie explains. But Franco's public neutrality in the war, together with his unyielding anti-Communism (something he shared with the other fascist dictators), made him a valuable ally to the United States during the Cold War. Now, says Bessie, it is only American money and military assistance that keep the regime in power. And Washington has been conspicuously silent about the recent reign of terror against the political opposition.

Time is running out for Franco, Bessie insists. "The Spanish people are fighting a good cause. It will soon be won. I just hope they handle it right."

The defeat of Franco will bring symbolic victories as well, and Alvah Bessie is waiting to share the triumph. He speaks about Dolores Ibarruri, "La Pasionaria," the spiritual leader of the Spanish Communist Party, now in her 80s and living in unhappy exile in Moscow. It was she, some 40 years ago, who proclaimed "*Vale mas morir de pie que vivir de rodillas*"; "It is better to die on your feet than to live on your knees."

"I hope," says Bessie, with tears in his eyes, "that she will live to see the Republic restored, that she will be able to go home at last."

"Mothers! Women!" La Pasionaria had preached during the war:

> When the years pass by and the wounds of the war are being stanched; when the cloudy memory of the sorrowful, bloody days returns in a present of freedom, peace and well-being; when the feelings of rancor are dying away and when the pride in a free country is felt equally by all Spaniards, then speak to your children. Tell them of these men of the International Brigades.
>
> Tell them how, coming over seas and mountains, crossing frontiers, bristling with bayonets . . . these men reached our country as crusaders for freedom, to fight and side for Spain's liberty and independence which were threatened by German and Italian Fascism. They gave up everything: their lives, their countries, home and fortune; fathers, mothers, wives, brothers, sisters and children, and they came and told us: "We are here. Your cause, Spain's cause, is ours—it is the cause of all advanced and progressive mankind."

"You know," Bessie remarks softly, "when it is over and Franco is gone, I will be an honorary citizen of the Republic."

In San Rafael, California, Alvah Bessie is waiting.

AN OPEN LETTER FROM ALVAH BESSIE TO FRANCISCO FRANCO

Senorito:

Your murder yesterday of five heroic antifascist Spaniards signed the death-warrant of your putrescent regime.

World leaders and the Secretary-General of the United Nations appealed for clemency; you paid no heed. Pope Paul VI, leader of the religion you have ostentatiously professed (since 1939) appealed to you three times. "Unfortunately," he said, "we were not listened to." You are consistent, *senorito;* only two months ago you advised some of your followers that, "You give too much importance to barking dogs."

You say these young men killed policemen? We have no evidence they did. We know your military courts need no such evidence. We know they operate under "emergency" decrees where due process is nonexistent and accusation brings automatic conviction. We know torture is common practice in your jails and *el garrote vil* is your favorite medieval instrument of torture and death.

We understand your panic, El Puto. We understand why your own people applied this epithet to you in 1936; you had just sold yourself to Hitler and Mussolini. They apply it to this day, because you sold them again—to the money-power in the USA—in 1953. To our everlasting shame we also know that it is that power alone and the arms "we" have supplied since then that have kept your regime alive. Now it will die.

You can spare your people of the shame of using your favorite instrument on you—though many would forgive them if they did. You can die quietly now and be buried temporarily in the monstrous vulgarity called The Valley of the Fallen which you erected in your own memory some years ago—with the prison labor of thousands of Spanish Republican soldiers whose only crime was defending their country against you and your foreign allies.

Or you can appeal for sanctuary for the brief time remaining to you, to the only friend you have left on the international scene: he pardoned Richard Nixon for any crimes "he might have committed" against us. He will surely pardon you for all the crimes you have committed against the Spanish people, because he is a law-and-order man himself and his name was conspicuously absent when many other heads of state expressed outrage over your latest atrocity.

We honor and cherish the memory of Juan Paredes Manotas (21) and Angel Otaegui (33, Basque patriots); of Jose Humberto Baena Alonso (23), and Jose Sanchez-Bravo Sollas (21, students), and of Ramon Garcia Sanz (27, metal-worker).

We despise the memory of El Senorito Don Puto Francisco Franco y Bahamonde, last fascist dictator in Europe, traitor to his country whose republican constitution he swore to uphold, butcher of the Spanish people for the last 39 years.

▷ **CHAPTER 12**

Foreword to Alvah Bessie's *Men in Battle*

Alvah Bessie, bounced out of Hollywood on his rear end, settled in the San Francisco area in the 1950s. Nearly everything he wrote reflected his craft as a screenwriter, cutting between characters, between past and present, and revealing, I think, his continuing desire to return to his glory days at Warner Brothers. Meanwhile, he remained a political radical with an obvious chip on his shoulder. We came to like each other. I assigned him and edited his book reviews and produced a two-hour interview about his career for KPFA, Pacifica Radio. I tried for years to persuade various publishers to re-issue his classic book, Men in Battle, *about the Lincoln Brigade. I even had a contract with a university press, for which I wrote this foreword. And then the marketing department intervened. It's published here for the first time.*

▷ *Men in Battle* is a memoir of war—indeed, it is a masterpiece of that genre. Ernest Hemingway, who knew a thing or two about the subject and who had met the author, Alvah Bessie, in 1938 during a lull in the fighting in the Spanish Civil War, called the work "true, honest, fine." Foreign correspondent, Vincent Sheean, who also met Bessie at the front, applauded the book's "terrifying impression of exact truth that . . . [makes] readers lie there and hide our heads beneath the moaning of the shells." Bessie obviously appreciated this praise, but later in life he grumbled that his book had first appeared in September 1939, in the week that World War II began, and the good reviews were buried beneath the rubble of more current war news.

Bessie's blistering description of frontline combat is not just a military memoir. Despite the autobiographical perspective, the work expresses political and ideological themes that are usually ignored in battlefield writing. The Spanish Civil War, in which Bessie participated, was not just a military match-up between reactionary generals and the legal government, it involved fundamental choices between fascism and democracy. Contemporaries understood that what was at stake in Spain was the future of Europe, perhaps the world.

The war had begun as a military insurrection when the army, led by Francisco Franco, rebelled against the elected Spanish Republic in July 1936. Within weeks the uprising exploded into a tense international drama. As the army renounced constitutional government and civilians spontaneously rallied to defend their country, the rebels began to receive vital military assistance from Nazi Germany and Fascist Italy. The Republic appealed for support from anti-fascist countries. In this era of "appeasement," Britain, France, and the United States refused to intervene. The Soviet Union, fearing that the inertia of the Western Allies indicated their willingness to see Hitler succeed, extended limited military aid to Spain and urged communists around the world to send volunteers to form an International Brigade to fight for the Republic. In the end, such appeals drew some 35,000 volunteers from 52 countries, men and women who left their homes to halt the fascist legions. Of these volunteers, about 3,000 were residents of the United States, who formed various battalions and medical groups that collectively were known as the "Abraham Lincoln Brigade."

What started as a local conflict emerged as a war of annihilation. Soon, the Spanish Civil War foreshadowed the horrors of World War II, including aerial bombardment of civilians, population upheavals, and brutal concentration camps. Those, like Alvah Bessie, who fought to save the Republic, warned presciently that a fascist victory in Spain would quickly lead to a second world war. His narrative depicts the growing frustration and rage of those who watched helplessly as the fascist juggernaut tore through the Spanish people. In the 1930s, therefore, the word "Spain" symbolized not only a place on a map or an agonized landscape, but also a line drawn in the earth, a cause, a commitment. Spain became a reason to fight or to die.

Alvah Cecil Bessie—novelist, journalist, literary critic—was already an outsider when he departed for Spain in 1938 to join the Lincoln Brigade. As *Men in Battle* makes clear, the war intensified his alienation from politics as usual. Like many survivors of tragedy, he could never forgive and forget. He came home with grudges as well as obligations to the living and the dead. But his conscience, which was both political and personal, also aroused the suspicion and hostility of the powers that be. They, too, could not forgive or forget that Bessie, and his comrades in the Lincoln Brigade, had stepped outside the political mainstream to participate in a foreign war. This commitment to antifascism in the age of isolationism had exceeded the boundaries of acceptable dissent. And they would pay a price for their obstinacy and pride, even though leaders like Roosevelt later acknowledged that they had been right. Bessie, consequently, spent a good part of his life after Spain trying to get back at, as well as back into, respectable circles without bending his principles. He was therefore not a happy man; he had a tendency to grouch. But he was supremely loyal to his friends and people he liked. He was a superb raconteur. And what he had to say was passionate, intelligent, and important.

Bessie had not always lived outside the cultural or political norm. He was born in New York City to an assimilated Jewish family in 1904 (and so, at age 33, was slightly older than most of the Lincoln volunteers). He also enjoyed a more privileged background than most. Having received a liberal arts education at Columbia College (Class of 1924), he had proceeded to indulge thespian fantasies on the New York stage, written drafts of two unpublished novels, and translated Pierre Louyes's *Songs of Bilitis* from the French. Still searching for his calling, Bessie sailed to France in 1928, hoping to become part of the "lost generation" of expatriate writers. He published his first short story in Paris the next year. Then, feeling homesick, he abruptly returned to New York. He found small jobs on the fringes of publishing, but each disappeared as the great Depression spread through the industry.

"My life did not go from Point A to Point B," he told me in a radio interview in 1984. "I did what I had to do." Despite his comfortable background, he identified with society's less fortunate. In 1930, Bessie married Mary Burnett, a painter, puppet maker, and writer, and the economic knots tightened. To cut expenses, they moved to rural Vermont, first to work as servants, then to become tenant farmers on rocky land. They had two sons, Dan and David. Amid extreme poverty and malnutrition, Bessie continued to write short stories, achieving substantial critical success and inclusion in the "best" annual anthologies. His stories frequently depicted couples living on the edges of starvation. He also wrote his first novel, *Dwell in the Wilderness*, which described several generations of a single family. Its publication in 1935 enabled Bessie to win a prestigious Guggenheim Fellowship. But by the end of the decade, he would inscribe a copy of the book to his Spanish Civil War colleague, Edwin Rolfe, calling it "this memoir of my dead life."

After 1935, Bessie's literary outlook underwent a vast change.[1] "For the first five years of my life as a writer I wrote short stories," he later explained.

> I was chiefly interested in . . . examining my own emotions, my own reactions to the world and my surroundings, my personal relationships with my wife and other people. To understand how a grown man could be so narrow . . . has something to do with the fact that I was brought up in a well-to-do family, sheltered from the hard facts of life.

But the Depression experience taught Bessie other lessons that, as he put it,

> literally saved my life and made me, I believe, a useful human being instead of a man who juggled with words. . . . For I learned that my problems as a writer were exactly the same as the problems of the farmer who lived down the road from me . . . when he could not get a living for his children out of the potatoes he grew (and I helped to pick) at such expense of labor.

Returning to New York City in 1935, Bessie's political development accelerated, part of a broader metamorphosis that affected many intellectuals of his generation. Working as a reporter for the *Brooklyn Eagle,* he found himself engaged in discussions about "communism, fascism, and the need for social change . . . by people who, only a few years ago, considered politics beneath the attention of an adult intellect." Bessie circulated among literary radicals and communists. He became involved in a bitter East Coast waterfront strike, working behind the scenes to persuade the *Eagle* to reverse its anti-strike editorial position. Soon afterward, Bessie joined the Communist Party. (Meanwhile, his wife had an affair with one of the striking seamen, and Bessie left the marriage.) His journalistic efforts now became overtly political, addressing such subjects as the student antiwar movement, the lynching of African Americans, Soviet films, and the League Against War and Fascism.

When the French novelist André Malraux toured the United States in 1937 to gain support for the Spanish Republic, Bessie interviewed him and came away dazzled. "He is that rare being," wrote Bessie of his ideal role model, "an artist and a man of action, the one inseparable from the other."[2] Bessie's editor disagreed with such praise. In the ensuing argument, Bessie quit his job, finding more agreeable work creating publicity for the Spanish Information Bureau in New York. He also followed Malraux's example by taking flying lessons to acquire some practical skills that might assist the Spanish Republican army. By the end of the year, he was making plans to enlist. "I came to know other people for the first time in my life," Bessie later wrote of his political awakening in this period. "And I have been concerned since that time, more with the problems of other people than with my own problems. . . . For the people and the words have become one."

When Bessie sailed for Spain (via Paris) in January 1938, he carried a pocket notebook (eventually he would have four) in which he kept a daily diary of his ten-month experience in the Spanish Civil War.[3] He had had just five weeks of training at Tarazona when a major fascist offensive required all able-bodied soldiers to move to the front. Bessie joined the Lincolns at the worst of times. Forced into chaotic retreats, the battalion suffered heavy casualties, long night marches, terrifying encounters with an unseen enemy in the dark, the loss of commanders, rearguard actions, and a desperate flight across the Ebro River. Later, in July 1938, he would participate in the recrossing of the Ebro River, as the Republic launched a counteroffensive and recovered some of the territory lost the previous spring. However, as Bessie bitterly records, there were never enough supplies and ammunition to overcome the superiority of Franco's military machine. His depiction of the fascist bombardment of Hill 666 is a poem to terror. Appreciating the value of Bessie's literary skills, battalion leaders decided to spare him further military exposure. They appointed him editor of the weekly newspaper, *The Volunteer for Liberty,* and sent him away from the front lines.

Men in Battle reflects the frustration and despair of a defeated army. Backed by his contemporary notebooks, Bessie reported what he saw and heard. But some of Bessie's comrades, particularly his battalion commander, Major Milton Wolff, have objected to the gloomy depiction of morale in the ranks. "Alvah's notes, though brief, reek with the stink of defeat," wrote Wolff, but "not everyone was demoralized, nor did everyone delight in the rumored withdrawal of the I[nternational] B[rigades]." One soldier's vantage, Wolff insisted, "is not necessarily the way it was for everybody."[4]

Bessie's perspective nevertheless had lasting effects on his life and work. "I knew, about myself," writes Bessie in *Men in Battle,* "that the historical event of Spain had coincided with a long-felt compulsion to complete the destruction of the training I had received all through my youth." And, as he had predicted, Bessie acquired in Spain personal obligations that would follow him for the rest of his life. In a political sense, the defeat of the Spanish Republic left Bessie and the other Lincoln veterans sad, frustrated, and angry about the failure of the Allies to intervene. Moreover, as the U.S. government viewed the Lincoln volunteers as potential subversives, their decision to go to Spain in violation of federal laws targeted them for government investigation. More profoundly, Bessie emerged from the war with a deep sense of loss—what commentators of later wars have labeled "survivor guilt"—because others had died while he continued to live. His recurring nightmare, a vision of the dead Aaron Lopoff beckoning to him (which Bessie added in the epilogue of the 1975 edition of *Men in Battle*), captures that feeling. The only way Bessie could assuage his survivor's guilt was to stick fast to the principles that had sent him to Spain in the first place.

Spain changed him forever. After returning to New York in 1938, he determined to fulfill his identity as a communist intellectual, a writer who blended literary craft with radical ideology. Besides writing *Men in Battle* and a second novel, *Bread and a Stone* (1941), about an illiterate man guilty of murder, he became the drama critic of the left-wing journal *New Masses* and wrote a regular column for the *Weekly Review,* published by the Young Communist League. Among his essays was a bitter criticism of Hemingway's Spanish Civil War novel *For Whom the Bell Tolls.* "What emerges from your book," wrote Bessie on behalf of the Veterans of the Abraham Lincoln Brigade, "is a picture so drastically mutilated . . . as to slander the cause for which we fought."[5]

Bessie's search for a larger audience flowered in 1943 when the Warner Brothers studio gave him a lavish salary to become a Hollywood screenwriter. Of course, his modest efforts to politicize the movies soon collided with the unyielding conservatism of the studio system. Bessie wrote a few good scripts, including *Objective, Burma,* for which he was nominated for an Academy Award. Five weeks after moving to Hollywood, however, the Federal Bureau of Investigation opened an intensive surveillance of Bessie's activities, as it did for most Spanish Civil War veterans, and placed his name on a list of "dangerous" individuals who would be arrested in the event of a national emergency. Bessie's thick FBI dossier shows him to have been especially concerned with Spanish issues, such as the treatment of Republican refugees and U.S. support of the Franco dictatorship.

Bessie paid for his dissident politics. When the House Committee on Un-American Activities summoned a group of Hollywood writers, producers, and directors to testify about their political beliefs in 1947, Bessie refused to cooperate on the grounds that the investigation violated First Amendment rights of free speech. He was soon placed on an industry blacklist that effectively ended his employment in Hollywood. Moreover, he was convicted of contempt of Congress and received a one-year sentence in a federal prison.

Devastated by the ordeal, Bessie vividly depicted the situation in a novel titled *The Un-Americans* (1957), a book he later considered his best work. In the style of a screenplay, the story cuts between two autobiographical narrative lines, one set in Spain in 1938, the other in Hollywood in 1947. Just nine years separated the shells of Spain from the HUAC witch hunt. A careful reading of *Men in Battle* discloses how Bessie's real-life friends, Aaron Lopoff and Joe Hecht, killed in battle in Spain and World War II, respectively, would surface as fictionalized characters to haunt the author's conscience. No other work of fiction better links the Spanish Civil War to the Cold War. But, as Bessie had feared, the novel received little attention. He then wrote a non-fiction account, *Inquisition in Eden*, which appeared in 1965.

Bessie's literary shortfalls mirrored the futility of his struggle to resume a Hollywood career after the blacklisting finally ended in the 1960s. In one essay, he described himself as "the non-existent man" and painfully lamented what he could not overcome: "to be skidded out of the economic system on your backside." Despite considerable talent—and Bessie was a skilled, engaging narrator—he could never suppress his didactic voice or the pleading for his personal cause. He wrote three additional books—*The Symbol* (1967), a Hollywood novel based loosely on the life of Marilyn Monroe; *Spain Again* (1975), an account of his return to Spain in the 1960s; and *One for My Baby* (1980), a fictional rendering of his years as the stage manager at a San Francisco nightclub, the hungry i. All revealed the same frustration at the deprivation of his livelihood and the silencing of his words. Each, moreover, suffered from the use of a screenplay format that imposed a choppy structure. In the end, his indignation drained his creative juices, but kept him alive politically. It was perfectly characteristic of the man that at the time of his death in 1985 he was embroiled in a legal case against his publisher for inadvertently shredding unsold copies of his last book (the publisher settled one day after Bessie died). And he was editing a collection of stories written by his comrades in the Lincoln Brigade, *Our Fight* (1986).[6]

Bessie remained an outspoken critic of American foreign policy, opposing U.S. intervention in Central America just as he once protested isolationism in the 1930s. One of his last public acts was to endorse the shipment of ambulances to Nicaragua, a project sponsored by the Veterans of the Abraham Lincoln Brigade to protest a U.S. embargo imposed by President Ronald Reagan.

When I first met Alvah Bessie to interview him on the reissue of *Men in Battle* and the publication of *Spain Again* in 1975, he plied me with gin and tonics in his poolside backyard in stylish Marin County and charmed me with personal stories and anecdotes. He did not spare his didacticism or his passion for justice; he remained an engaged intellectual. That day he gave me an open letter he had written to protest the execution of Basque nationalists by the still-reigning Franco dictatorship. Spain remained his primary interest, "a morbid obsession," he said. He also gave me an invitation to a private screening of a film about the Lincoln Brigade and added my name to a short roster of recipients of his frequent postcards that presented pithy advice and opinions about history and politics. "Keep warm and dry," he advised me one winter. "Worse weather is coming, both meteorological and political." In this way, he guided my interest in the Spanish Civil War. After he died, his widow, Sylviane, allowed me complete access to his papers, which I read at his untouched desk in his office. Without Alvah Bessie, my own writing about the Spanish Civil War would be much diminished. When I assess his thwarted career, I think: he was a writer of principle; he stuck to his guns. And that is a very good reason, if anyone needs one, to be a writer.

▷ **CHAPTER 13**

Foreword to Hank Rubin's *Spain's Cause Was Mine*

When I met Hank Rubin in the 1980s, he was well-known in the San Francisco area for starting one of the first "California-style" restaurants, The Pot Luck, in Berkeley, as well as writing a wine column for the San Francisco Chronicle *and* Bon Appetit *magazine, and for hosting a wine talk show on KPFA, Pacifica radio. He was also teaching cooking to high school students and planning a volume called the* Kitchen Answer Book. *None of this seemingly had to do with his time in the Lincoln Brigade, except, perhaps, that he gained an appreciation for a square meal. (Most of the volunteers remembered dire plates of garbanzo beans.) What brought Spain and cooking together, I think, was Hank's remarkable personality: he was a caretaker by nature, concerned about the comfort of others. I was pleased when he asked me to write the foreword for his memoir, and happy to put him in touch with Rick Stetter, director of Southern Illinois University Press, which published* Spain's Cause Was Mine *in 1997.*

▷ For college students of the 1930s, no less than for those today, the choices of the day sometimes boiled down to simple decisions, such as "to blow my almost empty wallet on a hamburger for lunch," as one UCLA undergraduate put it, or, as his lab partner replied, to "go into the library and do the research for Dr. Webb's paper."

So much for appearances. On one April day during the spring semester of 1937, Hank Rubin chose to do neither. And then, just a few minutes later, while sunbathing on the steps of the UCLA library, another student came along with a better proposition: How would you like to go to war in Spain?

"Sure."

Reading the plain and honest recounting of this conversation, one is tempted to seek psychological understanding: the young man's conflicts with his father; the fear of failure during the nation's economic depression; ambivalence about his Jewish heritage; a bad love life. There is plenty of grist in this narrative for speculation.

But psychology is not the point—or the methodology. When Hank Rubin replied, "Sure," and embarked on the road that would take him to Spain as a volunteer in the International Brigades fighting to save the legally elected government, he was participating in a worldwide political movement that attracted college students and alumni from every corner of the United States, not to mention men and women from innumerable occupations, economic backgrounds, and educational attainments.

Exact numbers are difficult to establish. Besides the 2,600 men who volunteered for military service, some 150 North American doctors, nurses, and medical technicians also enlisted in the ranks. Hank Rubin's recollections of his work in hospital laboratories are especially valuable because the Spanish Civil War proved a testing ground not only for weapons of war but also for military medicine used during World War II. It was in Spain, for example, that the Canadian doctor Norman Bethune developed techniques for preserving blood that made possible indirect frontline transfusions. Nor were medical personnel spared the hardships or dangers of war. Two U.S. physicians were killed during bombings, and one nurse was severely wounded. Indeed, ambulance drivers learned to remove medical insignia from their vehicles because fascist pilots seemed to be drawn to such targets. And while the medical staff was well trained in civilian medicine, the shortage of personnel, hospital equipment, and even food placed all patients at risk.[1]

Especially significant is the extent of Hank Rubin's duties. The fact that a UCLA undergraduate was given so much medical responsibility and so little training underscores the severe shortages facing the embattled Republic. While Germany and Italy amply supplied the rebellious Franco forces, the non-intervention policies of Britain, France, and the United States literally starved both soldiers and civilians in towns and cities held by Republican forces. In that age of isolationism, Hank Rubin's willingness to defy U.S. neutrality laws illuminates the deep political passions of the times. While leaders of the Western democracies adopted strategies of appeasement toward the fascist peril, many informed citizens understood that another world war loomed ahead, unless international aggression could be stopped. Hank Rubin's quick decision on the library steps reflected less the impetuosity of youth than it did the sound realization, sadly proved prophetic, that Hitler meant to embroil Europe in war.

The first International Brigade volunteers arrived in Madrid in November 1936, participating in the dramatic defense of the city. The first U.S. recruits sailed from New York the day after Christmas. The organization of the Brigades—from enlistment to passage—remained under Communist Party supervision. As Hank Rubin's memoir attests, the recommendation of a party member was the surest way of enlisting. (The failure of the Socialist party to field a "Debs Column" showed the difficulty of handling such a complicated international operation.) Once in Spain, however, communist soldiers enjoyed few special privileges. Noncommunists served as officers, even occasionally as political commissars, providing educational and morale assistance to the soldiers.

Hank Rubin's ideological leanings also reflected his ethnic background. Most Lincoln volunteers, born just before World War I, came from urban areas with high immigrant populations. About one-third, maybe more, were Jews, though seldom Orthodox. Given the international orientation of immigrant families and the obvious Nazi threat, the high participation of Jewish volunteers might be expected. Sketchy evidence from other countries suggests that Jewish refugees from Germany and central Europe appeared in disproportionate numbers. Among medical volunteers, Yiddish often served as the common language in hospitals.

Unlike Hank Rubin, nearly eight hundred U.S. volunteers died and were buried in Spain. Those who survived could never forget the loss of their comrades. Though many proceeded to follow successful careers—Hank Rubin as a restaurateur, wine columnist, and teacher—Spain remained the central ingredient of their lives.[2] During the long nightmare of the Franco dictatorship, Lincoln veterans agonized over the cost of their defeat. And in 1996, to mark the sixtieth anniversary of the outbreak of the war, the Spanish government offered a token of thanks by granting the rights of citizenship to all the surviving veterans. Now more than eighty years old, Hank Rubin could claim that honor in return for his youthful commitment.

▷ **CHAPTER 14**

War Stories

The Fiftieth Anniversary of the Spanish Civil War

The veterans of the Abraham Lincoln Brigade who met regularly in the San Francisco area invited me and four other "young" people to become associate members in 1984. I saw this as an opportunity to pursue my historical research while working on political projects that dovetailed with my own interests. Not everyone in the brigade welcomed outsiders, but as I participated with them in a campaign to send ambulances to embattled Nicaragua, I established a personal rapport with many veterans that I think is indispensable for good oral history. Over the years, the "subjects" of my interviews became friends, people with whom I could share ideas and emotions, despite the age gap between us. As the fiftieth anniversary of the Spanish Civil War approached, I was able to use my early interviews to build a story that appeared in the Sunday magazine supplement of the San Francisco Examiner *in April of 1986.*

▷ Half a century ago, Milton Wolff was a young military officer known as "Abe Lincoln incarnate"—partly because of his tall, dark, lanky resemblance to Honest Abe and partly because Wolff took so literally Lincoln's idea that government should be of, by, and for the people. In the name of Lincoln, as a fighter with the Abraham Lincoln Battalion of the International Brigades during the Spanish Civil War, Wolff went on to risk his life many times, both in the Spanish Civil War and during World War II.

Now, after a lifetime of struggle, the 70-year-old El Cerrito, California, resident is still tall and lanky—and just as dedicated to the proposition that all men are created equal. He has not retired from politics: At the first of this year [1986], he was part of a group taking medical supplies to aid and support the Sandinista government in Nicaragua.

Wolff, at six-foot-two and a little more than 180 pounds, still moves with the dash and spirit of the young soldier who rose through the ranks to become the last military commander of the legendary volunteers known as the Abraham Lincoln Brigade.

The brigade's 2,800 American fighters put their lives on the line to defend—unsuccessfully, as it turned out—the Spanish Republic against the armies of Franco, Mussolini, and Hitler. They provided the first American volunteers in the war against fascism. One-third of them died in Spain—a sacrifice that haunts the remaining survivors. None can forget the loss of a friend, a comrade, or the anguish of defeat.

The intervening years have added to the toll. Only about 350 veterans survive, including 60 who live in northern California. These Bay Area Veterans of the Abraham Lincoln Brigade (VALB) will gathered on April 27, in Berkeley, to commemorate the 50th anniversary of the outbreak of the Spanish Civil War. The reunion events, jointly sponsored by the Abraham Lincoln Brigade Archives (ALBA), will include a celebrity-studded program and memorial exhibitions—all part of the international revival of interest in the Spanish Civil War, the Lincoln Brigade, and their legacy in the modern world.

In an exhibit of photographs from the era currently on display at the Bancroft Library at the University of California, Berkeley, one of the most striking is Robert Capa's unceremonious shot of Milt Wolff and Ernest Hemingway, taken between actions on the Aragon front in 1938.[1] Hemingway and Wolff symbolize quite different attitudes—the fleshy novelist craving romantic adventure; the lean officer impatient to get on with the war. But there's another story behind the picture: the story Milt Wolff didn't tell his family.

A millinery worker from Brooklyn, Wolff went to Spain at age 21, informing his unsuspecting mother that he would be working in a factory in Barcelona. With a small group of volunteers, he sailed to La Havre and then traveled by train to southern France. Since the Spanish border was closed (because of an official policy of non-intervention on the part of the European powers), the Americans had to enter Spain by climbing the Pyrenees at night.

By the time Wolff arrived, the first Lincoln volunteers had already sustained heavy casualties in the Jarama Valley. So the new recruits were swiftly trained (five shots with live ammunition) and thrown into the front lines. Through all the fighting Wolff dutifully wrote letters to his mother, assuring her of how much he liked his work in the factory.

When the Robert Capa photograph appeared in the New York Yiddish-language newspaper, the *Daily Forward,* it held a different message for Wolff's mother. She discovered her son was no factory worker.

"Blew my cover," Wolff says today with a chuckle. "But by then what could she do?"

Wolff had first met Hemingway between battles at the Café Chicote in Madrid. The novelist, already famous, with *The Sun Also Rises* (1926) and *A Farewell to Arms* (1927) under his belt, was committed to the cause of the Spanish Republic and was gathering material for what was to be his masterpiece about the civil war, *For Whom the Bell Tolls.* There are those who believe that Hemingway saw in the tall, mustached Captain Wolff a partial prototype for his fictional hero, the American volunteer he named "Robert Jordan."

"Hell, no," Wolff exclaims. "Robert Jordan was a WASP, university educated, romantic about the whole business. I was just a Jewish kid from Brooklyn."

Wolff and Hemingway established a peculiar wartime friendship, quite distinct from the camaraderie within the brigade: It was circumstantial, intermittent, irreverent, and held together by rivalry. "I stole his girlfriend at the Hotel Florida in Madrid," Wolff recalls with a grin. "Either that, or he set me up. Anyway, I had a ball."

Next to the photograph of Wolff and Hemingway in the Bancroft exhibit is another piece of evidence in the Hemingway-Wolff relationship: an open letter from the Lincoln veterans criticizing the novelist's "slander [of] the cause for which we fought." Wolff remembers the angry meeting in New York at which they dissected the political failings of *For Whom The Bell Tolls.*

"The anarchy that reigned on the republican side at the beginning of the war was spontaneous and lasted only until the government could restore law and order," Wolff explains. "But the violence on the fascist side was organized terror that was designed to break the back of any republican sentiments. Thousands and thousands of people—teachers, mayors, councilmen, trade union leaders, socialists, republicans, communists, anarchists—were killed summarily." His voice rises as he recounts the blood baths that occurred in Spanish bull rings whenever Franco captured a town. "Hemingway never made that distinction. He treated all the terror as the same."

"I called him 'a tourist in Spain,'" Wolff recalls.

The Lincoln Brigade was withdrawn from the war in 1938. Wolff remembers the dramatic farewell parade in Barcelona, when Dolores Ibarruri, "La Pasionaria"—the woman who said, "It is better to die on your feet than to live on your knees"—at last acknowledged the political necessity of sending the volunteers home. "You can go proudly," she exhorted. And the Spanish people threw flowers to the soldiers like rice at a wedding.

"It was very upsetting to me," Wolff remembers. "The war was still on. I didn't want to leave at all, much less in defeat." But La Pasionaria's words inspired a commitment to fight on. "The parade, the speech . . . gave me the feeling that the war was continuing on another front. I didn't feel like I was leaving. I felt that I was going into a fight. So that helped."

The fall of the Spanish Republic in 1939 nonetheless dealt a crushing blow to the anti-fascist crusade. Wolff admits he never got over Spain. "Once you put your life on the line you're committed," he declares. "In Spain, it was sealed in blood." The 800 Americans buried in Spanish soil serve as a constant reminder of his special obligation—call it "survivor guilt"—to prove that their deaths were not in vain. "You can't let them down," he says.

After Spain, the Lincoln veterans received a hostile reception from their countrymen. At a time when American public opinion embraced isolationism and neutrality, the Lincoln volunteers were often considered "un-American" and were subpoenaed by Congress to explain their illegal travel to Spain.

"He was a second-rate citizen in his own country," Wolff wrote of himself in an unpublished piece during this period. "He was denounced as a false prophet, an adventurer, a bloodthirsty killer of priests and nuns, an anti-God pagan. He was hunted and persecuted, jailed and beaten, but Spain was still with him and he never wavered."

After Pearl Harbor, the open persecution ended, for a time at least. But the American army described the Lincoln veterans as "premature anti-fascists," stamped their papers "suspected of disloyalty," and blocked their enlistment. For example, Archie Brown, a brigade veteran and longtime San Francisco labor organizer, had to sign up three times before the army accepted him; then it assigned him to digging ditches in northern California until he befriended a sympathetic officer who approved his transfer to the European theater. In the end, nearly every able-bodied Lincoln veteran served in some branch of the U.S. armed forces or the merchant marine during World War II, many of them winning citations and medals in combat.

"I had to fight my way to the front," says Wolff. After numerous petty assignments that kept him out of combat, he obtained a transfer to General "Wild Bill" Donovan's Office of Strategic Services—predecessor of the Central Intelligence Agency—and fought behind enemy lines in Italy. But at the war's end, he was abruptly denied assignments with political significance, such as a role in the establishment of the new government in Italy in 1945.

"The Cold War was already on," he explains.

After World War II, the Lincoln veterans continued to advocate the overthrow of the Franco dictatorship in Spain, but by then American policymakers were more concerned with shoring up the regime as part of the anti-communist alliance in Western Europe. Individual veterans, including Wolff, were ordered before congressional committees and state investigatory agencies to testify about their political beliefs and affiliations. "We were not only premature anti-fascists," Wolff says indignantly, "we were premature McCarthyite victims." The U.S. Supreme Court eventually upheld the legality of VALB. But meanwhile, the FBI routinely placed the Lincoln Brigade members under surveillance.

"The FBI would ask the boss to keep an eye on Milt Wolff," explains Wolff, who for years supported his wife and two children at assorted low-paying jobs, "but the boss didn't want to keep an eye on Milt Wolff. It was easier to fire me.

"I might have become a millionaire in the garment industry," he says with a hearty laugh—as if anyone who knew his feisty political career would believe it—"but instead I volunteered to fight in Spain in 1937. After that, all I could get were lousy jobs."

His brow furrows; his dark eyes search for understanding. "But I didn't care," he adds. "It was the political work that mattered."

Through those bleak postwar years, Lincoln veterans distinguished themselves in the civil rights movement in the south. Wolff worked for the Civil Rights Congress and remembers traveling through Mississippi, Georgia, and Alabama with a loaded gun in his glove compartment. Among his crusades was the unsuccessful effort to gain support for Willie McGee, a black man eventually executed in Mississippi on flimsy evidence for raping a white woman.

"The Lincoln Brigade," Wolff explains with pride, "was the first American army fully integrated from top to bottom without regard to race." About 90 black Americans served in Spain; for many of them it was their first experience outside a racist environment. (The last surviving black brigader in California, Luchelle McDaniels, known as "Fantastico" for his ability to throw hand grenades ambidextrously, died in Sacramento last December [1985].)

"We're all part of the history," says another San Francisco veteran, Bill Sennett, a retired trucking executive who is coordinating the fiftieth anniversary events on the West Coast. Sennett, whose weekly letters from Spain constitute a unique historical source at the Bancroft Library, wants to set the record straight. "We all need to remember the tragic lesson of Spain. It wasn't just a romantic escapade. That's what these commemorations are all about."

During the tumultuous 1960s, Lincoln veterans were again in the vanguard of dissent. In San Francisco, Archie Brown's refusal to testify to HUAC precipitated a violent clash between spectators and the police. The incident appeared in the documentary *Operation Abolition*. When shown on college campuses around the country, it helped discredit the excesses of anti-communism. VALB also participated regularly in anti–Vietnam War demonstrations. Wolff even offered his services to the North Vietnamese government, but was "politely" turned down.

Such tenacity gives the Lincoln Brigade unassailable prestige among younger generations of activists. At the vast nuclear freeze demonstration in New York in 1983, the men marching beneath the VALB banner were greeted with a standing ovation from the hundreds of thousands of protesters in Central Park. And so it is fitting that the veterans can now rely on their renown to substitute for their diminishing numbers.

"We are anti-fascists," declares Wolff. "When we identify an issue that is anti-fascist, we're involved."

Today this involvement focuses on Central America, Nicaragua, in particular. Ted Veltfort, an ambulance driver in Spain and now a retired engineer in Berkeley, visited Nicaragua in 1984 and learned about a critical shortage of medical supplies there. Remembering the fund-raising drives of the 1930s to help American soldiers in Spain, he proposed that VALB raise money to send an ambulance to Nicaragua. The Bay Area veterans recruited a group of younger "associates," drafted a public appeal, bought a newspaper ad, and, within six months, raised more than $140,000, enough to send ten ambulances to Nicaragua.[2]

"It was natural for us to go in and help," explains Wolff. "Just as the people of Spain voted to come out of the dark ages, so have the people of Nicaragua. We went to Spain to stop the aggressors and to avert World War II. And we were right. We could have stopped them in Spain. And what happened in Spain is happening in Central America. Once again, we've got to stop the aggressors." He pauses to size up the situation. "Only this time, we're the aggressors."

Nothing so well captures the undaunted spirit of the Lincoln veterans as this commitment to Nicaragua. They are too old to fight, of course. But having launched the successful fund-raising campaign, having shipped the ambulances, they wanted—indeed felt obliged—to add a moral force to the war against the U.S.-backed Contras.

"Nicaragua today is a nation under siege, like Spain was in 1936," declares San Francisco's Ruth Davidow, who served as a nurse on the Ebro front nearly 50 years ago. Now she is spearheading a campaign to send a Mobile Ambulance and Surgical Hospital (M.A.S.H.) unit to Nicaragua. "When a hospital or a maternity clinic is bombed," she asks, "where do the Nicaraguan people go?"

A few months ago, a delegation of Bay Area veterans journeyed to the embattled country to see the war-in-progress and to endorse the gift of ambulances. "It was a gratifying experience," says Wolff. As they left for Nicaragua, a bon voyage rally was staged at Longshoreman's Hall. They were greeted in Nicaragua as heroes. "Fantastic," explains Wolff. "It was like a dream materializing." The veterans crowded aboard the shiny blue ambulances, sat in the drivers' seats, worked the gear boxes, sprawled on the beds in the back. "We were like kids who had gotten a toy at Christmas. We were laughing, crying, speechless all at the same time." Each ambulance bears the words: *"Brigada Abraham Lincoln; Solidarios Con Nicaragua."*

While the 50th anniversary celebrations allow ample time for history and reminiscence, the veterans indulge less in nostalgia than in proving their relevance today. According to Wolff, proceeds from the events this month—VALB expects to raise as much as $50,000—will be used to "extend material, humanitarian aid to the people of Central America." Meanwhile, he adds, "we've got to end the bloodshed there. We need to find a peaceful political solution."

Despite his energy and enthusiasm, however, Wolff is not necessarily optimistic about the outcome. It seems that the Lincoln veterans can never forget the lessons of defeat. "There's not enough movement in this country," he observes. "We don't identify sufficiently with the death count in Central America. It's not like Vietnam.

"No man is an island," he continues, reciting John Donne's line, the epigraph of Hemingway's Spanish novel. "If you support terrorism in Nicaragua, then terrorism will surface in your back street. If there's terrorism in the barrio, there will be terrorism in Noe Valley or the Sunset. We have to make that linkage."

This image of a global community will culminate next fall in another huge reunion in Spain. Dolores Ibarruri, who just celebrated her 90th birthday in Madrid, forecast such a homecoming back in 1938 when she bade farewell to the Lincoln Brigade in Barcelona:

"We shall not forget you, and when the olive tree of peace puts forth its leaves again, entwined with the laurels of the Spanish Republic's victory—come back!

"Come back to us. With us those of you who have no country will find one, those of you who have to live deprived of friendship will find friends, and all of you will find the love and gratitude of the whole Spanish people. . . ."

Milt Wolff hears these lines and smiles.

"I feel I'm putting out new green leaves, too," he says. "I feel victorious."

▷ **CHAPTER 15**

Ralph Fasanella Limns the Life of the Workingman

Ralph Fasanella served as a truck driver in the transport unit known as the Regiment de Tren. I first interviewed him for my book about the American volunteers, and he delivered salty stories of his struggles as a young man in the Bronx—in fact, in the same neighborhood where I grew up. Already well-known as a painter of working-class life, he was particularly bothered by his inability to produce a work of art about his time in Spain. He asked me to brainstorm with him about possible subjects, but none seemed to develop. Meanwhile, a former labor organizer named Ron Carver created a project called Public Domain to arrange for the purchase and display of Fasanella's works in public places, where they would be accessible to ordinary people. To promote the plan, Carver invited me to collaborate with photographer Matt Herron for an article in Smithsonian Magazine. *(The museum was in the process of acquiring one of the paintings.) We all spent two days with Ralph as he visited various sites of workers in action, including a picket line, a machinist plant, and a high school, where the artist spoke to the students. The article is quoted extensively on a panel near Fasanella's "Family Supper," a painting that celebrates immigrant life, at the Ellis Island Museum in New York harbor.*

▷ On a warm spring day in New York in May 1991, five hundred art-loving dignitaries and ordinary citizens clambered aboard a ferry at the foot of Manhattan and sailed past the Statue of Liberty to the new Ellis Island museum. There, in the historic Great Hall, where millions of foreigners first set their feet on terra firma in the United States, the entourage witnessed the formal installation of a humble, haunting painting commemorating the immigrant experience. "I became the immigrant again," said the artist Ralph Fasanella in presenting *Family Supper,* a 70-inch-by-50-inch oil canvas, to the American people.[1] As schoolchildren sang Woody Guthrie's "This Land Is Your Land," spectators applauded not only the

Ralph Fasanella, a self-taught artist, stands in front of one of his paintings. He served as a truck driver in the Regiment de Tren and remained a labor activist all his life. He died in 1997. (Photo by Jeannette Ferrary. Author's collection.)

painter but the historic traditions he represents. The occasion also celebrated an imaginative approach to the exhibition of art. An organization called Public Domain has helped to place nearly 20 of his works where they can be seen—from museums and libraries to a Congressional hearing room and, soon, even a subway stop in New York City.

Fasanella's reputation is growing. As Lynda Roscoe Hartigan, a curator at the Smithsonian's National Museum of American Art (NMAA), says, "Ralph Fasanella is an accomplished artist whose vivid, detailed paintings always challenge our conscience and imagination."[2]

And yet Fasanella's entry into the art world happened almost by chance only 21 years ago. A sharp-eyed collector, intrigued by one of his big, bright, effervescent "folk" paintings in a group show, was fascinated to discover that its creator was a self-taught 58-year-old service station attendant. He tipped off a reporter, and the resulting article splashed Fasanella's face on the cover of *New York* magazine. "This man pumps gas in the Bronx for a living," the headline exclaimed. "He may also be the best primitive painter since Grandma Moses."[3]

Fasanella personified the workingman stereotype. Short and stout and earthy, he was a grade school dropout who spoke with wisdom and humor in the idiom of the street. Yet his paintings revealed a poetic spirit and an unvarnished joy in the pleasures of everyday life. If art, as the philosopher John Dewey stated, accentuates what is valuable in ordinary experience, Fasanella's 150 large canvases extolled the natural beauty of urban life in America.[4]

Since 1944, the artist had struggled in obscurity to master his craft, laboring patiently, obsessively, to capture the soul of working-class life in America. Despite a sprinkling of exhibitions over the years, Fasanella had sold only two significant paintings. But after the article appeared that autumn, Fasanella's solitary passion became, overnight, his profession. A show at Automation House in New York City drew a thousand spectators a day, and his canvases found patrons by the carload. For the first time, Fasanella heard the praise of critics and customers, and he began to imagine a career outside the gas station.

Fasanella had seldom traveled far from his roots in Greenwich Village, where he was born, appropriately, on Labor Day, 1914. His parents, both natives of Bari, a province in southern Italy, had met and married in the city of immigrants. Joe Fasanella, the painter's father, delivered ice from his horse-drawn wagon; his mother, Ginevra, raised six children while working as a buttonhole maker in a coat factory. Their struggle would become the meat and potatoes of their son's art.

Family Supper, one of the most moving paintings, was completed just before his rise to fame in 1972. It is a bittersweet reminiscence of the artist's early life, expressing the pride and the anguish of an immigrant family battling to preserve its heritage amid the daily struggle of earning a living. "It brought back the image of my mother, the working woman," remarks Fasanella. "It gave me the sense of a family tradition." He recalls the cleanliness and order of his mother's kitchen, the warmth that came from the gas stove (fed by quarters in the gas meter on the back wall), his mother's uncomplaining efficiency as she prepared breakfast before she left for work. "She had no time to become neurotic," he asserts. Yet there is no sentimental nostalgia in the scene. On one wall hangs the portrait within the painting of the artist's father, crucified by the ice tongs that symbolized his working life. "The good old days," says Fasanella ironically; "I know the hardship besides."[5] The motto etched on the red bricks of the tenement wall proclaims the driving force of all his art: "Lest We Forget."

Fasanella's earliest works were plainly autobiographical. A tough street kid who knocked around the sidewalks of New York, he acquired a pedestrian's-eye view of the urban landscape. Massive buildings dwarf the multitudes that populate his paintings. But Fasanella's city is a happy place. It breathes vitality and motion—from the omnipresent stickball diamonds chalked on the asphalt to the unique interior decorations that peek through the open windows. "I don't reject the slums," Fasanella explains. "I take the best out of them. They are not negative views." Nor are the city dwellers anonymous. "This guy here," the painter says, pointing to a newspaper vendor in a recent paining, "I used to see him every day. And this one is an old buddy, and this one," he taps a portly figure in the foreground, "is me."[6]

Fasanella's love of the city and its feisty inhabitants reflects his intimate connections to the immigrant worker's experience. Just before the Depression he was in and out of reform school several times; in his late teens, he got involved in the burgeoning labor union movement, which defined his life's work. "I never did a painting for myself," he says. "I was always trying to uplift other people, to show them who they are and where they came from." As Fasanella participated in unemployment demonstrations, served a stint as a truck driver in the Spanish Civil War, and eventually settled down as a union organizer in New York, he gained a point of view that later would give his art a unique edge. "My job is not only to record American history," he declares, "but to record the feelings of American workers as honestly as possible."[7]

"The thing that comes through," observes Gerard C. Wertkin, director of the Museum of American Folk Art in New York, "is his commitment, his passion, for what is right. Fasanella is not just offering a personal vision. He is committed to recognizing the place of labor in American history." This commitment distinguishes Fasanella's art from that of so-called "primitive" painters and "outsider" artists. "A lot of people in the art world do not realize how integrated Fasanella's work is with the labor community," remarks NMAA curatorial associate Andrew Connors. "His paintings about labor and injustice portray the struggle of powerless people to change their situations. His work shows a deep understanding of contemporary social issues."[8]

For Fasanella, art and labor were thoroughly intertwined from the beginning. Near the end of World War II, before he ever considered painting, he was involved in unionizing electrical workers when he began to experience a curious itching and aching in his fingers. "I thought I had arthritis," he says. To ease the discomfort, he would rub his hands across tabletops or the surface of newspapers.[9] One day a colleague handed Fasanella a soft pencil and a pad and suggested he try sketching. Within minutes, he had managed his first drawing. Soon Fasanella was copying everything in sight. Finally, he had to admit that he was more interested in drawing his fellow workers than in organizing them. Yet when he attended an art class, he felt so out of place that he walked out and never went back.

So began the education of the artist. He dabbled with watercolors and poster paints until he got the nerve to stretch some canvas and dip his brushes in oil. "I put the paint on directly," he told an interviewer in 1972. "I just did it. Just put it on."[10] Those early works—a lonely subway kiosk in New York's Sheridan Square, the interior of his Greenwich Village apartment, the street he was born on—betray a "primitive" style and a decorative intent. But obsession overcame Fasanella's inexperience. He began to paint regularly, constantly, breaking off only to sleep or to go to the Whitney Museum or the Museum of Modern Art, where he could scrutinize the masters and endeavor to learn the principles of organization and unity. Much of the art confused him. "You've got to be an intellectual to understand," Fasanella remarks of Picasso's *Guernica*. "The guy in the street will never understand it."

He followed his own visions. "I worked and I painted, and I painted and I worked," he says, "and the world owes you nothing." To support himself, Fasanella took temporary jobs, relied on his brothers and sisters and his wife Eva, whom he married in 1950. Eva became the bulwark of his private life and, later, his business manager.[11]

To encompass his grandiose views, Fasanella turned instinctively to large canvases. The 50-inch-by-80-inch *May Day* took six sleepless months to complete, but its subject extends from the diverse heritage of American workers—white and black, immigrant and native born—to a utopian future where honest labor is rewarded with ample recreation and unencumbered delight. The workers' militant slogans—"Fight for Peace, Democracy, Security"—are matched with the patriotic iconography of Jefferson, Lincoln, Frederick Douglass, and Franklin Delano Roosevelt. "Americanism is what it's all about," says Fasanella.

At first glance, the story seems simple. But to focus only on the social message is to obscure Fasanella's subtle genius. For the paintings exude a feeling of warmth and playfulness. The eye follows the labor parade past the crowded buildings toward the gates of Eden; the throng gives way to paradise. "It's the form that gets them," Fasanella exclaims, "then the content. The inner feelings, the color, the design, pull people into the paintings. And then they see the inner story. My paintings look easy, but they're very complicated. That's why they're so big; that's why people like them."[12]

He calls it "monumental simplicity." The paintings are accessible, inviting, and fresh. "Here I show the subway riders at night after a hard day's work," Fasanella observes of *Subway Riders*, completed more than 40 years ago. "Everyone is separate, alone, but very much together. It's noisy with the creaks and squeals of the wheels, but peaceful too because we move to a rhythm and cadence that gets inside us; that's comforting, like the noise of the city itself."[13]

So Fasanella painted for more than two decades: a day at the gas station, home for dinner, conversation with his wife and two children, a nap—and then the creative work extending through the dark hours of night. His output was prodigious; his subjects explored the richness of working people's culture. He portrayed baseball games and union meetings, political rallies and election campaigns. *American Tragedy*, a combining of story and symbol, articulated the grief and suspicion surrounding the assassination of President Kennedy. "What a challenge to paint the big story," he declares. "Somebody's got to tell the people what's going on. I don't run away from it."

Fasanella's rapid ascent in the early 1970s nonetheless challenged his creative imagination. After the news stories and the exhibition and an elegant coffee-table book (*Fasanella's City* by Patrick Watson), the artist still had to face his daily foe—the empty canvas—and he no longer had the excuse of running the gas station. "It was dead as a doornail," he recalls, "and I was bored stiff. I had to get a new vision."[14] On impulse, he decided in 1975 to head for Boston, which he remembered fondly from his organizing days; but just before he departed, a friend suggested he first visit the old mill city, Lawrence, Massachusetts, birthplace of America's industrial revolution.

For Fasanella, that little detour to Lawrence proved to be the shortest way home. For the next three years, he rented a room at the YMCA for $18 a week, commuted to his family in New York on weekends, and systematically immersed himself in the history and culture of one of the most dramatic labor movements in the twentieth century, the "Bread and Roses" textile strike of 1912. He haunted the public library, studying old newspapers and books and examining drawings of mill life by Winslow Homer. He roamed the streets like a pilgrim, fondling the old red bricks at the mills, chatting with factory workers at the gate, exploring the ethnic traditions of the Italians, French Canadians, and Greeks, who had been not only clothed but also fed by New England textiles. He even persuaded the mill owners in nearby Lowell to allow him inside so he could draw the massive pulleys and gears and the machinery that tugged the soft tufts of cotton and wool into threads and yarn and fabric.

"I had to live like a monk," says Fasanella of his lonely sojourn, "and I had to be in a state of grace." And then he began to paint. The result, a series of 18 canvases, is a veritable history of the American immigrant labor experience, told with the accuracy and detail of a historian. The newspaper headlines are precise; the mini-anecdotes that compose the paintings—for example, the "pots and pans brigade" of the women workers, the mounted policeman in the foreground pummeling a child—are authentic. But Fasanella strove, too, to infuse his story with compassion for the ordinary worker who came to Lawrence to fulfill the American dream. "This is what really happened," Fasanella explains.[15]

The Lawrence series brought the artist to maturity. He had moved beyond personal recollections and nostalgia; he had escaped the limits of New York. "Lawrence introduced me to the variety of the labor experience," Fasanella declares. "I learned about the machinery, the different people, the role of women." He also acquired a fresh self-confidence. Back in New York, he focused on his favorite pastime and produced a series of canvases, including *Night Game—Yankee Stadium* and *Night Game—'tis a Bunt,* that depict the drama of the game and highlight the vitality of the fans. "People keep wanting to pin it down to a time and place," he says of these works. "Is it Yankee Stadium, is it Fenway Park, is it Ted Williams, is it Willie Mays, is it Casey Strengel? The answer is yes."[16]

Fasanella's populist instincts would soon lead to a remarkable experiment in public art. One day, Eva Fasanella mentioned to a Massachusetts union organizer, Ron Carver, that her husband had been offered six figures for one of his paintings of the Bread and Roses strike. The labor leader was aghast. "I realized that most of his great paintings were owned by private collectors," Carver remembers. "They represented the spiritual heritage of the labor movement. They belonged in the public domain. My position was transparently absurd. I told Ralph not to sell it."[17]

While Fasanella listened skeptically, Carver outlined a proposal to raise funds to purchase the painting and donate it to a museum. With the help of local politicians, newspaper editorials and several sympathetic labor unions, the coffers began to fill. "I undertook that in 1988 when I was working to save a plant from shutting down," Carver recalls. "It was a good year. We saved the plant and we saved the painting." *Lawrence 1912: The Bread and Roses Strike* hangs today in the Heritage State Park Visitors Center in Lawrence, Massachusetts.

That success inspired Carver to create Public Domain, a nonprofit organization dedicated to bringing other Fasanella paintings into public arenas. "It was absolutely wrong that the man's greatest paintings should be hidden away in the living rooms of wealthy folks," Carver asserts, "and the people whose heritage they celebrate would have no access to them." To broaden his appeal, Carver persuaded schoolteachers to include labor history in the curriculum and invite the artist into the classroom to explain the purposes of his art. Fasanella proved an adept instructor; his unpretentious style, recently captured on video in Glen Pearcy's award-winning *Fasanella,* appealed to streetwise students. "He's one of us!" exclaimed a surprised 15-year-old African American at Oakland Tech High School in California.[18]

Public Domain printed and sold almost 50,000 color posters to raise money so that his paintings could be purchased and put into public spaces. "It is entirely unique," says Museum of American Folk Art director Wertkin, with admiration. "Ron Carver is involved in an extraordinary crusade to assure that the contributions of organized labor not be lost to American history."[19]

The commitment to bring Fasanella's art back to its cultural roots has also prompted some innovative exhibitions. "Most working people don't go to museums," Fasanella explains. "They are frightened at the bigness. They feel left out. Going to a museum is like going into a rich man's house. They may have a lot of respect for art, for culture, but museums are like an obstacle course for them."[20]

Fasanella and Carver opted for alternative sites. Thus *Family Supper,* among Public Domain's first buy-back efforts, will always hang in one of America's most widely visited tourist locations, Ellis Island. *The Great Strike—Lawrence 1912,* a salute to ethnic diversity, is hanging in the Rayburn House Office Building on Capitol Hill in Washington, D.C. *Welcome Home, Boys,* Fasanella's tribute to labor's contribution to World War II, now greets a new generation of multicultural workers at the main library in Oakland, California. And *Subway Riders,* soon to be owned by the Museum of American Folk Art, will reside in a specially designed protective case in a Manhattan subway station at Fifth Avenue and 53d Street. "It was pretty obvious, wasn't it?" deadpans the resourceful Ron Carver.

Fasanella, at age 78, claims to be slowing down, but evidence is scant. As he takes a visitor into his basement studio in Ardsley, New York, he points to three recent medium-sized paintings about the 1990 *Daily News* strike and a massive work-in-progress depicting the rise and fall of socialism in the twentieth century. Later, he drives to a nearby Nathan's restaurant, which he visits almost every day, and sketches the regular patrons who, over the years, have become his friends and ardent fans. The artist, now in his element, solicits their opinions, measures their criticism, relishes their praise.

Fasanella chatters incessantly as he draws their faces, peering with soft, brown eyes through his thick glasses. "Most people live a life of beauty," he says, warming to the subject. "Not the Hollywood beauty, but the nice dish on the table, the beauty of a body. I'm observant about that and I put it down in my painting." He tears off a sheet from his sketch pad and hands it to a pleasantly surprised middle-aged man drinking coffee.

When a jazz musician tells him, "You paint like we play music," Fasanella feels he's communicating. "I look and I look and I look," he explains. "I see all these beautiful things. And I've got to put it on canvas." He pauses to make the point. "The painting's got to sing to me."[21]

▷ **CHAPTER 16**

From War Hero to Blacklist

The Lonely Odyssey of Sergeant Edward Carter

The shift in American cultural values since the Spanish Civil War can be measured in the story of Edward A. Carter, Jr., an unknown African American volunteer in the Lincoln Brigade who was awarded posthumously the Congressional Medal of Honor by President Bill Clinton for his heroism in World War II. U.S. Army policy in the 1940s had denied the nation's highest military honor to black soldiers, but by the end of the twentieth century the government made efforts to remedy the injustice. What has intrigued me about Carter's story, however, is whether he would have received the same justice and appreciation had the White House known in 1997 that he had served in the Spanish Civil War. It's a question that can't be answered, of course, but suggests strongly that even the most severe ideological splits may eventually be healed. A hero, after all, is a hero.

▷ Ever since Bill Clinton awarded posthumous Congressional Medals of Honor to seven African American heroes of World War II, including Staff Sergeant Edward A. Carter, Jr., the administration could take credit for correcting the racial injustice that had deprived black soldiers of equal treatment in the war against fascism. But what the public—and the president—did not know was that the celebrated Sgt. Carter had been twice victimized: once because of racial discrimination in the Army and a second time because of the color of his politics. Carter had dared to fight in the Spanish Civil War.[1]

In 1998, Carter's family allowed me to examine a suitcase full of documents that tell the story of his long, lonely, and ultimately futile effort to overcome the stigma of having served in Spain. On Memorial Day, 1999, the release of Carter's FBI and military intelligence files prompted *U.S. News and World Report* to put Carter's picture on the cover with the caption: "Sgt. Eddie Carter was a hero. But when he came home, the Army accused him of treachery. It was a lie—one that took 50 years to expose."

Carter's problems began in September 1949, when he learned that that the Army had rejected his application for reenlistment. He then journeyed to Washington, D.C., to plead his case with the Adjutant General, but his request for an interview was denied. He appealed for assistance to the legal department of the NAACP, but they declined to help because his case involved civil liberties not civil rights.

Carter took his case to the American Civil Liberties Union, which agreed to make a private inquiry to the White House. In 1950, one of President Harry Truman's personal advisors reported that the Carter case was officially closed. No charges were ever filed; Carter was never allowed to learn what he had been accused of.

The release of Carter's FBI files, however, clarified his problem. As *U.S. News* reported, there were two grounds for questioning the sergeant's loyalty in 1943. First, "Subject reportedly was a member of the Abraham Lincoln Brigade, having served for two and a half years [sic] with said Brigade in Spain." Second, "Potentially adverse—Subject is seemingly potentially capable of having connections with subversive activities due to the fact that he spent his early years (until 1938) in the Orient and has a speaking knowledge of Hindustani and Mandarin Chinese."

Although the story in *U.S. News* depicted Carter as a political naïve, he certainly knew that in going to Spain, he had violated State Department rules. Other Lincoln vets were treated by the U.S. Army as "premature anti-fascists"—a euphemism for "communist"—and were denied officer promotions and overseas service.

Why had Carter gone to Spain?

His odyssey began when he followed his father's missionary call to India and China in the 1920s and '30s. As a teenager in Shanghai, he studied the military arts at a Chinese academy and had volunteered to fight against the Japanese invaders of China between 1931 and 1935. From China, he had returned home to Los Angeles and soon afterward went to Spain. His family believes he joined the International Brigades as a professional soldier to fight the good fight.

Evidence of Carter's service in Spain remains sketchy. Aside from his listing on the official VALB roster, there is no other mention of his name yet found in the archives. In a 1942 interview, Carter referred to his frozen feet in Spain, suggesting that he had participated in action around Teruel during the winter of 1938. In 1946, he told an interviewer for *People's World,* a West Coast communist newspaper, that when the fascists broke through the Republican lines in March 1938, he had retreated all the way to the French border and been arrested in France. Thus his service in Spain probably lasted only a few months. We have not found information about which units he served with and no surviving Lincoln veteran can remember him in Spain.

By 1939 Carter was back in Los Angeles, where he married and had the first of his two sons. When World War II began, he enlisted in the U.S. Army. His service in the segregated army was limited to menial assignments. After his unit was shipped overseas, he repeatedly volunteered for a combat assignment. His application was finally accepted in 1945.

Downgraded to a private, he got his chance to fight in March 1945. When the tank he was riding on came under fire from a farmhouse in Germany, Carter led a three-man squad to locate the enemy. Almost immediately Carter's two comrades were shot. He was left in an exposed position, targeted by sprays of machine gun fire. He was shot five times, yet he used his marksman skills to take out an unknown number of German soldiers.

Finally, the Germans sent eight soldiers to capture him. Carter killed six of them and took the other two prisoners. Bleeding from his wounds, Carter walked across a German field with his bayonet stuck against the neck of one German, his rifle pointing at the back of the other. Carter was recommended for the Medal of Honor; he got the Distinguished Service Cross instead.

After the war, Carter returned to Los Angeles, trying unsuccessfully to start a small business. He also assumed leadership of a local black business association, aimed at ending racial discrimination.

Ebony magazine featured Carter with six other African American DSC winners. The article quoted him saying that black soldiers in World War II proved that racial cooperation was possible. He also said the army might benefit from some improvement—"about 99 percent improvement."

In 1947, Carter accepted recognition from a local group of the American Youth For Democracy and attended their "Welcome Home Joe" party. Other guests included Hollywood celebrities, such as Ingrid Bergman, and political radicals, including Lincoln veteran and screenwriter Alvah Bessie (soon to achieve notoriety as one of the Hollywood Ten) and Paul Robeson. Carter's attendance at this event is verified by the report of an FBI informant.

By 1947, Carter decided to reenlist in the army. The military overlooked his alleged offenses and assigned him as a weapons instructor in a newly created National Guard unit for black soldiers. But when the Guard published their roster of instructors, Carter's name was missing, foreshadowing his future problems.

Carter served well during the next two years, receiving no warnings about impending problems. One day before his reenlistment was expected, the army instead gave him an honorable discharge. His papers were stamped "Not permitted to reenlist without approval of the adjutant general."

When neither a personal appearance nor the NAACP nor the ACLU could persuade the army to reverse its decision, Carter's life turned sour. Letters to his attorneys reveal a frustrated and angry man. He even sent his DSC to a lawyer with the request that he return it to the White House.

When *Ebony* magazine prepared to publish a sequel to the earlier article about black DSC winners in 1950—asking where are they now?—Carter could barely respond. He finally sent a lame response that his work was "confidential." The accompanying photograph shows the despair that clouded his life.

When further appeals to the government brought no response, Carter's anger turned to bitterness and depression. He began to drink heavily, neglected his appearance, and seemed to become a problem for his family. In 1958, a friendly physician wrote once more to the ACLU, pleading for a reopening of Carter's case in hope that the restoration of his military career would restore his self-respect. The ACLU could offer no hope.

In 1963, at the age of 46, Staff Sergeant Edward Carter, Jr. died in Los Angeles. No obituary appeared in the newspapers; only his family visited the grave.

There the Carter case rested until President Clinton moved in 1996 to amend the errors of military justice for African Americans. The White House ceremony blazed Carter's name on the front pages. World War II comrades came forward to recall his heroism and mourn his early death. Only his family knew what the government had done to this proud veteran of two wars. "We need to end the hurt," his daughter-in-law told me, "to show the American people just what the army did to Edward Carter. We wish to restore his dignity."

Veterans of the Lincoln Brigade, who won many medals for courage during World War II and who shared with Carter the honor of being called "premature anti-fascists," welcomed him into their ranks.

Notes

PREFACE

1. I tell the story in more detail in *Keeping Time: Memory, Nostalgia, & the Art of History* (Athens: Univ. of Georgia Press, 2011), ch. 14–16. Because of privacy issues, I disguised the names of specific veterans of the Lincoln Brigade who can now be identified: "Red" was Jack Lucid; "Jonesy" was Don MacLeod; "Magnifico" was Elouard Luchelle McDaniels (aka Fantastico).

1. FROM GUERNICA TO HUMAN RIGHTS

1. Katz and Frankson letters, see Cary Nelson and Jefferson Hendricks, eds., *Madrid 1937* (New York: Routledge, 1996), 31–35; for Geiser, see Peter N. Carroll and Fraser Ottanelli, eds., *Letters from the Spanish Civil War: A U.S. Volunteer Writes Home* (Kent, Ohio: Kent State Univ. Press, 2013), 21–22.
2. Peter N. Carroll, *The Odyssey of the Abraham Lincoln Brigade: Americans in the Spanish Civil War* (Stanford, Calif.: Stanford Univ. Press, 1994), 374–75.
3. Richard Crossman, ed., *The God That Failed* (New York: Columbia Univ. Press, 1950), 11, 185.
4. Thomas S. Kuhn, *The Structure of Scientific Revolutions* (Chicago: Univ. of Chicago Press, 1962), 150.
5. Arthur Koestler, *Spanish Testament* (London: Victor Gollancz, 1937).
6. Ibid., 41.
7. Koestler wrote another book in early 1941, *The Scum of the Earth* (London: Jon athan Cape, 1941), adding an "Author's Note" [p. 13]: "To smuggle in elements of a later knowledge when describing the mental pattern of people in an earlier period is a common temptation to writers, which should be avoided." But in the preface to the 1955 edition of that book, he wrote: "Fascism' has to be replaced by its contemporary equivalent, 'Totalitarianism'" (8).
8. Arthur Koestler, *Dialogue with Death* (1946; Chicago: Univ. of Chicago Press, 2011), 2, ix.
9. George Orwell, *A Collection of Essays* (Garden City, N.Y.: Doubleday, 1954), 209.
10. See *The Complete Works of George Orwell*, ed. Peter Davison (London: Secker & Warburg, 1998), 18:360–62.
11. *New Masses*, Nov. 5, 1940, 25.

12. Carroll, *Odyssey*, 237
13. Ernest Hemingway, "Preface," Gustav Regler, *The Great Crusade*, trans. Whittaker Chambers and Barrows Mussey (New York: Longmans, Green, 1940), ix.
14. Carroll, *Odyssey*, 224–34.
15. Ernest Hemingway, *For Whom the Bell Tolls* (New York: Charles Scribner's Sons, 1940), 163.
16. Ernest Hemingway to Milton Wolff, Jan. 1941, *American Dialogue* (Oct.–Nov. 1964): 11.
17. Ernest Hemingway to John Dos Passos, March 26, 1938, in Carlos Baker, ed., *Ernest Hemingway: Selected Letters* (New York: Scribner, 1981), 463–64.
18. Martha Gellhorn to Eleanor Roosevelt [Apr. 1938] in Franklin D. Roosevelt Library, Hyde Park, N.Y.; see also Martha Gellhorn to Eleanor Roosevelt, July 8, 1937, in Caroline Moorehead, ed., *The Letters of Martha Gellhorn* (London: Chatto & Windus, 2006), 55–56, 59–61. Eleanor Roosevelt, "My Day," *Washington News*, July 10, 1937.
19. William Braasch Watson's four-part article, "Investigating Hemingway," *North Dakota Quarterly* (Summer 1991–Spring 1992).
20. Ernest Hemingway to Edwin Rolfe [Jan. 1940]. Copy in author's possession; original at University of Illinois Library, Urbana, Ill. This extract is printed with permission of The Ernest Hemingway Foundation.
21. Ernest Hemingway to Donald Friede, March 16, 1942, printed in Peter N. Carroll, "Ernest Hemingway, Screenwriter," *Antioch Review* (Summer 1995). For Hemingway's further response, see Chapter 8.
22. Robert T. Dallek, *Franklin D. Roosevelt and American Foreign Policy, 1932–1945* (New York: Oxford Univ. Press, 1979), 148; William E. Leuchtenburg, *Franklin D. Roosevelt and the New Deal* (New York: Harper & Row, 1963), 226.
23. Dominic Tierney, *FDR and the Spanish Civil War: Neutrality and Commitment in the Struggle that Divided America* (Durham, N.C.: Duke University Press, 2007), 109–10, 138–39; Stimson quoted in Godfrey Hodgson, *The Colonel: The Life and Wars of Henry Stimson* (Hanover, N.H.: Knopf, 1992), 217.
24. FDR to Ambassador Norman Armour, March 10, 1945, printed in Jon Cowan, ed., *Modern Spain: A Documentary History* (Philadelphia: Univ. of Pennsylvania Press, 2003), 223; see http://www.albavolunteer.org/2011/02/wikileaks-avant-la-wiki-fdr-on-franco-in-1945/.
25. Carroll, *Odyssey*, 230–31. See also Chapter 9.
26. FBI files of the Veterans of the Abraham Lincoln Brigade are now deposited at the Tamiment Library at New York University. This author used these government records before they were catalogued and indexed. The quoted document of 1942 is numbered NY No. 100–2545, pp. 16–17.
27. FBI files, March 30, 1944, No. 100–1162, p. 2 (No. 166129) and June 29, 1944, p. 3 (No. 106194).
28. Author's interviews with Sydney Levine and Jack Bjoze; FBI files of Felix Kusman.
29. See Peter N. Carroll, Michael Nash, and Melvin Small, *The Good Fight Continues: World War II Letters from the Abraham Lincoln Brigade* (New York: New York Univ. Press, 2006), Chapter 2.
30. Carroll, *Odyssey*, 242–44.

31. Charles A. Beard and Mary Ritter Beard, *A Basic History of the United States* (New York: New Home Library, 1944), 465.
32. Anthony Geist, "Documentaries of the Lincoln Brigade," *The Volunteer* (Dec. 2011): 5–6; http://www.albavolunteer.org/2011/12/documentaries-of-the-lincoln-brigade/.
33. See Alvah Bessie's *Men in Battle,* and Milton Wolff's *Another Hill.* Both have been cited in student papers I have seen.
34. See Peter N. Carroll and James D. Fernandez, *Facing Facism: New York and the Spanish Civil War* (New York: New York Univ. Press, 2007); Eric R. Smith, *American Relief Aid and the Spanish Civil War* (Columbia: Univ. of Missouri Press, 2013).
35. Paul Preston, *The Spanish Holocaust: Inquisition and Extermination in Twentieth-Century Spain* (New York: Norton, 2012).
36. Carroll, *Odyssey,* 285–88. Barsky's memoir remains unpublished at the Tamiment Library of New York University, except for a chapter in Carroll and Fernandez, *New York and the Spanish Civil War.*
37. For the text of the Atlantic Charter: http://www.nato.int/cps/en/natolive/official_texts_16912.htm.

2. FACING FASCISM

1. Caroline Bird, *The Invisible Scar* (New York: McKay, 1966), Chapter 2.
2. For background to the Spanish Civil War, see Helen Graham, *The Spanish Civil War: A Very Short Introduction* (New York: Oxford Univ. Press, 2005).
3. Daniel Kowalsky, *Stalin and the Spanish Civil War* (New York: Columbia Univ. Press, 2004).
4. See Patrick J. McNamara, "Pro-Franco Sentiment and Activity in New York City," in Peter N. Carroll and James D. Fernandez, eds., *Facing Fascism: New York and the Spanish Civil War* (New York: New York Univ. Press, 2007).
5. Peter N. Carroll, *The Odyssey of the Abraham Lincoln Brigade: Americans in the Spanish Civil War* (Stanford, Calif.: Stanford Univ. Press, 1994), 10.
6. Carroll, *Odyssey,* 18.
7. Ernest Hemingway, "On the American Dead in Spain," *New Masses* (Feb. 1939).
8. See Eric R. Smith, *American Relief Aid and the Spanish Civil War* (Columbia: Univ. of Missouri Press, 2013).

3. AMERICAN WOMEN IN THE SPANISH CIVIL WAR

1. Author interviews with Mildred Rackley Simon, Sept. 25, 1989; Apr. 6, 1991. See also Peter N. Carroll, *The Odyssey of the Abraham Lincoln Brigade: Americans in the Spanish Civil War* (Stanford, Calif.: Stanford Univ. Press, 1994), 80–81. Unless otherwise noted, these are the sources for Rackley's story.
2. Langston Hughes, *I Wonder as I Wander,* 2d edition (New York: Hill and Wang, 1993), 382. For an introduction to African Americans in the Spanish Civil

War, see http://www.alba-valb.org/resources/lessons/african-americans-in-the-spanish-civil-war.

3. *San Francisco Chronicle,* Feb. 10, 1977, 10.
4. Hughes, *I Wonder,* 382. See also the pamphlet, *A Negro Nurse in Republican Spain* (New York: Veterans of the Abraham Lincoln Brigade, Bay Area Post, 1938), and Danny Duncan Collum and Victor Berch, *African Americans in the Spanish Civil War: This Ain't Ethiopia But It'll Do* (New York: G. K. Hall, 1992).
5. Author interview, Nov. 1, 1989; see also Carroll, *Odyssey,* 47; Esther Silverstein Blanc, *Wars I Have Seen: The Play, in Three Acts, with Selected Short Stories* (Volcano, Calif.: Volcano Press, 1996). For additional Silverstein interviews, see Julia Newman's documentary film *Into the Fire* (2002).
6. Frances Patai, "Heroines of the Good Fight," *Nursing History Review* III (1995): 79–104.
7. See note 5.
8. The Union's magazine, *Art Front,* printed articles and artwork by left-wing writers and painters, some of whom would find their way to Spain.
9. Information about Kea comes from an unpublished memoir, titled "While Passing Through," held by the Abraham Lincoln Brigade Archives collection at New York University's Tamiment Library.
10. See Kea's interviews in the documentary *The Good Fight* (1984), directed by Noel Bruckner, Mary Dore, and Sam Sills. Outtakes can be found at the Tamiment Library.
11. *San Francisco Chronicle,* Feb. 10, 1977, 10.
12. One other African American woman volunteered for service in Spain, social worker Thyre Edwards. See Rima Lunin Schultz and Adele Hast, eds., *Women Building Chicago: A Biographical Dictionary, 1790–1990* (Bloomington: Indiana Univ. Press, 2001), 244–48.
13. Esther Silverstein Blanc, *Berchick* (Volcano, Calif.: Volcano Press, 1989). See also her *Long Johns for a Small Chicken* (Volcano, Calif.: Volcano Press, 2003).
14. See note 5.
15. Ibid.

4. PSYCHOLOGY AND IDEOLOGY IN THE SPANISH CIVIL WAR

1. Edwin Rolfe, "City of Anguish," *First Love and Other* Poems (Los Angeles: Larry Edmunds, 1951), 19. The poem is reprinted in the anthology *The Wound and the Dream: Sixty Years of American Poems about the Spanish Civil War,* ed. Cary Nelson (Urbana: Univ. of Illinois Press, 2002).
2. Peter N. Carroll, *The Odyssey of the Abraham Lincoln Brigade: Americans in the Spanish Civil War* (Stanford, Calif.: Stanford Univ. Press, 1994), 3, 15–17.
3. John Dollard, *Fear in Battle* (New Haven, Conn., 1943), 7. See also Carroll, *Odyssey,* 251.
4. William Aalto interview, Fear in Battle Mss, Abraham Lincoln Brigade Archives collection, Tamiment Library, New York University.
5. Leland Stowe, "Evelyn the Truck Driver," *Harper's* 178 (Feb. 1939): 279–80. Carroll, *Odyssey,* 69, 117.

6. Carroll, *Odyssey,* 117.
7. Ibid., 118.
8. Carroll, *Odyssey,* 118–19; see also Bill Bailey's interview in the documentary film, *The Good Fight* (1984).
9. Carroll, *Odyssey,* 119
10. Ibid. See also *Alvah Bessie's Spanish Civil War Notebooks,* ed. Dan Bessie (Lexington: Univ. Press of Kentucky, 2002).
11. Carroll, *Odyssey,* 119–20.
12. Ibid., 120; originally in Sidney Kurtz to Wilson Morris, Nov. 19, 1937; Jan. 13, 1938, David M. White Mss., New York Public Library.
13. Ibid., 120–21.
14. Author interview with Dr. William Pike, May 8, 1990; see also Carroll, *Odyssey,* 121–22.
15. Pike interview, May 8, 1990; Paul Margolis, "Dr. Pike's Spanish War," unpublished major project, Bard College, 1976, privately held; *Letters from the Trenches from Our Boys in Spain* (New York: Workers' Alliance of New York, 1937), 25–26; Stowe, "Evelyn," 281.
16. See Stowe, "Evelyn"; Carroll, *Odyssey,* 146, 117.
17. For McCarthy's story, see Carroll, *Odyssey,* 179–80.
18. Bill McCarthy interview for "The Good Fight," transcription, ALBA Collection, Tamiment Library, New York University; Bill McCarthy to Milton Wolff, Aug. 16, 1985, Veterans of the Abraham Lincoln Brigade Mss., Bancroft Library, University of California, Berkeley.
19. For Amery, see his unpublished memoir mss., Tamiment Library, New York University.
20. Carroll, *Odyssey,* 178.
21. Ibid., 181–83.
22. White's statement: Fond 545, Opis 6, file 1012, Russian Center for the Preservation and Study of Recent Historical Documents, Moscow, Russia.
23. A fictionalized version of this execution is found in Milton Wolff, *Another Hill: An Autobiographical Novel* (Urbana: Univ. of Illinois Press, 1994). Wolff, however, was not the executioner, as some of his readers have assumed. My interviews and oral histories, including one with the actual shooter (given with assurances that I would not identify anyone alive), confirm that the man responsible was a volunteer named Saul Shapiro.
24. Printed in Alvah Bessie, ed., *The Heart of Spain: An Anthology of Fiction, Nonfiction and Poetry* (New York: Veterans of the Abraham Lincoln Brigade, 1952), 345–47.

5. THE SOCIAL ORIGINS OF THE ABRAHAM LINCOLN BRIGADE

1. Peter N. Carroll, Michael Nash, and Melvin Small, eds., *The Good Fight Continues: World War II Letters from the Abraham Lincoln Brigade* (New York: New York Univ. Press, 2006), 5–6, 36–38.
2. See Peter N. Carroll, *The Odyssey of the Abraham Lincoln Brigade: Americans in the Spanish Civil War* (Stanford, Calif.: Stanford Univ. Press, 1994), Chapters 19–20.

3. The last elected officers of the Veterans of the Abraham Lincoln Brigade, Moe Fishman and Abraham Smorodin, legally transferred all assets and rights of VALB to the Abraham Lincoln Brigade Archives (ALBA), an educational nonprofit organization created by six veterans in 1979. ALBA continues to publish the quarterly journal, *The Volunteer,* and hosts annual reunions for friends and family in New York and northern California. As of September 2014, one veteran, Delmer Berg, was still alive.
4. See, for instance, Cecil D. Eby, *Comrades and Commissars: The Lincoln Battalion in the Spanish Civil War* (University Park: Pennsylvania State Univ. Press, 2006).
5. Harvey Klehr, John Earl Haynes, Fridrikh Igorevich Firsov, *The Secret World of American Communism* (New Haven, Conn.: Yale Univ. Press, 1995); Ronald Radosh, Mary R. Habeck, Grigory Sevostianov, *Spain Betrayed: The Soviet Union in the Spanish Civil War* (New Haven, Conn.: Yale Univ. Press, 2001).
6. Anthony Beevor, *The Battle for Spain: The Spanish Civil War, 1936–1939,* rev. ed. (New York: Penguin, 2006); Sam Tanenhaus, "Innocents Abroad," *Vanity Fair* (Sept. 2001).
7. Carroll, *Odyssey,* 15–17.
8. *Investigation of Un-American Activities in the United States. Hearings Before a Special Committee on Un-American Activities* XIII (1940), 7785–93.
9. *Wisconsin State Journal,* Oct. 26, 2009.
10. Carroll, *Odyssey,* 17–18. Originals in Hyman Katz to Ma, Nov. 25, 1937, in Cary Nelson and Jefferson Hendricks, eds., *Madrid 1937: Letters of the Abraham Lincoln Brigade from the Spanish Civil War* (New York: Routledge, 1996), 31–33. The second quotation, while accurately transcribed from the personnel files of the archives in Moscow, Fond 545, Opis 6, cannot be identified by the writer's name because research material has disappeared from this author's files.
11. Fraser Ottanelli, "Anti-Fascism and the Shaping of National and Ethnic Identity: Italian American Volunteers in the Spanish Civil War," *Journal of American Ethnic History* (Dec. 2007), 22.
12. For an introduction to African Americans in the Spanish Civil War, see http://www.alba-valb.org/resources/lessons/african-americans-in-the-spanish-civil-war; Danny Duncan Collum and Victor A. Berch, *African Americans in the Spanish Civil War: This Ain't Ethiopia But It'll Do* (New York: G. K. Hall, 1992); and Harry Haywood, *Black Bolshevik: Autobiography of an Afro-American Communist* (Chicago: Liberator Press, 1978).
13. Cary Nelson and Jefferson Hendricks, eds., *Madrid 1937: The Letters of the Abraham Lincoln Brigade from the Spanish Civil War* (New York: Routledge, 1996), 33–35.
14. Carroll, *Odyssey,* 18. Original in author interview with Vaughn Love, Apr. 7, 1978; *People's World,* Feb. 13, 1939, p. 3.
15. Carroll, Nash, Small, *Good Fight Continues,* Chapter 3.
16. Hutchins interview in Dollard Mss., Abraham Lincoln Brigade Archives, Tamiment Library, New York University; see also Hutchins interview in the documentary film, *The Good Fight* (1984).
17. Charles E. Schamel and Wynell B. Schamel, "The Inquiry into the Education of Don Henry and His Subsequent Death in the Spanish Civil War," Social Education LXII (March 1998): 135–41.

6. AMERICAN TOURISTS IN SPAIN

1. Ernest Hemingway, "Milton Wolff," in Jo Davidson, *Spanish Portraits* (New York: Georgian Press, 1938).
2. Vincent Sheean, *Not Peace but a Sword* (New York: Doubleday, Doran, 1939), 65.
3. Peter N. Carroll, *The Odyssey of the Abraham Lincoln Brigade: Americans in the Spanish Civil War* (Stanford, Calif.: Stanford Univ. Press, 1994), 78.
4. George Orwell, *A Collection of Essays* (Garden City, N.Y.: Anchor, 1954), 209. See also Chapter 1, above.
5. André Malraux, *Man's Hope,* trans. Stuart Gilbert and Alastair Macdonald (New York: Bantam, 1968), 174, 318; André Malraux, "Help Spain!" *Artfront* III (1937): 8.
6. Carroll, *Odyssey,*, 87–88.
7. Alvah Cecil Bessie, *Men in Battle: A Story of Americans in Spain* (New York: Scribner, 1939), 7.
8. Carroll, *Odyssey,* 78.
9. John Miller, *Voices Against Tyranny: Writing of the Spanish Civil War* (New York: Scribner, 1986), 202.
10. Carlos Baker, ed., *Ernest Hemingway: Selected Letters* (New York: Scribner, 1981), 463–64. See also Paul Preston, *We Saw Spain Die: Foreign Correspondents in the Spanish Civil* War (New York: Skyhorse, 2009), Chapter 3; Paul Preston, *The Spanish Holocaust: Inquisition and Extermination in Twentieth-Century Spain* (New York: Norton, 2012), 393–96. See also Chapter 1, above.
11. Edwin Rolfe, Diary, Nov. 10, 1937, Rolfe Mss, University of Illinois, Urbana; Edwin Rolfe, *The Lincoln Battalion; The Story of the Americans Who Fought in Spain in the International Brigades* (New York: Random House, 1939), 70.
12. Carroll, *Odyssey,* 78–79.
13. Gellhorn to Eleanor Roosevelt [Spring 1938], FDR Library, Hyde Park, NY. See also Chapter 1, above.
14. Carroll, *Odyssey,* 151.
15. Carroll, *Odyssey,* 151; Arthur H. Landis, *The Abraham Lincoln Brigade* (New York: Citadel Press, 1967), 328.
16. Carroll, *Odyssey,* 152–53.
17. Bessie, *Men in Battle,* 136; James Neugass, *War Is Beautiful: An American Ambulance Driver in the Spanish Civil War,* ed. Peter N. Carroll and Peter Glazer (New York: New Press, 2008), 194.
18. Rolfe, Diary, Rolfe Mss.
19. Sheean, *Not Peace,* 241.
20. Carlos Baker, *Ernest Hemingway: A Life Story* (New York: Charles Scribner's Sons, 1968), 415, 426.
21. *New Masses* (Feb. 1939).
22. See note 1.
23. Baker, *Hemingway: Selected Letters,* 476.
24. Carroll, *Odyssey,* 236.
25. Ernest Hemingway, *For Whom the Bell Tolls* (New York: Scribner, 1940), 163.
26. Hemingway to Wolff, January 1941, *American Dialogue* I (Oct.–Nov. 1964): 11.
27. Carroll, *Odyssey,* 237; Bessie to Edwin Rolfe, Sept. 8, 1939, Rolfe Mss.

28. Alfred Kazin, *Starting Out in the Thirties* (Boston: Little, Brown, 1965), 140.
29. Ernest Hemingway, "Preface," in Gustav Regler, *The Great Crusade,* trans. Whittaker Chambers and Barrows Mussey (New York: Longmans, Green, 1940), ix.
30. Carroll, *Odyssey,* 237–40.
31. For the full text of Hemingway's critique of the screenplay, see Chapter 7.
32. Aalto to Edwin Rolfe, Sept. 1, 1943, Rolfe Mss.
33. See Chapter 9, below.
34. The text, together with an audio tape recording, is in Cary Nelson, ed., *Remembering Spain: Hemingway's Civil War Eulogy and the Veterans of the Abraham Lincoln Brigade* (Urbana: Univ. of Illinois Press, 1994).
35. Hemingway to Milton Wolff, May 7, 1950, *American Dialogue* I (Oct.–Nov. 1964): 13.
36. Milton Wolff to Ernest Hemingway, Aug. 8, 1950, Ernest Hemingway Mss., JFK Library, Boston, Mass.
37. See Carroll, *Odyssey,* 315–19.
38. Hemingway to Wolff, May 7, 1950: see note 25.
39. These and following quotes: Carroll, *Odyssey,* 318–19.
40. Milton Wolff to Alvah Bessie, Aug. 15 1981, Bessie Mss., Wisconsin Historical Society; Milton Wolff to Joseph Brandt, Feb. 15, 1980; Wolff to Herbert Matthews, Aug. 27, 1975, VALB Mss., Bancroft Library, Berkeley, Calif.
41. Milton Wolff to Alvah Bessie, Aug. 15, 1981, Bessie Mss., Wisconsin Historical Society.
42. Alvah Bessie and Albert Prago, eds., *Our Fight: Writings by Veterans of the Abraham Lincoln Brigade* (New York: Monthly Review Press, 1986), 23–24.

8. "NOT VALID FOR TRAVEL IN SPAIN"

1. Martha Gellhorn to Eleanor Roosevelt [April 1938], Eleanor Roosevelt Mss., Franklin Delano Roosevelt Library, Hyde Park, New York.
2. Peter Glazer, *Radical Nostalgia: Spanish Civil War Commemoration in America* (Rochester, N.Y.: Univ. of Rochester Press, 2005), 72–74.
3. Peter N. Carroll, *The Odyssey of the Abraham Lincoln Brigade: Americans in the Spanish Civil War* (Stanford, Calif.: Stanford Univ. Press, 1994), 211.
4. See James Neugass, *War Is Beautiful: An American Ambulance Driver in the Spanish Civil War,* ed. Peter N. Carroll and Peter Glazer (New York: New Press, 2008), 3.
5. See Carroll, *Odyssey,* passim.
6. Carroll, *Odyssey,* 217.
7. Ibid., 226.
8. Ibid.
9. Ibid., 230–31.
10. The release of the FBI records of the Veterans of the Abraham Lincoln Brigade (VALB) to the Abraham Lincoln Brigade Archives (ALBA) is largely completed. These unpublished documents can be found at the Tamiment Library of New York University, but they were not indexed when I read them. Quotations from these documents in this paper are not further footnoted.
11. For more on this topic, see also Chapter 1, above.

12. See Veterans of the Abraham Lincoln Brigade, FBI files, NY No. 100–2545, pp. 16–17 and passim; 100–7060–215.
13. Besides the VALB files, the FBI files on Felix Kusman are particularly illuminating; these papers are now held by the Tamiment Library.
14. Peter N. Carroll, Michael Nash, and Melvin Small, eds., *The Good Fight Continues: World War II Letters from the Abraham Lincoln Brigade* (New York: New York Univ. Press, 2006), 42.
15. Carroll, Nash, and Small, *Good Fight Continues,* 44.
16. Ibid., 72.
17. Ibid., 89–92.
18. See Carroll, *Odyssey,* 262–64.
19. Carroll, Nash, and Small, *Good Fight Continues,* 46.
20. Ibid., 101.
21. FBI files HQ File 100–7060, Section 27.
22. See Rolfe's *The Lincoln Battalion: The Story of the Americans Who Fought in Spain in the International Brigades* (New York: Random House, 1939) and Bessie's *Men in Battle: A Story of Americans in Spain* (New York: Charles Scribner's Sons, 1939).
23. George Orwell, *A Collection of Essays* (Garden City, N.Y.: Doubleday, 1954), 193–215.
24. Adam Hochschild, "Orwell: Homage to the 'Homage,'" *New York Review of Books* (Dec. 19, 2013): 62–64; see also Chapter 1, above.
25. See for example, Harvey Klehr, John Earl Haynes, Fridrikh Igorevich Firsov, *The Secret World of American Communism* (New Haven, Conn.: Yale Univ. Press, 1995); Ronald Radosh, Mary Habeck, and Grigory Sevostiano, *Spain Betrayed: The Soviet Union in the Spanish Civil War* (New Haven, Conn.: Yale Univ. Press, 2001); Cecil D. Eby, *Comrades and Commissars: The Lincoln Battalion in the Spanish Civil War* (University Park: Pennsylvania State Univ. Press, 2006); Anthony Beevor, *The Battle for Spain: The Spanish Civil War, 1936-1939* (New York: Penguin, 2001). For a critique of Cecil Eby's account of the death of Oliver Law, see Grover Furr, "Anatomy of an Anticommunist Fabrication: The Death of Oliver Law, An Historiographical Investigation," *Reconstruction: Studies in Contemporary Culture* 8 (2006).
26. See *The Volunteer* XXVIII (Sept. 2006): 4 and private correspondence with the author.
27. Peter N. Carroll, *Keeping Time: Memory, Nostalgia and the Art of History* (Athens: Univ. of Georgia Press, 2011), 207–9; Glazer, *Radical Nostalgia,* 131.
28. Edwin Rolfe, *First Love and Other Poems* (Los Angeles: Larry Edmunds Book Shop, 1951), 53.
29. Quoted in Glazer, *Radical Nostalgia,* 31–32.

9. PREMATURE ANTI-FASCISTS, AGAIN

1. John Earl Haynes and Harvey Klehr, *In Denial: Historians, Communism and Espionage* (San Francisco: Encounter Books, 2003), 121–34.
2. *Daily Worker,* January 18, 1945, 8.
3. Bernard Knox, *Premature Anti-Fascist* (New York: s.n., 1998).

4. Archie Brown to Esther Brown, August 24, 1945, Archie Brown Mss, Tamiment Library, New York University.
5. Peter N. Carroll, *The Odyssey of the Abraham Lincoln Brigade: Americans in the Spanish Civil War* (Stanford, Calif.: Stanford Univ. Press, 1994), 234.
6. Ibid., 242.
7. For the Lincolns in World War II, see Peter N. Carroll, Michael Nash, and Melvin Small, eds., *The Good Fight Continues: World War II Letters from the Abraham Lincoln Brigade* (New York: New York Univ. Press, 2006).

10. THE MYTH OF THE MOSCOW ARCHIVES

1. Peter N. Carroll, *The Odyssey of the Abraham Lincoln Brigade: Americans in the Spanish Civil War* (Stanford, Calif.: Stanford Univ. Press, 1994), 374–75.
2. See Harvey Klehr, John Earl Haynes, and Fridrikh Igorevich Firsov *The Secret World of American Communism* (New Haven, Conn.: Yale University Press), 222.
3. The most thorough research appears in Grover Furr, "Anatomy of a Lie: The Death of Oliver Law," published in the on-line journal *Reconstruction* [Feb. 2008] http://reconstruction.eserver.org/Issues/081/furr.shtml. An abridged version of this article appears in *The Volunteer* (June 2010). See http://www.albavolunteer.org/2010/06/anatomy-of-a-lie-the-death-of-oliver-law/.

11. SPAIN AND "SPAIN AGAIN"

1. Bessie exaggerates the number. Approximately 425 veterans of the Lincoln Brigade served in U.S. armies during World War II and another 100 in the merchant marine.

12. FOREWORD TO ALVAH BESSIE'S *MEN IN BATTLE*

1. The following quotations come from a document Bessie titled "Your Honor: Ladies & Gentlemen of the Jury." He subsequently penciled in "Undelivered because un-tried (1948)," a reference to the fact that he never had the opportunity of a trial following his indictment for contempt of Congress for refusing to testify in 1947. See Speeches, Miscellaneous, Bessie Mss. I read his papers in his house after his death and they were subsequently deposited at the State Historical Society in Madison, Wisconsin. These papers are a goldmine for a study of his life and work.
2. *Brooklyn Eagle*, March 7, 1937; Articles Scrapbook, Bessie Mss.
3. Dan Bessie, ed., *Alvah Bessie's Spanish Civil War Notebooks* (Lexington: Univ. Press of Kentucky, 2002).
4. *The Volunteer* (June 2002).
5. Peter N. Carroll, *The Odyssey of the Abraham Lincoln Brigade: Americans in the Spanish Civil War* (Stanford, Calif. : Stanford Univ. Press, 1994), 237–38.
6. Carroll, *Odyssey*, 332–34.

13. FOREWORD TO HANK RUBIN'S *SPAIN'S CAUSE WAS MINE*

1. The best description of frontline ambulance work is James Neugass, *War Is Beautiful: An American Ambulance Driver in the Spanish Civil War*, ed. Peter N. Carroll and Peter Glazer (New York: New Press, 2008).
2. See Hank Rubin, *The Kitchen Answer Book* (Sterling, Va.: Capital Books, 2002); Jeannette Ferrary, "Hank Rubin: Wine and Food Maven," *The Volunteer* XXV (March 2003); Barry Glassner, "The Only Place to Eat in Berkeley': Hank Rubin and the Pot Luck," *Gastronomica* II (Fall 2002).

14. WAR STORIES

1. Although Milton Wolff remembered Robert Capa as the photographer who took his picture, archivists at the International Center of Photography in New York cannot confirm that the photo can be attributed to Capa. Nor can the Bancroft Library at the University of California, Berkeley, though no other likely suspects have emerged.
2. Full disclosure, as one of the West Coast VALB "Associates," the author participated in these campaigns. Ultimately, we sent twenty ambulances as well as funds for wheelchairs, hospital generators, and other medical supplies.

15. RALPH FASANELLA LIMNS THE LIFE OF THE WORKINGMAN

1. *Fasanella,* video by Glenn Pearcy (1992).
2. Fasanella interview, Oct. 20, 1992.
3. *New York,* Oct. 30, 1972.
4. John Dewey, *Art as Experience* (New York: Capricorn Books, 1958), 11.
5. Fasanella interview, Oct. 29–30, 1992.
6. Ibid.
7. Fasanella interviews, Oct. 27 (phone), Oct. 29–30, 1992.
8. Interviews, Oct. 1992.
9. Fasanella interview, Oct. 29–30, 1992.
10. Patrick Wilson, *Fasanella's City* (New York: Knopf, 1973), 14. Since the publication of this article in 1993, Wilson's pioneering volume has been joined by Paul S. D'Ambrosio, *Ralph Fasanella's America* (Cooperstown, N.Y.: Fenimore Art Museum, 2001).
11. Fasanella interviews, Oct. 1–2, 1989.
12. Fasanella interview, Oct. 29, 1992.
13. Fasanella poster statement.
14. Fasanella interview, Oct. 29, 1992.
15. Ibid.
16. Fasanella to author, Nov. 16, 1990.
17. Ron Carver interview, Nov. 7, 1992.
18. Interview, Oct. 5, 1989.
19. Werkin interview, Oct. 29, 1992.
20. Fasanella interview, Oct. 29, 1992.
21. Ibid.

16. FROM WAR HERO TO BLACKLIST

1. The best biography of Carter appeared after the publication of this article. See Allene G. Carter and Robert L. Allen, *Honoring Sergeant Carter: Redeeming a Black World War II Hero's Legacy* (New York: Amistad, 2003). See also Carter's letters in *The Good Fight Continues: World War II Letters from the Abraham Lincoln Brigade*, ed. Peter N. Carroll, Michael Nash, and Melvin Small (New York: New York Univ. Press, 2006).

Index